The Superpowers and the Third World

The Superpowers and the Third World

Turkish-American Relations and Cyprus

Suha Bolukbasi

Volume 15

Exxon Education Foundation Series
on Rhetoric and Political Discourse

Series Editor

Kenneth W. Thompson

White Burkett Miller Center of Public Affairs
University of Virginia

University Press of America

Lanham • New York • London

The Miller Center

University of Virginia

4720 Boston Way
Lanham, MD 20706

3 Henrietta Street
London WC2E 8LU England

Printed in the United States of America

British Cataloging in Publication Information Available

Library of Congress Cataloging-in-Publication Data

Bolukbasi, Suha.
The superpowers and the Third World : Turkish-American relations
and Cyprus / Suha Bolukbasi.
p. cm. —(Exxon Education Foundation series on rhetoric and
political discourse ; ʋ. 15)
Bibliography: p.
1. United States—Foreign relations—Turkey. 2. Turkey—Foreign
relations—United States. 3. Cyprus—Politics and government—1960—
I. White Burkett Miller Center. II. Title III. Series.
E 183.8.T8B65 1988
956.45'04—dc 19 88–10343
ISBN 0–8191–6977–3 (alk. paper)
ISBN 0–8191–6978–1 (pbk. : alk. paper)

The views expressed by the author(s) of this publication do not necessarily represent the opinions of the Miller Center. We hold to Jefferson's dictum that: "Truth is the proper and sufficient antagonist to error, and has nothing to fear from the conflict, unless by human interposition, disarmed of her natural weapons, free argument and debate."

Co-published by arrangement with
The White Burkett Miller Center of Public Affairs,
University of Virginia

All University Press of America books are produced on acid-free paper which exceeds the minimum standards set by the National Historical Publications and Records Commission.

TO MY FATHER AND MOTHER

Acknowledgements

I am particularly grateful to Professor Kenneth W. Thompson without whose continuous encouragement and support this book would not have been published. Professor Thompson furthermore undertook a critical examination of the text and helped me to revise some parts of it significantly. The manuscript was also read by Professors R.K. Ramazani and Michael J. Smith who made valuable suggestions.

Further, I am pleased to acknowledge that grants from the White Burkett Miller Center at the University of Virginia and the Institute for the Study of World Politics in New York made it possible for me to start the process of thought and study which led to this volume.

I owe a special dept to my wife, Yeshim, who helped ease the task of writing and proved to be indispensable in the preparation of this book. Though many have provided assistance to improve this work, the views expressed here are, of course, entirely my own responsibility.

Preface

KENNETH W. THOMPSON

Discussions of contemporary international politics tend to focus on great power relationships. Indeed some analysts speak of superpower relations as the only relationships that count. The disparity between the superpowers and the lesser powers is far greater than between comparable states at any time in the history of the state system.

The Miller Center has published a volume in the Exxon series on rhetoric and political discourse on the superpower dialogue (Kenneth W. Thompson, Dialogue of the Superpowers: Soviet-American Discourse, Lanham, Maryland: University Press of America, 1988). From the discussion in that volume, the dominance of the superpower role in the minds of well-respected observers is apparent. The present volume offers an alternative portrait of contemporary international politics. It is a viewpoint that deserves discussion and elaboration.

Dr. Suha Bolukbasi is a brilliant young scholar from Ankara University in Turkey. He holds the Ph.D. from the Department of Government and Foreign Affairs at the University of Virginia. On completion of his degree, he returned to take up a university appointment in Turkey. He is already well launched as a scholar and teacher in his native country and has achieved worldwide recognition for his research. Few if any Third World scholars have done the exacting empirical research he has undertaken in the archives of foreign policy materials.

Dr. Bolukbasi's major thesis is that the study of power and influence on the contemporary world scene requires attention to both the influence of the superpowers on the lesser powers and the influence of the latter on the former. A process of mutual influence is established that requires attention to the two sides of the equation. In the present study, the United States unquestionably exerts a significant influence on Turkey but particularly in the 1970s Turkey succeeded in influencing American foreign policy. The author keeps his eye on the factors most responsible for such influence including domestic politics, the strategic views of leaders, other events taking place in the world and the context of the relationship at a particular moment in history.

It should be clear that this study has primary value for the understanding of Turkish-American relations. It may also be important in a more general sense. The question that can be raised is whether the approach that undergirds the Bolukbasi study may not have relevance for all or most studies of superpower-Third World country relations. Is the intellectual framework provided here relevant for a whole category of foreign relations studies? Is the interaction and political dialogue described in this study one which recurs in similar relations of other superpower-Third World countries? Are we in the presence of a set of concepts and ideas that can carry over into the study of similar patterns of world politics and relationships?

To be quite specific, Dr. Bolukbasi has contributed an important foreign relations case study. He also has given us a way of thinking about superpower-Third World dialogues and relationships. For this reason, the Miller Center is proud to include his work in this important series of studies of rhetoric, dialogue and political discourse.

Table of Contents

Introduction

On 5 June 1964, U.S. Ambassador to Turkey Raymond Hare delivered a diplomatic note to Turkish Prime Minister Ismet Inonu. The note, signed by President Johnson, urged Inonu not to intervene in Cyprus and threatened that the U.S. might reconsider its commitment to Turkey's defense if a Turkish landing took place. Johnson stated:

> I hope you will understand that your NATO allies have not had a chance to consider whether they have an obligation to protect Turkey against the Soviet Union if Turkey takes a step which results in Soviet intervention without the full consent and understanding of its NATO allies.[1]

Johnson's warning was a substantial blow to Turkey's confidence in the reliability of American support to Turkish national security. Nevertheless, Inonu complied with Johnson's "request" and "postponed" the intervention. It *seemed* that Johnson's warning was almost solely responsible for the cancellation of the operation. A decade later, however, the U.S. was not as successful in deterring Turkey's landing. After Turkey established control on 36 percent of Cyprus in 1974, the U.S. Congress imposed an arms embargo on Turkey which remained in force for nearly four years. Congress justified its action by contending that Turkey should be ineligible for further assistance because it used American arms for aggressive purposes.

The disagreements and frictions between the U.S. and Turkey which intensified during the Cyprus crises, reflect a problem that besets similar alliance relations between the superpowers and their regional allies. Often the geopolitical interests of the superpowers clash with the regional interests of their smaller allies. Superpowers then strive to induce "orderly" behavior on the part of these states by using their power and/or influence. The alliance relationship remains intact if a compromise can be worked out. Yet sometimes the differences are so unbridgeable that the smaller partners try to lessen their dependency on the superpowers in order to have a freer hand in a future contingency.

Before 1964 Turkey had assumed that its geopolitical and regional interests were identical with those of the U.S. Both post-World War II leaders, Inonu and Menderes, considered Turkey's alliance with the U.S. essential for Turkey's security, and hence, tried to cooperate with the U.S., even in areas thought unimportant to Turkish national security interests. Turkey was eager, for instance, to associate itself with American Middle East policies during the 1950s.

The three Cyprus crises significantly altered Turkish perceptions of America's importance to Turkish national security. Turkey realized that its NATO membership did not assure the protection of its interests in Cyprus. Therefore, the Turkish Governments strove to adopt a "flexible" foreign policy which would lessen Turkey's reliance on the U.S. for the settlement of the Cyprus problem. The "flexible" or "multi-faceted" foreign policy led to an improvement in relations between Turkey and the Soviet Union and other regional states. This development, in turn, further shaped the American-Turkish influence relationship.

The major purpose of this study is to contribute to an understanding of the American-Turkish influence relationship. The Cyprus crises of 1964, 1967 and 1974 are examined to understand how the respective parties desired the crises to end and why their efforts were or were not successful. It is expected that the answers to these questions will demonstrate how an influence relationship between two unequal allies works. It is also hoped that the conclusions of this study will indicate why U.S. alliances with some countries failed, and how the U.S. could avoid making the same mistakes. This study is also relevant to American-Soviet relations because the latter was able to capitalize on the errors committed by American policymakers in the eastern Mediterranean. The Turco-Soviet rapprochement has been modest so far, but it is still too early to determine exactly how it will affect the balance of power between the superpowers.

An influence relationship is neither easy to define nor easy to identify. There are several definitions of influence and most of them are ambiguous regarding the differences between power, influence and control. Identifying an influence relationship may also be difficult because of the various circumstances. This question will be examined later. Let us start by looking at a number of definitions.

Carl J. Friedrich suggested that influence may be characterized "by saying that it usually exists when the behavior of [the influenced state] B is molded by and conforms to the preferences of [the influencer] A, but without the issuance of a command."[2] A similar definition is provided by Jack Nagel who stated that "[i]nfluence is a relation among actors such that the wants, desires, preferences, or intentions of one or more actors affect the actions, or predispositions to act, of one or more other actors."[3]

A more elaborate definition is given by Morton Baratz and Peter Bachrach. They have argued that "[o]ne person has influence over another within a given scope to the extent that the first, without resorting to either a tacit or an overt threat of severe deprivations, causes the second to change his course of action."[4] As in the preceding definitions, there are as many unknowns in this definition as there are knowns. A major loophole is the fact that we do not know why B would accommodate its actions to the desires of A.

The inadequacy of these definitions is due to the fact that influence relations comprise a variety of aspects of state-to-state relations which can not be sufficiently explained in one or two paragraphs. There are a number of variables which further shed light on the intricacies of influence and also pertain to the American-Turkish influence relationship. These shall be examined shortly. First, the confusion surrounding the distinction between power and influence should be briefly discussed.

Hans J. Morgenthau and Kenneth W. Thompson suggested that:

> [p]olitical power is a psychological relation between those who exercise it and those over whom it is exercised. It gives the former control over certain actions of the latter through the impact which the former exert on the latter's minds. That impact derives from three sources: the expectation of benefits, the fear of disadvantages, the respect or love of men or institutions. It may be exerted through orders, threats, the authority or charisma of a man or of an office, or a combination of any of these.[5]

Influence, on the other hand, means mainly the ability to move others through promises or grants of benefits.[6] It should be added that this construction is an oversimplification. The above authors do not suggest that power operates exclusively through coercion while influence relies entirely on persuasion. As Arnold Wolfers maintained, "[i]n practically every instance in which these means achieve significant political results, there is present both an element of persuasion and an element of pressure or constraint bordering on coercion."[7]

The term influence is always indicative of power and control for the influencer and dependence for the influenced. Yet influence is not identical with either power, control or dependence. If power corresponded to influence, the U.S. or the U.S.S.R. would automatically convert their power to influence in third states.[8] Thus, one should state that not all power is usable or convertible to influence. As Morgenthau and Thompson suggested, an increase in a state's power does not necessarily bring influence over other states.[9] It is necessary, however, "to remind oneself...that 'coercive power in the background' usually deserves a major part of the credit" for successfully influencing others.[10]

States are inclined to resort to coercive power to attain highly valued objectives, and yet, as Wolfers maintained, the usefulness of influence

> as an instrument of policy is far from negligible and in some situations, especially where demands are to be made on friendly nations, it outstrips power. A nation can often be persuaded by its ally to see the common interest more clearly, or to yield for the sake of benefits from continued solidarity.[11]

During each of the three Cyprus crises, the U.S. relied on influence as an instrument of its policy to discourage Turkey from landing forces on Cyprus. The appeal to reason, to allied solidarity, to self-interest, and the hint of support or opposition on other issues played a substantial role in U.S. influence attempts. Needless to say, the U.S. power lent credibility to American mediation efforts; yet it was not sheer American power which was taken into account by Turkey, but rather, *how* it was used and for *which* purposes. In other words, there were times when the greater power of the U.S. translated into greater influence over Turkey, but there were also times when it did not.[12]

Let us now briefly consider the influence variables which constitute the analytical framework of this study, and which help explain the working of the Turco-American influence relationship during the Cyprus crises. There are three essential variables which affect the exercise of influence. First, "[t]he amount of influence a state wields over others can be related to the capabilities *mobilized* in support of *specific* foreign policy objectives."[13] If a state does not utilize its resources in support of *specific* objectives, it may not be able to influence others, no matter how powerful it is. In addition to mobilization, the resources of the potential influencer should be *relevant* to a particular situation.[14]

Second, the success or failure of acts of influence is determined by the "extent to which there are needs between the two countries in any influence relationship."[15] A country that needs something from another is vulnerable to its influence. Third, "the ephemeral quality of responsiveness" determines the effectiveness of acts of influence.[16] Receptivity or responsiveness is defined by Holsti as

> . . . a disposition to receive another's request with sympathy, even to the point where a government is willing to sacrifice some of its own values and interests in order to fulfill those requests; responsiveness is the willingness to be influenced.[17]

Robert Dahl proposed two more factors to explain why actors—in our case, states—exercise different degrees of influence. He suggested that there are variations in the skill or efficiency with which individuals—or statesmen—use the resources available to them. Second, there are variations in the extent to which individuals stress influencing others.[18] This proposition explains why a different amount of pressure was exerted on Turkey by the

Johnson Administration in 1964 than was exerted by the Nixon Administration in 1974.

As David Singer maintained, B's expectation of A's potential reaction to B's compliance or non-compliance also affects B's decisions.[19] Singer assumed that "A is attempting to influence B by the use of threatened punishment in order to deter B from pursuing a certain goal." A may succeed or fail depending on the importance of the issue for B and B's perception of the probability of "A carrying out the threatened punishment." If B estimates that A would very likely not punish B, then it would almost certainly act without considering A's desires. Even if B expects that A would actually carry out its threat, B may go ahead with its original plan if it attaches a high value to the outcome.[20] In short, states take into account two additional variables: utility of actions and probability of reactions.

Singer suggested that the above explanation excludes the relative weight which a given set of decision-makers might assign to each of the two dimensions (utility and probability). Each nation and decision-maker differs "in the degree to which they emphasize either the probability or the preference element in their appraisal of an outcome." Moreover, policymakers tend to exaggerate the probability of an outcome if they value it highly. "... [C]onversely, when a probability looks very low, the tendency will be to downgrade the attractiveness of the associated outcome."[21]

Another assumption which is relevant to the Cyprus crises was offered by Friedrich. He suggested that influence is usually negative in its impact upon those influenced. This is to say that influencers usually uphold the existing state of affairs and therefore would object to a change in the *status quo*.[22] As we shall see, the U.S. insisted on the preservation of the *status quo* during each of the three Cyprus crises.

The tendency to favor the *status quo* is closely related to probability calculations. As Karl W.

Deutsch argued, A can prevent a moderately improbable outcome

> by the application of even a relatively limited amount of power . . . The same degree of power produces far less impressive results, however, when it is applied to promoting an outcome which is fairly improbable in the first place.[23]

The so-called "rule of anticipated reactions"[24] also proved to be relevant to the three Cyprus crises. Many times, B behaves in a way desired by A, even though A has not tried to pressure B. Often it is the case that B's policymakers anticipate the reactions of the influencer and behave in ways which would not evoke hostile reactions.[25] Sometimes, however, states fail to anticipate the reactions of other states due to "possible errors in anticipation,...to oversight, incomplete information, lack of insight and the like..."[26]

The Cyprus crises also bore out the proposition that failing to provide alternatives "is to call for a probable showdown."[27] Instead, if A, the influencer, provides an alternative besides prohibiting B's, the influenced state's, proposed action, B would very likely try the alternative and not ignore A's advice.

The discussion of crises as criteria of influence may be questioned. It is correct that crises are usually of short-term duration and that they may not reflect the overall state of the relationship between two countries. On the other hand, there are very few instances which would indicate the parameters of influence. Turkey's support of American diplomacy in Latin America is certainly not indicative of the influence relationship between the U.S. and Turkey because the issue is irrelevant to Turkey's security. As Rubinstein suggested, a state adapts to the preferences of the other when the issue is of marginal importance to it. "Minimal adaptations are part of the overall influence relationship; they are the 'payoffs' for services rendered and are usually made since the costs are negligible."[28] Crises provide us with the opportunity to see whether states are influential enough to affect each other's policies, especially when they have different opinions on how to settle the conflicts.

Still, even in times of crises, one cannot be sure why states behave the way they do. This is especially true in cases when the small state heeds the advice of its great power partner. In such cases, factors other than the influence exerted by the great power may play a more important role. As Rubinstein suggested, "[w]hat often seems to be influence turns out instead to be joint interests of the two parties."[29] In both 1964 and 1967 Turkey chose to comply with the U.S. mediation partly because the Turkish Government believed that it was in Turkey's interest to do so.

The discussion of the three case studies indicates that domestic, geopolitical, and functional factors affected the influence variables discussed above. These in turn shaped the American-Turkish influence relationship and determined the outcomes of the Cyprus crises. An example will suffice to clarify this proposition. In 1974, Ecevit was less responsive to American influence attempts because: (1) He believed in the political virtue of assertiveness (domestic factor); (2) The U.S.S.R. was perceived no longer as a threat to Turkey's security (geopolitical factor); (3) Turkish armed forces were capable of undertaking a military intervention in Cyprus. (functional factor)

The domestic factor, which included the influence of not only the Turkish but also the American policymaking process, had an important effect on the outcomes of the three crises. The post-World War II consensus enabled President Johnson to deal with the 1964 and 1967 crises without effective congressional interference. Kissinger had to deal with an enraged Congress in 1974 which blamed the Cyprus debacle on his ineptitude. The Greek lobbying of the Congress and the White House, the weakening of the Presidency, and the assertiveness of the Congress in the post-Vietnam era significantly affected the administration's flexibility to solve the crisis in 1974.

Turkey dealt with the 1964, 1967 and 1974 crises with three different governments and prime ministers. Each of these governments had different goals as to the final settlement of the Cyprus problem. Moreover, Inonu (1964), Demirel (1967) and Ecevit's (1974) different personalities were reflected in the decisions they made. It is no wonder that the "cautious" Inonu, the "pragmatist" Demirel and the "risk taker" Ecevit acted the way they did. When discussing Turkish domestic politics' impact on Turkey's Cyprus policy, one also must talk about public opinion and its influence on Turkish governments. We will see that the Turkish policymakers took into account not only domestic but also world public opinion when they were trying to decide what to do in Cyprus.

The geopolitical factor involved does not so much refer to the relaxation of tensions between the two superpowers in the latter part of the 1960s and early 1970s as it does to Turkey's normalization of its relations with the Soviet Union and the Middle Eastern countries during the same period. Turkey-U.S.S.R relations could be characterized in terms of hostility even during the early 1960s. Likewise, Turkey's relations with many Middle Eastern states were not friendly until the first Cyprus crisis in 1964. By 1974 Turkish relations with the Soviets and the Middle Eastern states became normal if not cordial. This study suggests not only that the normalization of Turkey's relations with countries mentioned was a result of its frustration with the lack of U.S. support on Cyprus, but also that Turkey's ability to adopt an assertive Cyprus policy in 1974 was partly due to this normalization.

The functional factor, or Turkey's ability to conduct a successful naval and aerial landing in Cyprus, also affected the decisions of Turkish policymakers in all three crises. During the first two crises the Turkish armed forces were not prepared to undertake a landing on the island. Hence, both Inonu and Demirel feared that Turkey's intervention would fail to achieve its military objectives. In 1974 the Ecevit Government felt that Turkey was in a much better position to successfully complete a military intervention. This further contributed to Ecevit's inclination to be assertive in Cyprus.

The first chapter of this study examines the Cyprus problem during the 1950s and Britain's, Turkey's, Greece's and the U.S.'s Cyprus policies during the same period. The Greek Cypriot *enosis* (unification with Greece) campaign, as well as Britain's reform proposals to deal with the Greek Cypriot revolt, are discussed. This chapter ends with the negotiation and conclusion of the 1959 Zurich-London Agreements which granted independence to Cyprus.

The second chapter deals with the 1964 Cyprus crisis and the preceding friction between the two Cypriot communities. It examines Turkey's and America's reactions to the violence which flared up in Cyprus throughout 1964. The London Conference (January 1964), Undersecretary of State George Ball's mission to Ankara, Athens and Nicosia (February 1964), the Johnson Letter (5 June 1964), Geneva negotiations between Turkey, Greece and the U.S., the Acheson Plan (July-August 1964), and Turkish aerial bombing of Cyprus (8-9 August 1964) are discussed.

The third chapter focuses on Turkey's adoption of a "flexible" foreign policy after 1964, and analyzes Turkey's and America's actions throughout the 1967 Cyprus crisis. It examines the mediation efforts of Cyrus Vance (November 1967) as well as Turkish Prime Minister Demirel's handling of the crisis.

The fourth chapter deals with the 1974 crisis and Turkish and American responses to it. The Sampson coup (15 July 1974), Turkey's military interventions (20 July 1974 and 14 August 1974) and the Geneva Conferences (25-30 July and 9-14 August

1974) are examined. This chapter also deals with Kissinger's "telephone-diplomacy" and the interference of the American Congress in the crisis.

Needless to say, throughout the study the above-mentioned three propositions (domestic politics, geopolitical and functional factors) and influence variables are discussed wherever relevant. The final chapter once more focuses on them in light of the facts presented in the preceding chapters.

NOTES

1. "President Johnson's Letter to Prime Minister Inonu," *The Middle East Journal*, Vol. XX, No. 3 (1964), p. 386.

2. Carl Joachim Friedrich, *Man and His Government: An Empirical Theory of Politics* (New York: McGraw-Hill, 1963), p. 200.

3. Jack H. Nagel, *The Descriptive Analysis of Power* (New Haven: Yale University Press, 1975), p. 29.

4. Peter Bachrach and Morton S. Baratz, *Power and Poverty* (New York: Oxford University Press, 1970), p. 30.

5. Hans J. Morgenthau and Kenneth W. Thompson, *Politics Among Nations* (6th ed., New York: Alfred A. Knopf, 1985), pp. 32-33.

6. *Ibid.*, Arnold Wolfers, *Discord and Collaboration* (Baltimore: The John Hopkins University Press, 1979), p. 103.

7. *Ibid.*, p. 104.

8. Shirin Tahir-Kheli, *The United States and Pakistan: The Evolution of an Influence Relationship* (New York: Praeger, 1982), p. xii.

9. Morgenthau, *op. cit.*, p. 33.

10. Wolfers, *op. cit.*, pp. 108-109.

11. *Ibid.*, p. 108.

12. See R. K. Ramazani, *The United States and Iran: The Patterns of Influence* (New York: Praeger, 1982), p. xvi.

13. K. J. Holsti, *International Politics: A Framework for Analysis* (Englewood Cliffs, N.J.: Prentice-Hall, 1983), p. 149.

14. *Ibid*., p. 151.

15. *Ibid*.

16. *Ibid*., p. 153.

17. *Ibid*.

18. Robert Dahl, *Modern Political Analysis* (Englewood Cliffs, N.J.: Prentice-Hall, 1976), p. 33.

19. David Singer, "Inter-Nation Influence: A Formal Model," in James N. Rosenau, ed., *International Politics and Foreign Policy* (New York: The Free Press, 1969), p. 386.

20. *Ibid*.

21. *Ibid*., p. 387.

22. Friedrich, *op. cit*., p. 202.

23. Karl W. Deutsch, *The Analysis of International Relations* (Englewood Cliffs, N.J.: Prentice-Hall, 1968), p. 260.

24. Friedrich, *op. cit*., p. 203; Carl J. Friedrich, *Constitutional Government and Democracy* (New York: Harper and Brothers, 1937), pp. 16-18.

25. Dahl, *op. cit*., pp. 30-31.

26. Friedrich, *Man and His Government . . .*, pp. 204-205.

27. Singer, *op. cit.*, p. 391.

28. Alvin Z. Rubinstein, *Red Star on the Nile: The Soviet Egyptian Influence Relationship Since the June War* (Princeton, N.J.: Princeton University Press, 1977), p. xv.

29. Rubinstein, *op. cit.*, p. xvii.

I. Cyprus Until 1960

Turkey-U.S. Relations until 1960

The Turkey-U.S. alliance relationship dates back to 1952 when the U.S. agreed to accept Turkey's application to join NATO. This decision ended a long waiting period for Turkey whose applications previously had been rejected. Before 1952 the U.S. was convinced that Turkey's defense was not vitally important to the security of the Western bloc and hence was reluctant to make a commitment to support it. The U.S. did, however, provide military assistance under the Truman Doctrine between 1947 and 1952.

The Democratic Party (DP) Government, which ended the twenty-seven year rule of Inonu's Republican People's Party (RPP) in the 1950 elections, considered Turkey's participation in NATO a big victory for Turkey. Adnan Menderes, who headed the DP Government in 1950, had stated in 1948 that Turkey could not pursue a "neutralist" foreign policy but had to take its place among democratic nations.[1] In December 1951, two months after Turkey was invited to join NATO, the foreign minister of the DP Government, Fuat Koprulu, told the National Assembly that "[o]ur national interests are identical from every standpoint with the joint interests of the North Atlantic Treaty Organization and with its geographic and military requirements."[2]

The Menderes Government was so convinced about the identity of interests that it did not hesitate to accept a role for Turkey in the Middle East.

Menderes genuinely believed that the rest of the Middle East was also threatened by Soviet expansionism and that Turkey had to do its best to prevent it. On 20 July 1951, Foreign Minister Koprulu told the National Assembly that Turkey's security was part of European and world security. He added:

> I would also like to indicate that the defense of the Middle East is necessary for the defense of Europe as regards strategic and economic matters. Therefore, after joining NATO, we will enter into . . . negotiations with interested parties in order to execute the role due us in the Middle East.[3]

Between 1950 and 1960 Turkey interfered in the intra-Arab disputes on the side of the U.S. Menderes' pro-Western Middle East policy and his opposition to nonalignment thus alienated many Middle Eastern and Third World states. This policy was at least partly responsible for Turkey's isolation in the United Nations in the 1960s.

The perception of identical interests also prevented the Turks from looking for ulterior motives behind American actions affecting Turkey. On 15 July 1958, one day after General Abdul Karim Kassem overthrew the pro-Western Iraqi government, U.S. marines landed in Lebanon. During the landing, without prior consultation with Turkish authorities, the U.S. used the Incirlik base in southern Turkey to transfer some of its airborne troops to Lebanon. There is no indication that the Menderes Administration complained about the U.S. attitude.[4] Inonu, chairman of the opposition RPP, demanded a parliamentary debate on 26 July 1958 on the American use of Incirlik, but the DP's majority in the National Assembly defeated the RPP's motion and no debate took place. The RPP's objection to Menderes' handling of the 1958 Lebanon crisis was probably its first questioning of the DP's foreign policy. The RPP avoided, however, any criticism of American foreign policy, or of Turkey's relations with the U.S.[5]

Another significant event of the Menderes era was the 1 May 1960 shooting down of a U-2 reconnaissance plane which was flying over the Soviet Union and had taken off from Incirlik, Turkey. The Turkish public accepted the event as a matter of course. The commentator of the daily *Cumhuriyet*, which was not a pro-Menderes publication, argued that the Soviet Union's reaction to the U-2 incident was aimed at "disturbing the close relationship between the U.S and its allies." M. Piri added that

> the angry reaction of Khrushchev will lead to a closer relationship between the allies despite the differences which currently exist between them. The reason for the existence of NATO has never been more apparent than today.[6]

The same perception of the identity of interests also led Turkey to coordinate its Cyprus policy with that of Britain and the U.S. Turkey shared the American view that a Turco-Greek conflict over Cyprus would destabilize NATO and play into the hands of the Soviet Union. Therefore, during the 1950s Turkish decision-makers were anxious not to antagonize Greece. As we shall see in the next pages, Turkey's readiness to compromise led to a Cyprus settlement in 1959.

A Short Summary of Cypriot History

Cyprus, the third largest island in the Mediterranean, forty miles south of Turkey and sixty miles west of Syria, changed hands continuously throughout history. Because of its strategic geographic location and the richness of its copper mines, Cyprus was captured and ruled consecutively by Myceneans, Assyrians, Egyptians, Persians, Romans, the Ptolemies, Byzantines, Franks, Venetians, Turks and the British.[7]

The Greek Cypriots are descendants of Aegean colonists who came from Greece and Asia Minor between 1400 and 800 B.C. The Byzantine era (395-1192 A.D.) further consolidated the Greek culture on the island. In 1192, Cyprus was captured by the Franks.[8] During the rule of first the Franks and later the Venetians, feudalism was introduced and the people of the island became serfs. The Latins also forced the Greek Orthodox Church to go underground, but they failed to eliminate the people's allegiance to it.[9]

The Turkish conquest in 1571 had more fundamental consequences than the 400 year rule of the Latins. First, the Turks abolished feudalism. Second, they restored the Greek Orthodox Church to its former dominant position. Third, a number of Turkish settlers arrived, and gradually a sizeable Turkish Cypriot community formed.[10]

With the abolition of the aristocratic order, the Greek Orthodox Church became the central institution in the Greek Cypriot community. Its secular and spiritual powers were further strengthened by additional privileges granted by the Sultan. Despite the presence of an Ottoman governor, the Church was authorized to collect state taxes and the archbishop was elevated to the status of *milletbashi* (ethnarch), national leader or spokesman for the Greek population.[11] Throughout the period of Turkish rule "the church remained the central institutional sphere around which the political, intellectual and cultural life of Greek Cypriots revolved."[12] It is therefore not surprising that the Church played a prominent role in the fight for *enosis* [unity with Greece] under both Turkish and British rules.

Turkish control of Cyprus effectively ended in 1878 when the Ottoman Sultan transferred the administration of the island to Britain. Sultan Abdulhamid's decision came after Britain had forced Russia at the Berlin Conference in 1878 to give up some of the territories it captured during the 1876-77 Turco-Russian war. Abdulhamid realized that in order to keep the remaining Ottoman territories, he needed Britain's continued support. In exchange for British agreement to assist Turkey in its defense against Russia, the Ottoman Sultan accepted Britain's lease and administration of Cyprus. According to the "Convention of Defensive Alliance" of 1878, Britain would return Cyprus when Turkey recaptured three of its eastern territories lost to Russia in the 1876-77 war.[13]

The Greek Cypriots welcomed the change of administration, and many believed that the British rule would be a step toward *enosis.* In July 1878 Archbishop Sophronios greeted British High Commissioner Sir Garnet Wolseley by stating that the Greeks "believe that Great Britain will help Cyprus, as she helped the Ioanian Islands to become united with her Mother Greece..."[14] Throughout the British rule the Greek Cypriots continued calling for *enosis.* As one Greek Cypriot writer puts it:

> [t]o be a Greek, aware of one's Greekness, and not support the union of Cyprus with the free Greek state, is more than just paradoxical; it is an impossibility. A 'true' Greek of Cyprus is, by definition, a supporter of enosis.[15]

The Turkish Cypriot community feared that it would be unable to protect its rights as a community if Cyprus united with Greece. Turkish Cypriot leaders frequently protested against the *enosis* movement. In one such protest, a former Turkish member of the Legislative Council sent a telegram to the Committee of Supply of the British Parliament suggesting that the Moslems were unanimously opposed to cession of the island to Greece, which would amount "to deliver[ing] peaceful people into the hands of wild beasts and ruin[ing] and destroy[ing] them."[16] The

Turks argued that if Britain decided to give up Cyprus, it should return it to Turkey.

Despite the heated atmosphere, there were few instances of intercommunal or anti-British violence until the 1950s. A major anti-British riot took place in 1931 after the Greek members of the Legislative Council issued a manifesto and called for *enosis*. At the same time pro-*enosis* crowds demonstrated and burned down many official buildings.[17]

At the outset of World War I, Britain renounced the 1878 Convention and annexed the island. Turkey and Greece recognized British sovereignty over Cyprus by the Treaty of Lausanne in 1923.[18] Ismet Inonu, who was Turkey's negotiator at Lausanne, later stated that he did not even bring up the question of Cyprus at Lausanne because the most important problem he had to tackle was eliminating the economic and juridicial capitulations. Raising the issue of Cyprus would provoke the British to be intransigent on the question of capitulations.[19] Ataturk had already renounced Turkey's claims over areas inhabited by non-Turkish majorities in 1920.[20] Inonu's behavior at Lausanne (1923) was therefore in compliance with foreign policy goals of the new Turkish regime.

According to the Treaty of Lausanne, those Cypriots who wanted to retain their Turkish nationality were required to do so within two years.[21] Within the next two years 9,310 out of 62,000 Turkish Cypriots emigrated to Turkey. While the Turkish Government encouraged the emigration, the British created a variety of bureaucratic difficulties in order to retain a sizeable Turkish community in Cyprus. Turkey's policy was in accord with its overall policy of exchanging the Greek minority in Turkey for the Turkish minorities in Greece and elsewhere. Britain opposed Turkish emigration because it did not want to face in the future a pro-*enosis* Greek population with no Turkish community to oppose it.[22]

During the interwar years, both Turkey and Greece adopted a hands-off attitude toward Cyprus. A statement made by Greek Premier Venizelos in 1931, after the anti-British riots in Cyprus, explains why Greece did not interfere in Cypriot politics until the 1950s:

> Crucial and more than crucial interests of Greece impose the necessity of undisturbed friendship with Great Britain . . . In fact we have the right to demand of the Greek inhabitants of these islands [Cyprus, Dodecanese] that they be less egotistical.[23]

Venizelos assumed that Britain eventually would grant self-government to Cyprus and that this would lead to *enosis.* He spoke against "untimely" *enosis* attempts which could cost Greece Britain's support.[24]

The Cyprus Question After World War II

Greek Governments abided by the Cyprus policy of Venizelos until the early 1950s. They did not actively support the *enosis* struggle of Greek Cypriots, but they made it clear that they looked favorably upon *enosis.* Greek Prime Minister Emmanuel Tsouderos, for instance, sent a memorandum to the U.S. Administration in 1942 asking for American support of the right to self-determination for Cypriots.[25]

In the latter part of the 1940s, public opinion in Greece was overwhelmingly pro-*enosis*, and a wide spectrum of political forces including the communists and the church campaigned in favor of it. Yet Greek governments were facing civil war and political instability at home and thus were not in a position to strive for the unification of Cyprus with Greece. In 1950, George Papandreou, then Interior Minister, discouraged a pro-*enosis* Cypriot delegation by saying that Greece was "breathing today with two lungs, one British and one American, and therefore it could not allow the Cyprus problem to cause her suffocation."[26]

Until 1954 Greece rejected Archbishop Makarios' suggestions that Greece should raise the Cyprus question at the United Nations (U.N.). When in 1952 Makarios threatened Greek Prime Minister Sophocles Venizelos by saying, "I shall expose you to the Greek people for your refusal [to have recourse to the U.N.]," Venizelos replied, "You may do whatever you wish ... but you shall not be allowed to dictate the foreign policy of Greece."[27] The Greek government was able to resist Makarios' pressures until 1954 when it finally decided to take up the issue with the U.N. This decision was inevitable given the fact that Makarios was viewed as a national hero in Greece and that Greek public opinion strongly favored *enosis*.

In Cyprus, the struggle for *enosis* had intensified when in 1948 the Greek Cypriots rejected a "home-rule" plan of Britain which would have granted self-government to Cyprus. Makarios, then Bishop of Kition, was among those who opposed the plan and started an enosis campaign by establishing the Ethnarchy Bureau.[28] After the Greek Cypriot rejection of the "home-rule" plan, thousands of Turkish Cypriots demonstrated in the major cities of Cyprus and sent a telegram to Ankara, stating:

> . . . Turkish Cypriots decided unanimously to reject the Greek demand for the annexation of Cyprus by Greece and for autonomy. They believe that annexation and autonomy would result in the annihilation of the Turkish community.[29]

On 15 January 1950, the Orthodox Church of Cyprus organized a plebiscite, and Greek Cypriots were asked to choose between the status-quo or *enosis*. Ninety-six percent of those voting preferred *enosis*.[30] Makarios hoped that the results of this informal plebiscite would convince the U.N. to force the British to grant self-determination to Cyprus.

In July 1952 Makarios and George Grivas, a former colonel of the Greek army, and a number of other Greek Cypriots established the "Struggle Committee" in Athens. Makarios was elected chairman. On 7 March 1953, "the members of the Committee took a pledge to dedicate their lives to the cause of *enosis* and to maintain the strictest secrecy about their activities." Makarios rejected, however, Grivas's suggestion that an armed rebellion should immediately be started. He was still hopeful that the U.N. would grant self-determination to Cyprus.[31]

Turkey's Initial Reactions

As suggested earlier, Turkey recognized Britain's annexation of Cyprus in 1923 and encouraged Turkish Cypriots to emigrate to Turkey. Because of the improvement in Turco-British relations in the 1930s, Turkey had little concern that the island might be used as a staging ground for attacks against itself.[32] Especially during the late 1940s and 1950s Turkey was in favor of British sovereignty over Cyprus because it believed that the British presence on the island would function as a deterrent against Soviet expansionism in the Middle East. Turkish governments also did not expect that Britain would ever decide to leave the island. It is not surprising that the foreign minister of the RPP Government, Necmettin Sadak, told the National Assembly on 30 October 1948 that "there is not a Cyprus problem as such."[33]

The foreign minister of the DP Government, Fuat Koprulu, made a similar statement on 20 August 1951: "We don't see any reason for a change in the *status quo* of Cyprus. But, if there would be a change . . . our rights have to be respected . . ." Koprulu added that under the current world conditions which "required unconditional solidarity of free nations," issues such as the Cyprus problem should not be raised.[34]

Koprulu's statement shows that given the Soviet threat, Turkey was against an internal quarrel within the Western camp over an issue as "peripheral" as

Cyprus. Second, Turkey did not propose an alternative to British sovereignty. Koprulu stated that Turkey's "rights" had to be respected, but he did not spell out what these "rights" were because neither he nor the rest of the Government had determined what Turkey's Cyprus policy should be. The opposition was in no better shape. Inonu said on 28 August 1954 that he was "against a revision of the *status quo* in Cyprus," but he, too, failed to offer an alternative.[35]

The initial uncertainty on the part of the DP Administration gave way to a search for alternative solutions in the mid-1950s. Three different solutions were subsequently adopted: (1) the return of the island to Turkey; (2) partition; (3) independence. The first two alternatives were as easily abandoned as they were adopted once it became clear that they were infeasible. Compared to its initial uncertainty, the DP's flexibility and resourcefulness may seem surprising. Yet one should remember that Turkey's "policy on Cyprus underwent changes because it was not a policy of active irredentism, but one of reaction to Greek irredentism."[36] As a result, Turkish Governments of the 1950s and 1960s were ready to compromise in Cyprus, provided they did not look like losers.

Greece Raises the Issue at the U.N.

On 22 September 1953, a meeting took place between British Foreign Secretary Anthony Eden and Greek Prime Minister Marshal Papagos in Athens. When Papagos brought up the Cyprus question, Eden refused to discuss it and told Papagos that as far as Britain was concerned there was no Cyprus problem.[37] As this event shows, Britain was not ready to give up its sovereignty over Cyprus, even though in 1948 it had proposed self-government or autonomy.

Greece was also unsuccessful with the U.N. Starting in 1954, Greece had sponsored draft resolutions calling for international support of Cypriot self-determination. Greece's attempts failed, however, due to opposition from NATO countries. Greece's first endeavor was defeated in the General Assembly on 17 December 1954 by a vote of fifty to none with eight abstentions.[38]

Turkish U.N. Representative Selim Sarper told the U.N. General Assembly on the same day that the status of the island had been determined by the Treaty of Lausanne in 1923 and that "Greece [was] equally a signatory of its own free will and without any reservations." Sarper added that the U.N. was not competent to revise international treaties. Three days earlier, Sarper had stated in the First Committee that the U.N. should not deal with the Cyprus question because it was an internal affair of Britain, and, the provisions of Article 2, paragraph 7 of the U.N. Charter excluded U.N. intervention in the domestic affairs of any state.[39]

The U.S. also sided with Britain at the U.N. in 1954 and in following years. The main U.S. goal was to prevent the Cyprus issue from destabilizing NATO's southeastern flank. U.S. policymakers believed that the best way to achieve that goal was through bilateral and, after Turkey's involvement, trilateral negotiations.[40] On 16 November 1954, Secretary of State John F. Dulles sent a message to Greek Premier Papagos and told him that since the U.N.'s "adoption of any resolution would harm good relations between some of our friends and allies, . . . [w]e shall be obliged to oppose the adoption of any substantive resolution."[41]

One year later the U.S. position had not changed. The U.N. Representative of the U.S., Henry C. Lodge, stated on 21 September 1955 that the Cyprus question could be solved more easily if the U.N. General Assembly did not debate the issue. Lodge added that the U.S. decision had not been an easy one: "To make a decision which may be contrary to the desires of our Greek friends to whom we feel so close is particularly painful to us . . . "[42]

Turkey Demands the Return of Cyprus

By the end of 1954 Makarios, who had earlier opposed armed rebellion, changed his mind. He told Grivas in January 1955 that the armed struggle of EOKA [National Organization of Cypriot Fighters] should begin in March 1955. The Greek Government, too, had reconsidered its position and in January 1955 agreed to supply the EOKA fighters in Cyprus.[43]

EOKA was established by Grivas with Makarios' approval as the "fighting arm of the Ethnarchy." Makarios believed that only a limited number of guerrilla operations would be necessary to convince the British to leave Cyprus. Nevertheless, EOKA gradually grew into a very strong and effective guerrilla organization.[44]

It was also in 1955 that the Turkish Cypriot community became politically active. As the Turkish Cypriot leader Denktash suggests, the Turkish Cypriots perceived *enosis* as "colonization, loss of all human rights and physical elimination [of Turks] from Cyprus."[45] The Cyprus Turkish National Party, established in 1945, was renamed in 1955 the Cyprus Turkish Party after EOKA started its rebellion. During this period a paramilitary organization, the TMT [*Turk Mukavemet Teshkilati*, or Turkish Resistance Organization] was established which effectively defended Turkish Cypriots against EOKA attacks.[46]

Faced with the initiation of guerrilla warfare in Cyprus, the Turkish Government quickly revised its previous Cyprus policy. Whereas it had argued earlier that Cyprus was an internal affair of Britain, it began to suggest in 1955 that if Britain were to give up Cyprus, possession of the island should revert to Turkey. On 24 August 1955 Prime Minister Menderes stated that the ethnic factor was not enough to determine "the fate of an area." He added:

> One should also take into account geographic, political, economic and military

> factors and historic events . . . Cyprus is a continuation of the Anatolian peninsula. It is very important for the security of Anatolia. If there would be a change in sovereignty of Cyprus it should correspond not to technical facts but to much more important realities . . . [T]he preservation of the status quo is the most Turkey could accept.[47]

At the London Conference (29 August-7 September 1955) convened by Britain, Turkish Foreign Minister Zorlu told his British and Greek counterparts that self-government, as proposed by Britain, was not acceptable to Turkey as long as *enosis* was not excluded as an eventual outcome of self-government. He added:

> If a change in the status quo is desired, Turkey would demand a return to *status quo ante*. . . . Cyprus should be in the hands of either Turkey or a Middle Eastern country allied to Turkey. This means that if Turkey enters a war, Cyprus should be on its side. Otherwise, the defense and supply of [Turkey's southern coast] cannot be realized.[48]

The conference ended in failure because both Greece and Turkey rejected Britain's offer of self-government for different reasons. Turkey objected because Britain failed to assure it that self-government would not lead to *enosis*. Greece objected because *enosis* was not clearly identified as an eventual result of self-government.[49] Turkey's and Greece's attitudes toward self-government would continue unchanged throughout the late 1950s when they rejected similar British offers of self-government, such as the Radcliffe Proposal (December 1956), the Foot Plan (December 1957), and the Macmillan Plan (June 1958).[50]

Turkey Adopts the Taksim [Partition] Thesis

Turkey made its 1955 demand for the return of Cyprus to Turkey as a reaction to Greece's *enosis* efforts. The Menderes Administration improvised the Turkish version of *enosis* as a means to oppose the *enosis* movement. Menderes did not seriously believe that Turkey would ever be sovereign over the whole island. Turkey never even presented the U.N. with draft resolutions calling for the return of Cyprus to Turkey. In 1956, Menderes gave a list to Nihat Erim, Turkey's representative at various Cyprus negotiations, that included Turkey's preferences for a Cyprus solution. They ranged from the best to the worst alternatives:

> (1) the British should stay in Cyprus; (2) if they left, Cyprus should revert to Turkey; (3) Cyprus should be partitioned; (4) self-government [under formal British sovereignty]; (5) the worst alternative is Cyprus's unification with Greece.[51]

This list clearly indicates that Turkey still believed that British sovereignty over Cyprus was the best solution, albeit infeasible in the long run. Since the second alternative was never seriously considered, Menderes started in 1956 to call for *taksim*, or partition, as a practical solution which might be acceptable to all interested parties. When the opposition RPP criticized this change, Menderes replied in the National Assembly on 28 December 1956:

> Cyprus is not the only problem Turkey has. Turkey cannot afford to spend all of its material and spiritual potential for Cyprus . . . Such a behaviour would create additional problems for us and for the world when the ways of life of nations are already threatened.[52]

Menderes' statement shows that despite the adoption of a more active Cyprus policy since the early 1950s, Turkey still considered the Soviet Union the most important national security threat. Therefore, it was not willing to create disunity within NATO in order to achieve its objectives in Cyprus. The Greek government, for which Cyprus was more of a national cause, shared the same sentiment with Turkey. Greek Prime Minister Karamanlis told the Greek Parliament on 14 March 1957:

> Greece is obligated to conduct the Cyprus struggle within the boundaries of her alliances. This last point renders the Cyprus problem an issue with dramatic contradictions. There are moments during which a policy that promotes the Cyprus problem could be damaging for Free Greece.[53]

However, Greece continued using peaceful methods and appealed to the U.N. in 1957 and 1958. In both cases Greece was turned down, and the U.N. adopted resolutions calling for negotiations among interested parties.[54] As in the previous U.N. debates, the members of the Commonwealth, NATO and the Baghdad Pact sided with Britain and Turkey, whereas the Soviet bloc and most Arab states supported Greece's appeals.[55]

After its initial criticism of the adoption of *taksim* as Turkey's official Cyprus policy, the RPP avoided discussing the issue further. This was not uncharacteristic of Inonu, the RPP chairman, who usually shunned public debate of foreign policy issues. Inonu stated at an election rally in October 1957 that he did not want to talk about Cyprus because he did not want the government to face difficulties at home when dealing with foreign governments. In December 1957 Inonu further revised his position and told the National Assembly that "we approve the settlement of the conflict between two friendly nations [Greece, Turkey] by partitioning Cyprus."[56]

The Birth of the Cyprus Republic

The British Government announced in 1958 that despite Greece's objection, Britain would implement the Macmillan Plan granting self-government to Cyprus. The British also concluded that the ongoing EOKA warfare made the continuation of British rule very costly. Therefore, Britain was ready to give up its sovereignty over Cyprus provided it received military bases in return.[57]

By 1959, Karamanlis, the Greek Prime Minister, and Makarios had adopted the belief that for the time being there was no possibility of achieving *enosis* through the U.N., and that the British attempt to unilaterally implement the Macmillan Plan could lead to unwanted results, including partition. As a result of these developments, the Greeks and Greek Cypriots began to consider independence an acceptable first stage solution of the Cyprus crisis.[58]

The Menderes Administration on the other hand had repeatedly called for negotiations among interested states. It demanded partition only in reaction to the *enosis* policy of Greece and EOKA. So when Greece opted for negotiations after the November 1958 U.N. debate, Turkey joined Greece without hesitation. On 18 December 1958 Turkish and Greek Foreign Ministers, Zorlu and Averoff, met in Paris and agreed to a meeting between the prime ministers of their countries.[59]

Turkish and Greek Prime Ministers, Menderes and Karamanlis, met in Zurich 5-11 February 1959 and agreed on a general plan for a settlement. This general plan contained almost all important aspects of the final settlement. On 17 February Turkish and Greek Cypriot representatives, Dr. Fazil Kucuk and Archbishop Makarios, joined British, Turkish and

Greek prime ministers for a final conference in London.

Before and during the London Conference, Makarios complained to Karamanlis about some parts of the Zurich Agreement. He especially opposed granting a veto right to the Turkish Cypriot vice-president and Turkey's right of intervention as stipulated in the Treaty of Guarantee. Makarios also objected to the stationing of Greek and Turkish troops in Cyprus as provided in the Treaty of Alliance. Nevertheless, he signed the Zurich-London Agreements as did the others on 19 February 1959.[60]

After the conference, Turkish, Turkish Cypriot, Greek and Greek Cypriot representatives drafted the Cyprus constitution. The Republic was proclaimed on 16 August 1960.[61] According to Art. 1 of the constitution "[t]he State of Cyprus is an independent and sovereign Republic with a presidential regime, the President being Greek and the Vice-President being Turk elected by the Greek and the Turkish Communities of Cyprus . . . "[62] Art. 48d provided the president or the vice-president with the "right of final veto on decisions of the Council of Ministers concerning foreign affairs, defence or security." The president or the vice-president could also veto the laws or decisions of the House of Representatives concerning foreign affairs, defense or security. (Art. 48f)[63]

The constitution also stipulated that the Council of Ministers would be composed of seven Greek and three Turkish ministers who would be designated respectively by the president and the vice-president. One of the posts of defense, foreign Affairs or finance minister would be reserved for a Turkish Cypriot. The decisions of the Council were to be taken by an absolute majority.(Art. 46)[64]

The legislative body of the Republic, the House of Representatives, would include 50 members, 70 percent of whom were to be elected by the Greek community and 30 percent by the Turkish community.(Art. 62)[65] The adoption of any law relating to the municipalities and of any law imposing duties and taxes required "a separate simple majority of the Representatives elected by the Greek and Turkish Communities respectively taking part in the vote."(Art. 78)[66]

The constitution also provided that "[t]he public service shall be composed as to seventy per centum of Greeks and as to thirty per centum of Turks"(Art.123)[67] The police force also was to be apportioned between Greeks and Turks on the principle of a seventy to thirty ratio.(Art. 130)[68] The army on the other hand would be composed of 2,000 men of whom 60 percent would be Greeks and 40 percent Turks.(Art.129)[69]

Article 173 of the constitution provided for the establishment of separate municipalities in the five largest towns of the Republic—Nicosia, Limassol, Famagusta, Larnaca and Paphos—by the Turkish Cypriots.[70] This article and the other previously mentioned articles were considered the "basic Articles" of the constitution. They guaranteed institutional protection of Turkish Cypriots' representation at many levels of the government and their veto power over some critical issues. Moreover, Article 182 of the constitution stipulated that these "basic Articles . . . cannot, in any way, be amended." The remaining provisions of the constitution could be revised with the approval of the two-thirds majority of the Representatives of each community.[71]

The Treaty of Guarantee and the Treaty of Alliance concluded in London between Britain, Greece and Turkey were annexed to the constitution. Article 181 of the constitution stated that these two treaties "shall have constitutional force."[72] After the intercommunal violence of 1964, these two treaties were repeatedly denounced by Makarios as encroaching upon the sovereignty of Cyprus. The Treaty of Alliance provided for the stationing of 950 Greek and 650 Turkish troops in Cyprus.[73] Article IV of the Treaty of Guarantee, upon which Turkey based its right of intervention in 1974, stipulated:

> In the event of a breach of the provisions of the present Treaty, Greece, Turkey and the United Kingdom undertake to consult together with respect to the representations or measures necessary to ensure observance of those provisions.
>
> In so far as common or concerted action may not prove possible, each of the three guaranteeing Powers reserves the right to take action with the sole aim of re-establishing the state of affairs created by the present Treaty.[74]

Another important feature of the 1959 settlement was that Britain retained sovereignty over two bases in Cyprus covering an area of ninety-nine square miles. The borders of these bases (Akrotiri and Dhekelia) were subsequently negotiated between the British Government and the representatives of two Cypriot communities, and an agreement was reached on 1 July 1960.[75]

Turkey Accepts the 1959 Settlement

When the Zurich-London Agreements came before the Turkish National Assembly, the opposition RPP considered them a failure. On 4 March 1959, Ismet Inonu, the RPP chairman, told the assembly that the DP Administration failed to implement the parliament's *taksim* (partition) resolution, and the 1959 settlement explicitly ruled out the partition of the island in the future.[76]

Inonu added that the independence of Cyprus limited the range of actions Turkey could undertake if new crises arose in Cyprus:

> Cyprus will become a U.N. member and in case of a conflict, the U.N. would deal with it. Therefore, Turkey could prevent *enosis*

> only if it acted quickly. However, no one can be sure that conditions would always enable Turkey to act quickly. Hence the possibility of *enosis* still exists.[77]

Inonu also prophesied that the Greek Cypriots would try to ignore those articles of the constitution which provided for the participation of Turkish Cypriots in the administration of the island: "As long as both communities are not convinced that *enosis* is not possible in the long run, we will have a difficult time to ensure that other articles of the constitution are implemented."[78] As we will see in the next chapter, the events in Cyprus followed a course quite similar to that described by Inonu.

Menderes considered the 1959 settlement neither a victory nor a defeat for Turkey. In a statement on 13 February 1959 he defended the Zurich-London Agreements as "a compromise which was not against Turkey's national interests and which respected the other party's rights and interests."[79] The vote in the National Assembly on 4 March 1959 was divided along party lines. All 347 votes cast in favor of the Zurich-London Agreements belonged to DP deputies; all of the 138 votes cast against it belonged to the RPP.[80]

The Turkish public seemed to accept Menderes' explanation that the 1959 Agreements were not contrary to Turkey's national interests. The flexibility with which not only the Government, but also the public, accepted compromises stemmed from the fact that Turkey did not have an irredentist Cyprus policy. The assurance given by the DP Government that the Turkish Cypriots would have constitutionally guaranteed rights, and that Turkey as a guarantor power would prevent any violation of these rights, convinced the Turks that Cyprus was not going to be "lost."[81] As a result, no demonstrations against the Agreements took place. Even Inonu, who initially opposed the Agreements, ceased to criticize them after their approval by the National Assembly.

Conclusion

Throughout the 1950s, Turkey's Cyprus policy evolved as a reaction to Greek and Greek Cypriot actions. During the early 1950s, Turkish policymakers refused to accept that there was a Cyprus question as such. Toward the middle of the decade, however, they became convinced that Cyprus was vitally important to the security of Turkey and that it should not fall into the hands of hostile powers. In order to ensure that, the DP Administration favored the return of the island to Turkey (1955) and later its partition (1956).

Between 1950 and 1960 Turkey was anxious to coordinate its Cyprus policy with Britain and the U.S. and to compromise on its stated objectives. The main reason for Turkey's flexibility was the conviction of most Turks that the Soviet Union continued to be the real threat, and that Turkey should not alienate its NATO allies. Second, since Turkey did not strive for a Turkish version of *enosis*, but only desired that Cyprus should not come under the control of a hostile power, it could afford to be tractable. Turkey's abandonment of the *taksim* thesis in favor of Cypriot independence was hence not a major policy change, but rather a liberal implementation of the same policy.

The U.S. adopted a passive role toward Cyprus during the same decade because it considered Cyprus within Britain's sphere of influence. The U.S. was mainly concerned that the Cyprus crisis would cause a deterioration of relations between three of its allies and weaken NATO. It did not object to *enosis* or *taksim per se*, provided that these solutions came as a result of trilateral negotiations. Hence, the U.S. opposed Greece's recourse to the U.N. and called for negotiations among interested parties.

The Zurich-London settlement and the declaration of Cyprus' independence was thus a welcome development for both Turkey and the U.S.

The U.S. was pleased with the compromise agreements which seemed to eliminate a serious friction point in the relations of three of its allies. For the moment the stability and viability of the Western Alliance seemed assured. Turkey was also pleased with the settlement because in return for its recognition of Cyprus' independence, Turkish Cypriots were granted constitutional guarantees which would not only enable them to exist as a community, but would also ensure their full participation in the administration of the state. Moreover, Turkey's fears that Cyprus could one day come under the control of a hostile state and become a threat to Turkish security were alleviated by the Treaty of Guarantee which accorded Turkey a right of intervention.

NOTES

1. *Cumhuriyet* [Turkish daily], Istanbul, 28 August 1948.

2. George Harris, *Troubled Alliance* (Washington, D.C.: American Enterprise Institute, 1972), p. 63.

3. *Cumhuriyet*, 21 July 1951.

4. For Foreign Minister Zorlu's statement see: *The New York Times*, 16 July 1958; Harris, *op. cit.*, p. 67.

5. See: *Akis* [Turkish weekly], 2 August 1958, p. 7.

6. *Cumhuriyet*, 18 May 1960, pp. 1,3.

7. Nancy Crawshaw, *The Cyprus Revolt* (London: George Allen & Unwin, 1978), pp. 19-20; Kyriacos C. Markides, *The Rise and Fall of the Cyprus Republic* (New Haven and London: Yale University Press, 1977), p. 2; Sir George Hill, *A History of Cyprus* (Cambridge: Cambridge University Press, 1952); Thomas Ehrlich, *Cyprus: 1958-1967* (New York, London: Oxford University Press, 1974), p. 1.

8. Crawshaw, *op. cit.*, p. 19; Markides, *op. cit.*, p. 3.

9. Crawshaw, *op. cit.*, p. 19.

10. Markides, *op. cit.*, p. 3; see: *U.N. Official Records of the General Assembly*, Ninth Session, First Committee, 1954, 749th meeting, 14 December 1954, p. 553; Richard Patrick, *Political Geography and the Cyprus Conflict* (Ontario,

Canada: University of Waterloo, 1976), p. 8; Sharon A. Wiener, "Turkish Foreign Policy Decision Making on the Cyprus Issue" (Ph.D. dissertation, Duke University, 1980), p. 48.

11. Hill, *op. cit.*, Vol. IV, p. 68.

12. Markides, *op. cit.*, p. 5.

13. They were Kars, Ardahan and Batum. See: Alvin Z. Rubinstein, *Soviet Policy Toward Turkey, Iran and Afghanistan* (New York: Praeger, 1982), p. 3; Ehrlich, *op. cit.*, p. 2. For the 1878 Convention see: "Convention of Defensive Alliance Between Great Britain and Turkey with Respect to the Asiatic Provinces of Turkey, 4 June 1878," *Accounts and Papers*, Vol. 82 (1878), pp. 3-4.

14. Zenon Stavrinides, *The Cyprus Conflict: National Identity and Statehood* (Wakefield: Stavrinides, 1976), p. 20.

15. *Ibid.*, p. 22.

16. Hill, *op. cit.*, Vol. IV, p. 510.

17. Stavrinides, *op. cit.*, p. 25.

18. See Art. 20 of the *Treaty of Peace with Turkey*, Cmd. 1929 (London: Her Majesty's Stationary Office, 1923), p. 22.

19. Nihat Erim, *Bildigim ve Gordugum Olculer Icinde Kibris* (Ankara: Ajans-Turk, 1975), pp. 1-2.

20. For the National Pact, see: J.C. Hurewitz, *Diplomacy in the Near and Middle East* (Vol. II, Princeton, New Jersey: D. Van Nostrand, 1956), pp. 74-75.

21. Art. 21 of the *Treaty of Peace with Turkey*, p. 22.

22. G. S. Georghallides, "Turkish and British Reactions to the Emigration of the Cypriot Turks to Anatolia," *Balkan Studies*, Vol. XVIII (1977), No. 1, pp. 43-52.

23. *Greek Parliamentary Record*, 18 Nov. 1931 in Michael A. Attalides, *Cyprus: Nationalism and International Politics* (New York: St. Martin's Press, 1979), pp. 59-60.

24. Markides, *op. cit.*, p. 123.

25. *Foreign Relations of the United States, 1942* (Vol. II, Washington, D.C.: GPO, 1962), p. 825.

26. Markides, *op. cit.*, p. 123.

27. Markides, *op. cit.*, p. 124.

28. Stavrinides, *op. cit.*, p. 67.

29. *Ibid.*, p. 27.

30. Dimitri S. Bitsios, *Cyprus: The Vulnerable Republic* (Thessaloniki: Institute for Balkan Studies, 1975), p. 40.

31. Stephen Xydis, "Toward 'Toil and Moil' in Cyprus," *The Middle East Journal*, Vol. XX, No. 1 (Winter 1966), p. 8.

32. Ehrlich, *op. cit.*, p. 18.

33. Sevket Sureyya Aydemir, *Ikinci Adam* ("Second Man") (Vol. III, Ankara: Remzi Kitabevi, 1975), p. 217.

34. Suat Bilge, "Kibris Uyusmazligi" ("The Cyprus Conflict"), *Olaylarla Turk Dis Politikasi* (Ankara: Ankara Universitesi, 1977), p. 351.

35. Mumtaz Soysal, *Dis Politika ve Parlamento* ("Foreign Policy and the Parliament") (Ankara: Siyasal Bilgiler Fakultesi, 1964), p. 240.

36. Andrew Mango, "The State of Turkey," *Middle Eastern Studies*, Vol. XIII (May, 1977), No. 2, pp. 171-172; See also Sharon A. Wiener, "Turkish Foreign Policy Decision Making on the Cyprus Issue" (Ph.D. dissertation, Duke University, 1980), p. 76.

37. Bitsios, *op. cit.*, p. 19; Christopher Hitchens, *Cyprus* (New York: Quartet Books, 1984), p. 37.

38. U.N., *Official Records of the General Assembly, Ninth Session: Plenary Meetings, 1954*, 514th meeting, 17 December 1954, p. 539.

39. U.N., *Official Records of the General Assembly, Ninth Session: First Committee, 1954*, 749th meeting, 14 December 1954, p. 544.

40. Theodore A. Coulombis, *The United States, Greece and Turkey: The Troubled Triangle* (New York: Praeger, 1983), P. 32.

41. Stephen G. Xydis, *Cyprus: Conflict and Conciliation, 1954-1958* (Columbus, Ohio: The Ohio State University Press, 1967), p. 599.

42. U. S. Department of State, *Department of State Bulletin*, Vol. XXXIII (July-December, 1955), p. 545.

43. United Nations, *Records of the General Assembly*, 11th Session (1956/57), Annexes, Vol. II, Document A/C.1/788, p. 6.

44. Bitsios, *op. cit.*, p. 43; Crawshaw, *op. cit.*, pp. 90-113.

45. Rauf Denktash, *The Cyprus Triangle* (Boston: George Allen & Unwin, 1982), p. 196.

46. Attalides, *op. cit.*, p. 46; Stanley Kyriakides, *Cyprus: Constitutionalism and Crisis Government* (Philadelphia: University of Pennsylvania Press, 1968), p. 28.

47. Bilge, *op. cit.*, pp. 354-355; Crawshaw, *op. cit.*, p. 133.

48. Bilge, *op. cit.*, p. 357.

49. *Ibid.*, Crawshaw, *op. cit.*, p. 134.

50. The Macmillan Plan was somewhat different from other plans in that it provided for a division of sovereignty of Cyprus among Britain, Greece, and Turkey at the end of seven years of self-government. After its initial rejection Turkey accepted the plan. Greece continued to object. See: Bilge, *op. cit.*, p. 375; Bitsios, *op. cit.*, pp. 70-71; Crawshaw, *op. cit.*, p. 667; Harold Macmillan, *Riding the Storm: 1956-1959* (London: Macmillan, 1971), p. 687. For other plans, see: Crawshaw, *op. cit.*, pp. 274-277; Bilge, *op. cit.*, p. 363; Ehrlich, *op. cit.*, pp. 26-27.

51. Erim, *op. cit.*, p. 17.

52. Bilge, *op. cit.*, pp. 368-69.

53. Markides, *op. cit.*, p. 63.

54. *U.N. General Assembly Official Records 1956/57, Annexes*, Agenda Item 55, p. 18; *U.N. General Assembly Official Records, 1958/59 Annexes*, Agenda Item 68, pp. 14-19.

55. *Ibid*., Bitsios, *op. cit*, pp. 59-60.

56. Bilge, *op. cit*., p. 371.

57. Ehrlich, *op. cit*., p. 20; Crawshaw, *op. cit*., p. 259; Kyriakides, *op. cit*., p. 141; Macmillan, *op. cit*., pp. 667-687.

58. Charles Foley, *A Legacy of Strife* (London: Penguin, 1964), p. 27; Markides, *op. cit*., pp. 36-37.

59. Bitsios, *op. cit*., p. 102; Crawshaw, *op. cit*., p. 340.

60. Crawshaw, *op. cit*., p. 345; Bitsios, *op. cit*., p. 102. For the text: *Conference on Cyprus: Documents Signed and Initialed At Lancaster House on February 19, 1959*, (London: Her Majesty's Stationary Office, 1959), Cmnd. 680.

61. Albert P. Blaustein, Gisbert H. Flanz, *Constitutions of the Countries of the World: Cyprus* (Dobbs Ferry, N.Y.: Oceana Publications, 1972).

62. *Ibid*., *p. 1.*

63. *Ibid*., p. 21.

64. *Ibid*., p. 20.

65. *Ibid*., p. 28.

66. *Ibid*., p. 33.

67. *Ibid*., p. 48.

68. *Ibid*., p. 51.

69. *Ibid*., p. 51.

70. *Ibid.*, p. 69.

71. *Ibid.*, p. 72.

72. *Ibid.*, p. 71.

73. *Ibid.*, p. 84.

74. *Ibid.*, p. 82.

75. Great Britain, *Cyprus*, Cmnd. 1093 (London: Her Majesty's Stationary Office, 1960).

76. *Cumhuriyet*, Istanbul, 5 March 1959, pp. 1,5.

77. *Ibid.*

78. *Ibid.*

79. Bilge, *op. cit.*, p. 380.

80. *Cumhuriyet*, Istanbul, 5 March 1959, pp. 1,5.

81. *Cumhuriyet*, 5 March 1959.

II. 1964 Cyprus Crisis

Turkish Foreign Policy, 1960-1963

When the Republic of Cyprus was proclaimed on 16 August 1960, Turkish Premier Menderes had already been overthrown (27 May 1960) by a military junta. This coup was the first indication of a period of political instability which lasted until the Justice Party's (JP) landslide victory in the 1965 elections and affected Turkey's response to the 1964 Cyprus crisis. During this period two coup attempts took place and four different coalition governments—excluding the military regime in 1960—came to power.[1] Moreover, the military often interfered in the domestic politics and manipulated the composition of coalition governments in order to prevent the accession of Menderes faithful to power.[2]

Until the fourth coalition (February 1965), which excluded Inonu's Republican People's Party (RPP), the military insisted on including the RPP in all coalition governments because the RPP was perceived as a reformist party with similar goals as the putschists of 1960. The right-wing parties, which captured a total of 63 percent of the vote in the 1961 elections, had to accept Inonu as Prime Minister even though his party received only 37 percent of the vote.[3]

Throughout this period, many cliques within the armed forces who were dissatisfied with the National Assembly's failure to carry out socio-economic reforms plotted to overthrow the Inonu coalition governments. Yet only twice did the planners of these coups dare to implement their plans. Both the coup attempts of 22 February 1962 and 21 May 1963, which were led by Colonel Talat Aydemir, failed. After his second attempt, Aydemir was tried and subsequently executed.[4]

Despite the various domestic controversies which plagued the period between 1960 and 1964, the main tenets of the Turkish foreign policy, including reliance on NATO to assure national security, remained unchanged, and all coalition governments indicated that they were not interested in revising them. Before the 1961 elections, Inonu stated that ". . . Turkey's foreign policy has remained the same for a long time. It is a national foreign policy. The RPP will not change it."[5] Even the military junta (June 1960-October 1961) whose agenda comprised giant socio-economic transformations had little to say on foreign policy. On the day of the coup (27 May 1960) the putschists announced that they respected Turkey's links with NATO and CENTO and were thus in conformity with the post-World War II consensus.[6]

Relations with the U.S.S.R. did not improve despite some Soviet overtures immediately after the 27 May 1960 coup. In a letter to President Cemal Gursel on 28 June 1960, Khrushchev stated that Soviet-Turkish relations would improve "if Turkey embarked upon the road of neutrality." Khrushchev added that Turkey's neutrality would benefit its economy because "Turkey would receive an opportunity to use her resources . . . for . . . the well-being of its people." Khrushchev added, however, that the Soviets would still be ready to normalize relations even if Turkey remained in NATO.[7]

Later it was disclosed that the U.S.S.R. also had urged the junta to remain in power and offered $500 million in aid. President Gursel replied that Turkey was ready to normalize relations, but rejected the aid offer.[8] The Soviets repeated the same offer to Inonu in 1961 when he became prime minister. Inonu, too, rejected the offer because he, like the junta, apparently believed that Soviet aid would be linked to political concessions on Turkey's part.[9]

Turkish-American relations continued to be as close as they were during the 1950s. Major events of this period—the Cuban missile crisis and the withdrawal of Jupiter missiles from Turkey—did not diminish Turkey's confidence in U.S. reliability and alliance solidarity. After receiving President Kennedy's request for solidarity on 22 October 1962, Inonu told the National Assembly the next day that "when we are in danger, we expect our allies to support us. Likewise, we have to stand by our allies if they are in danger."[10] As signs of solidarity, Turkish ships refused to deliver goods to Cuba until the end of the crisis, and on 25 October 1962 student organizations issued declarations supporting the U.S. policy toward Cuba.[11]

After the crisis the Government publicly supported the U.S. decision to remove the Jupiter missiles from Turkey.[12] Neither the press nor the Government raised any questions suggesting that the withdrawal of these missiles might be a result of an American *quid pro quo* with Moscow.[13] Instead, on 18 February 1963, Inonu's foreign minister, Feridun Cemal Erkin, assured the National Assembly that the Jupiters would be removed because they were outmoded and thus of little help to Turkey's security.[14] The press also refused to contemplate the possibility of a *quid pro quo.* Piri of *Cumhuriyet* wrote that the removal of Jupiters was a U.S. good-will gesture towards the Soviets in order to relax super-power tensions. Piri added somewhat naively that the U.S. decision was motivated by its desire not to make Turkey "a target of a Soviet nuclear strike."[15]

Constitutional Controversies in Cyprus, 1960-1963

After the Zurich-London Agreements in 1959, Makarios returned home believing that he had achieved the first stage of the *enosis* struggle. Makarios assumed that in the long run, the Turks would resign themselves to the gradual elimination of their constitutional rights and accept the status of a minority in a Greek-ruled state. On 1 April 1960, at the ceremonies commemorating the fifth anniversary of the start of the EOKA warfare, Makarios announced:

> The epic grandeur and glory of EOKA's liberation struggle has laid the foundation-stone of national freedom . . . National struggles never come to an end. They merely change their form, preserving deep down the same substance and the same content . . . The realization of our hopes and aspirations is not complete under the Zurich and London Agreements . . . Let us therefore work with faith for the future of our country and let us be certain that the task we began five years ago will soon be completed and bear fruit.[16]

As this statement shows, Makarios still adhered to the ideal of *enosis* even after independence. Given the fact that his traditional legitimacy was based on the understanding that as head of Greek Cypriot Hellenism he would struggle for *enosis*, Makarios often made it known that he regarded the constitution as a necessary evil to be tolerated temporarily.[17]

Between 1960 and the end of 1963, the relations between the two communities were marred by a series of controversies. One of them concerned the opposition of Turkish Cypriot members of the House of Representatives to a new income tax bill which was to replace the colonial law after independence. In order to have time to reach an agreement on the new bill, the old law was renewed until 31 March 1961. At the end of this period, however, Turkish Cypriots refused to go along with another period of extension. As a result of the deadlock the island was left without income tax legislation.[18] Later, the Greek and Turkish Communal Chambers adopted their own tax laws.[19]

Turkish Cypriots' refusal to accept the new law was a retaliation for the Greek side's failure to uphold the 70:30 ratio in the civil service as stipulated in the constitution. The Greek Cypriots argued that they were in favor of only a gradual implementation of the 70:30 ratio because there were not enough qualified Turks to fill 30 percent of the jobs.[20]

Another controversy arose over the establishment of the Cyprus army in January 1961. According to the constitution, "[t]he Republic shall have an army of two thousand men of whom sixty per centum shall be Greeks and forty per centum shall be Turks."[21] The constitution did not specify whether units of the army should be formed on a separate or mixed basis. The Greek members of the Council of Ministers insisted on mixed units. Turkish ministers, too, were in favor of mixed battalions, but they insisted that ethnic separation was necessary on the company level. Turkish ministers argued that religious, linguistic and disciplinary problems could be unmanageable in mixed companies. Despite these objections, the Greek-dominated cabinet passed a resolution establishing a mixed army. Turkish Vice-President Dr. Kuchuk vetoed the resolution, which led Makarios to declare that Cyprus should have no army at all if integration was not possible.[22]

The third controversy concerned the implementation of another "basic article" of the constitution. According to Article 173, "[s]eparate municipalities shall be created in the five largest towns in the Republic, that is to say, Nicosia, Limassol, Famagusta, Larnaca and Paphos by the Turkish inhabitants thereof."[23] Separate municipalities had existed since 1958, and in 1959 the Colonial Administration had recognized them. After independence the representatives of both communities met to determine the respective borders of separate municipalities. In the meantime, the Government renewed the colonial law recognizing separate Turkish municipalities.[24]

By 1962, it became clear that no agreement would be achieved. Makarios, who was against separate municipalities from the outset, proposed on 19 March 1962 the establishment of unified municipalities. According to his proposal the Turks would be represented in the administration of these municipalities in proportion to the whole population in each town.[25] On 2 January 1963, the Greek-dominated cabinet decided to abandon the establishment of separate municipalities.[26] Makarios explained this decision by saying that "the constitutional provision for separate municipalities in the five main towns is wholly inapplicable . . . Neither at present nor in the future will we ever accept geographical partition."[27] Later, the Supreme Court annulled the Government's decision, but the issue remained unresolved.[28]

The above-mentioned examples of intercommunal friction show that the Greek Cypriots believed that the constitutional powers of the Turks were excessive. Throughout 1962 and 1963, the Greek side expressed its desire to revise the constitution which assured Turkish Cypriots a partnership status in the administration of the island. The Greeks resented the fact that they had to share power with a 20 percent minority. Second, as long as the Turkish Cypriots preserved their partnership status, the Greek Cypriots believed that *enosis* would be impossible.

The Turkish Cypriots insisted on the full implementation of the constitution and could be blamed for being inflexible concerning revisions. Their insistence on the 70:30 ratio principle in civil service, for instance, unnecessarily antagonized the Greeks who were not very enthusiastic about the constitution in the first place. The Turks, for their part, feared that a revision of the constitution, however minor, would mean that the whole constitution was open to change. Eventually, they believed, the Turkish Cypriots would lose their communal rights and would become a small minority in a Greek-dominated state.

Toward the middle of 1962, Makarios decided to ignore the appeals of the Turkish Cypriots and achieve Greek Cypriot goals by doing "nothing". He ignored the question of a Turkish quota in civil service, the establishment of the army and separate municipalities. Makarios expected that if he held on long enough to his attrition tactics, the Turkish Cypriots would give up and accept a less prominent place in the administration. In June 1962 Makarios confided to Greece's U.N. Ambassador Bitsios: "I am the head of state and I shall implement my decisions. Let those who disagree appeal to the United Nations, and then we shall see . . . "[29]

Makarios also continued to assure Greek Cypriots that his long term goal was still *enosis*. On 4 September 1962 he made a speech at his birthplace, Panayia, and announced that "[u]ntil this small Turkish community that forms part of the Turkish race and has been the terrible enemy of Hellenism is expelled, the duty to the heroes of EOKA cannot be considered as terminated."[30] Needless to say, such statements were hardly reassuring to the Turkish Cypriots.

Turkey's and America's Reactions

During 1962 and 1963, the last two years preceding the total breakdown of the constitutional order in Cyprus, Turkey continuously urged Makarios and Greece to abide by the constitution. Between 13 February 1962 and 21 December 1963 the Turkish Government delivered fourteen notes to Makarios and eleven notes to Greece. Moreover, when Makarios visited Ankara (22-24 November 1962), Inonu told him that Turkey would not allow him to alter the constitution.[31] Turkish Government officials also publicly registered their opposition to Makarios' violations of the constitution. On 14 January 1963 Turkish Foreign Minister Feridun C. Erkin told the National Assembly that Turkey would not "cede one inch" of the Turkish Cypriots' rights arising out of the 1959 agreements.[32]

Inonu carefully avoided, however, presenting Makarios with an ultimatum. Despite public acknowledgment of the notes, neither he nor other Government officials tried to present the situation in Cyprus to the public as a crisis. Despite Makarios' repeated violations, Inonu perceived the problem as a natural outcome of an intricate constitution, and thus, as manageable if goodwill prevailed on all sides.

During the same period, the U.S. Administration considered the problems in Cyprus to fall into two categories. First, the U.S. was concerned about deteriorating intercommunal relations and did not want Cyprus once again to become a focus of tension between its NATO partners and cripple the alliance. Second, the U.S. disliked the growing influence of the communist AKEL party in Cyprus and Makarios' collaboration with it. Until 1963, the U.S. considered the second concern more urgent. A White House memorandum dealing with Makarios' June 1962 visit to Washington urged President Kennedy to pressure Makarios to establish his own party and lessen his reliance on AKEL.[33] Another memorandum dated 7 January 1963 complained that U.S. support for Makarios had not yet produced effective results and that communist victory in the 1965 elections was still a possibility.[34]

With regard to constitutional controversies between the two Cypriot communities, the U.S. sympathized with Makarios' demand that the constitution should be revised provided that all parties agreed to it. As early as December 1961, Secretary of State Dean Rusk told Cyprus Foreign Minister Kyprianou that "the U.S. Constitution would have been unworkable, too, without continual adjustment and interpretation to meet changing needs."[35]

Yet Rusk counseled moderation and insisted that the "liabilities [of the constitution] can be overcome by reasonable compromises without necessitating formal revision of the agreements."[36]

In February 1963 the State Department became alarmed at the prospect that the municipalities dispute could trigger fighting on the island. Dean Rusk was nevertheless reluctant to directly intervene in the dispute. In a cable sent to the U.S. Ambassador in London, Rusk stated: "We want Britain to emphasize to Greeks and Turks similarities [in] their present positions and guide them to a common stance and coordinated 3-power pressure on Cypriot communities."[37] The American reluctance to interfere with the intercommunal crisis continued until 1964 when the crisis threatened to engulf two NATO allies, Greece and Turkey, in a war.

Fighting Breaks Out: 21 December 1963

By the end of 1963 the intercommunal tensions had deteriorated and the constitutional deadlock seemed as unmanageable as ever. On 30 November 1963 Makarios submitted to Vice-President Kuchuk a list containing his "Proposals to Amend the Cyprus Constitution."[38] These proposals contained most of the Greek revision demands concerning the constitution articulated earlier. Makarios proposed that:

> [t]he right of veto of the President and the Vice-President of the Republic . . . be abandoned . . . The constitutional provisions regarding separate majorities for enactment of certain laws by the House of Representatives . . . be abolished . . . Unified municipalities . . . be established . . . The proportion of the participation of Greek and Turkish Cypriots in the composition of the Public Service and the

> Forces of the Republic . . . be modified in proportion to the ratio of the population of Greek and Turkish Cypriots.[39]

The proposals also included changes that could be considered favorable to Turkish Cypriots. Makarios proposed, for instance, that the Turkish vice-president should be able to deputize for the president.[40] According to the constitution, only the Greek president of the House of Representatives could deputize for the president. Yet as the above-quoted articles suggest, if adopted, the constitutional revisions would have eliminated the quasi-federal nature of the Cypriot state. The Turkish Cypriots would have lost their constitutionally guaranteed rights concerning separate majorities for passage of important legislation, the veto-power of the vice-president, separate municipalities and 30 percent representation in the public service.

It was hence no surprise that both Turkey and the Turkish Cypriots rejected Makarios' proposals out of hand on 16 December 1963. Vice-President Kuchuk argued that these proposals indicated the Greek Cypriots' "preconceived intention to abrogate the constitution and to undermine the present regime."[41] Kuchuk was justified in his suspicion because earlier, on 3 November 1963, Makarios told the congregation of the church of Paralimni: "What is our desire? We have proclaimed it many times: our union with the Motherland, eternal Greece. . . [T]he struggle will continue until complete fulfillment."[42]

As the above quote shows, Makarios was pro-*enosis* even in 1963. Makarios knew, however, that *enosis* was not feasible in the short run because if he moved prematurely to proclaim *enosis*: (1) Turkey might militarily intervene to prevent it; (2) Greece might desist from fighting Turkey if Turkey intervened in Cyprus; (3) the U.S. and NATO might support Turkey's intervention. As Makarios' proposals to amend the constitution suggest, he instead believed in a gradual disenfranchisement of Turkish Cypriots from the state apparatus. Makarios calculated that if he were able to make Turkey accept a Cypriot state dominated by Greek Cypriots, he would have less trouble achieving *enosis* in the long run, especially if Turkey were preoccupied with another security problem.

The intercommunal violence started on 21 December 1963 after Greek Cypriot policemen murdered two Turkish civilians at a checkpoint near the Turkish quarter of Nicosia. Within hours, Greek Cypriot policemen and ex-EOKA irregulars started an all-out attack against number of Turkish quarters throughout Cyprus, but the major assault took place in Nicosia.[43] During the first two days (21-23 December) ten people—nine of them Turks—died as a result of clashes. During the following week (23-30 December) an additional sixty-nine people—forty-nine of them Turks—were murdered.[44]

A number of sources claim that after the Turkish refusal to accept the constitutional amendments, Makarios ordered these attacks in order to achieve the changes by force.[45] As proof of their claim, these sources point to a secret plan published in the Greek Cypriot press.[46] They argue that Makarios set up a secret organization and appointed Interior Minister Yeorgadjis, an ex-EOKA member, as its head. The so-called *Akritas Plan* stated that in order to prepare the way for *enosis*, the Zurich-London Agreements should be revised. If the Turkish Cypriots resisted the revision, it would be necessary

> . . . to suppress this forcefully in the shortest possible time, since if we manage to become the masters of the situation within a day or two, outside intervention [by Turkey] would not be possible, probable or justifiable.[47]

Makarios never denied that he was associated with the *Akritas Plan*, and the events of December 1963 created the perception that the Greek Cypriots actually were trying to implement it. If that was the case, then they failed, because they were unable to establish effective control over the Turkish areas.

During this period, Turkey was experiencing a political crisis. The RPP-New Turkey Party-Republican Peasants' Nation Party coalition government had dissolved on 2 December 1963, and Inonu was trying to form a new government. Until the new RPP-Independents coalition government received a vote of confidence on 3 January 1964, Inonu remained in power as caretaker prime minister.

In an emergency session on 22 December 1963, the Council of Ministers decided that the violence in Cyprus was an isolated event. Inonu told reporters that "an accident" had happened and he hoped that "common sense would bring back the peace. . ."[48] Yet contrary to his public appearance, Inonu was apprehensive about the situation and met with the commanders of the armed forces and the chief of staff several times.[49]

The U.S. reaction was less ambiguous. The U.S. realized that the crisis could lead to a war between Greece and Turkey, destroying the southern flank of NATO. On 23 December 1963, Secretary of State Dean Rusk asked the U.S. Ambassadors in Ankara, Nicosia and Athens to "urge maximum restraint on three governments and on both communities in Cyprus."[50] The same day, when the Turkish military contingent of 650 troops took up positions to protect Turkish Cypriots in northern Cyprus, U.S. Ambassadors in Ankara and Athens went a step further and informed the Turkish and Greek Governments that the "use of MAP [Military Assistance Program] equipment by either [Greek or Turkish] contingent[s] on Cyprus . . . without clear prior consent of [the] U.S. [is considered] a violation of the letter and intent [of] MAP agreements."[51]

On 24 December 1963 violence continued and five more Turks were shot to death. By then it had become clear to Inonu that the Turkish Cypriots were faced with a serious threat. Upon Inonu's prompting, the British and Greek Governments joined Turkey in issuing a cease-fire call the same day. The Turkish Administration also told Britain and Greece that if a cease-fire did not work, a joint military intervention would be necessary.[52]

Since neither Greece nor Britain had yet accepted Turkey's offer of joint intervention, it was inevitable that Inonu engage in his dramatic role of brinkmanship and convince the U.S. and others of his seriousness. At the end of a meeting with a team of military and civilian government officials on 24 December 1963, including Chief of Staff Cevdet Sunay and Foreign Minister Feridun C. Erkin, Inonu ordered low-altitude warning flights over Cyprus. It was also decided that if Greek attacks did not stop, aerial bombings should take place.[53]

The flights, conducted by five aircraft on 25 December 1963, had the effect Inonu desired. Within two hours both Britain and Greece informed Turkey that they would join in a peacekeeping operation. On 26 December 1963 British, Greek and Turkish ambassadors proposed the joint peace-keeping plan to Makarios who accepted it. The so-called "joint peacekeeping operation" actually provided for British troop patrols, and Turkish and Greek contingents did not participate.[54]

The establishment of the "joint" peace force seemed to please all parties, though violence continued on a lower scale. Makarios was pleased because Turkish military intervention was avoided. The Turkish government also seemed pleased. Foreign Minister Erkin, in his address to the Senate, described the "joint" peacekeeping operation as Turkey's use of its intervention rights under article four of the Treaty of Guarantee of 1959.[55] In reality, the introduction of British troops was to keep order and prevent the outbreak of new hostilities. Contrary to Erkin's statements, they were not authorized to restore the constitutional order in Cyprus. On the other hand, the engagement of British forces could be considered a diplomatic success for Inonu given the fact that, as he later admitted, he had then no intent to intervene in Cyprus.[56]

Inonu justified his behavior by saying that "one shouldn't play into the hands of provacateurs. . . . We have to remain calm in order to examine the events."[57] Inonu also justified his decision by notifying the Senate on 3 January 1964 that when violence started in Cyprus, Turkey could not intervene immediately because the Treaty of Guarantee required consultations among guarantor powers. He added that when Britain and Greece offered the establishment of a joint peacekeeping force, he had no other option but to accept it. Inonu concluded that Turkey could not intervene before exhausting all other alternatives.[58]

Inonu's policy at the initial stage of the crisis was supported by his party and the pro-RPP press. *Milliyet's* editor in chief stated that Turkey's intervention at an early stage could be counterproductive and that world public opinion was not yet convinced that Turkey's cause was justified.[59] Another *Milliyet* writer, Cetin Altan, wrote that Inonu's method of solving crises by using his intelligence was superior to "brute force."[60] The main opposition party, the Justice Party (JP), was, however, critical of what it called "Inonu's passivity." Several JP deputies criticized Inonu for having missed an opportunity to intervene in Cyprus. The tone of criticism was conciliatory, though. Most of the speakers concluded that Turkey still had time to adopt an effective policy toward Cyprus.[61]

Inonu's decision not to intervene was also in accordance with American wishes. In one of his cables on 25 December 1963, the day Turkish planes overflew Nicosia, Dean Rusk stated that the U.S. was "urging Turks in both Washington and Ankara [to] avoid unilateral intervention."[62] The U.S. did not, however, choose to play a prominent role in solving the conflict. The State Department's policy directive to the U.N. representation of the U.S. on 27 December suggested:

> [the] U.K., Greece and Turkey have treaty responsibilities. We look to [the] U.K. to take [the] lead to keep debate in constructive channels. . . The U.S. should take a back seat during debate but should discreetly seek [to] keep discussion in [a] moderate key, particularly when chair. . . . We assume, however, it will be necessary for [the] U.S. to speak. Our statement should not discuss [the] merits of Cypriot complaint against Turkey or of background issues which brought on recent communal violence, but should stress [the] need for those concerned to work out their differences. . . . We would hope [that] the Security Council by consensus and without formal resolution would take note of consultation machinery under [the] Treaty of Guarantee and urge all parties [to] employ this machinery in [their] efforts [to] resolve [the] Cyprus problem.[63]

In the same cable the State Department argued that the Greek Cypriots were trying to abrogate the 1959 Treaties by "involving [the] U.N. in [the] Cyprus question and by involving the right of self-determination . . ." The cable further stated that the U.S. supported British efforts of facilitating negotiations among interested parties, though the U.S. did not want to "do anything to abet [the] Greek Cypriots in their efforts [to] bypass [the] treaties . . ."[64] As these statements show, the U.S. was reluctant to get involved in the Cyprus crisis, even though it considered the conflict a factor which could destabilize the southeastern flank of NATO. Hence, the U.S. supported the initiatives of Britain by asking Turkey and Greece to cooperate with Britain.

The London Conference (13 January-1 February 1964)

Despite the establishment of the "joint" peacekeeping force, violence did not end in Cyprus. Meanwhile, the breakdown of the constitutional order had convinced the Turkish Cypriots that the 1960 constitution needed change so as to grant them additional guarantees against violence. The Greek Cypriots, on the other hand, renewed their calls for a unitary state without the "fetters" of the 1960 constitution. Since all parties desired a change in the constitution of Cyprus, they readily accepted a British proposal to convene a conference in London.[65]

Greece and Turkey sent to London their foreign ministers, Costopoulos and Erkin, whereas Britain was represented by Secretary of State for Commonwealth Affairs Duncan Sandys. On 16 January, the representatives of the Greek and Turkish Cypriot communities, Klerides and Denktash, joined the conference. During the first phase of talks they discussed the political status of the island. Three different plans were proposed by Greek and Turkish Cypriots and Britain.

Greek Cypriots demanded the establishment of a unitary state and the elimination of special rights granted to Turkish Cypriots by the 1959 Treaties.[66] Denktash, too, called for the revision of the 1959 Treaties so that a bizonal or cantonal federation could be established. His plan envisaged the establishment of one or two Turkish cantons and the transfer of the Turkish population to these areas.[67] Denktash added that if federation were not accepted, partition would be the only alternative left.

As expected, the Greeks and Turks rejected each other's proposals. In order to save the conference, Duncan Sandys offered a compromise solution on 20 January 1964. The British plan contained several aspects which could be considered pro-Greek or pro-Turkish, such as the adoption of a parliamentary system without communal quotas or local autonomy.[68]

The British plan satisfied neither the Turkish nor the Greek side. After its rejection on 21 January, the conference was suspended for two days.[69] The same day, Secretary of State Rusk asked U.S. Ambassador Hare to assure the Turkish Government that if the London Conference failed, the NATO Council could take up the issue. He added that Turkey should be reminded that it was an integral part of the "NATO family" and that the U.S. would do its best to accommodate Turkey's interests.[70]

Rusk realized that the situation was getting out of hand and that if the U.S. wanted to prevent a debacle in NATO's southeastern flank, it had to act. Yet he still opposed assuming an active role in solving the crisis. On 24 January 1964, British Ambassador Sir David Ormsby Gore delivered a demarche to the State Department proposing the dispatch of a NATO force to Cyprus.[71] The next day Undersecretary of State George Ball told the Ambassador that the U.S. was not prepared to participate in an allied force. He added that the U.S. had heavy commitments in many parts of the world and:

> did not wish [to] move into another political problem with no end in sight . . . We [are] prepared to do what we could with Greeks and Turks but [we are] not sure what could be said that [is] new . . . [The] U.K. should understand that we viewed getting involved with greatest reluctance.[72]

The same day Numan Menemencioglu Turkish Ambassador to Washington, discussed the Cyprus crisis with Phillips Talbot Assistant Secretary of State. Menemencioglu said that Inonu wanted to know why the U.S. was "doing nothing" despite Turkey's repeated inquiries. Menemencioglu added that Inonu "needs something to help calm potentially serious public reaction to new Cyprus incidents."[73] Inonu's anxiety stemmed partly from his belief that the

Cyprus crisis could be solved to Turkey's advantage easily and with little risk if the U.S. intervened and forced the parties to negotiate. In an interview on 25 January 1964, Inonu stated that he wanted the U.S. to know all the facts about the crisis because "once the U.S. understood the facts, I could not imagine that it would ignore its responsibilities."[74]

Inonu was also anxious for a U.S. intervention because, as U.S. intelligence reports showed, the armed forces were dissatisfied with his passivity regarding the Cyprus crisis. In order to mollify the Turkish generals, Undersecretary of State George Ball asked General Lemnitzer Supreme Allied Commander in Europe (SACEUR), to go to Turkey and dissuade the armed forces from pressuring Inonu. Lemnitzer was instructed to "impress upon them [the] dire consequences [of a military operation] for [the] alliance as a whole . . ."[75] Lemnitzer went to Ankara on 28 January 1964.

We do not know if the coup rumors were accurate or whether or not Inonu was secretly distorting the news of the military's displeasure with his Cyprus policy in order to influence the U.S. Administration. On 28 January 1964, Inonu told U.S. Ambassador Raymond Hare that unless the U.S. gave him some kind of an assurance by the next morning, he would have to intervene.[76] This last warning had an effect. On 31 January, Britain, after receiving U.S. approval, proposed a 10,000-man NATO peace-keeping force which would serve in Cyprus for three months during which time Turkey would promise not to intervene. The U.S. promised to contribute 1,200 troops to the force.[77]

The American reversal of policy concerning the NATO force shows the effectiveness of Inonu's use of the leverage of invasion threats. Throughout January the U.S. Administration had repeatedly declined to join the NATO force proposed by Britain. America's change of policy in the face of the failure of the London Conference also indicates the U.S.'s desire to maintain control over developments on NATO's southeastern flank and to stop the escalation of the crisis.

Turkey and Greece accepted the NATO force proposal, though Turkey accepted more enthusiastically. Inonu stated that after the establishment of the NATO force, a negotiated settlement would be achieved more easily.[78] Inonu knew that the presence of a NATO force in Cyprus *per se* did not necessarily mean that it would be able to contain the violence on the island or that the parties to the dispute would become more conciliatory. It was, however, the U.S. decision to participate in the force that gave rise to Inonu's optimism. Inonu calculated that U.S. involvement in the crisis would make it easier for him to call for U.S. mediation and resist the pressures of pro-intervention circles, including the military. Makarios's rejection of the NATO force on 4 February 1964 seemed to be a setback for Inonu's plan to involve the U.S.[79] Inonu still possessed, however, his trump card: the threat of military intervention. Since the major U.S. objective according to President Johnson was "to prevent unilateral Turkish intervention," Inonu believed that he could manipulate American policy toward Cyprus by threatening an invasion.[80] As the U.S. State Department has admitted, on at least five occasions in 1963-1964 Inonu did use this trump card.[81]

Why Did Inonu Not Intervene in January 1964?

Before proceeding to the later stages of the 1964 crisis, the factors which affected Inonu's decision not to intervene in December 1963 and January 1964 and to seek U.S. mediation should be discussed. These factors were Inonu's personality, Soviet support for Makarios, and the lack of readiness of the Turkish armed forces to undertake an intervention in Cyprus.

The most important factor affecting Turkey's decision not to intervene was Inonu's characteristic cautiousness. This trait is important because Inonu almost always insisted on making the important foreign policy decisions of the governments he headed. These decisions were widely respected by a broad spectrum of the Turkish society which considered him a genius of diplomacy. Inonu's reputation as a great diplomat rested on the role he played during the war of independence and Lausanne negotiations in 1923 and his statesmanship during World War II which spared Turkey from the calamities of the war.

Throughout the 1964 crisis, Inonu stated that Turkey's military intervention in Cyprus would possibly result in a war between Greece and Turkey.[82] This view was also widely accepted by the press during the first half of 1964. Inonu often stated that he would try to avoid this eventuality as much as possible by first exhausting all the peaceful alternatives. Inonu's reluctance to get involved in a regional war stemmed from his abhorrence of war. In 1923 he had stated:

> . . . war is a holy act. It is undertaken for ideals . . . Yet, these ideals should be based on realities and wars should have clear-cut goals. We should not shed the blood of our children for temporary emotions . . . A decision which could end the life of a 25-year old youth requires a lot of thinking. This is a heavy responsibility . . .[83]

As this statement shows, Inonu took extreme care to make the right decision. Unlike Ataturk, who was known to be a risk taker, Inonu tried to make the most logical, legitimate and usually safest decisions. It was hence no surprise that Inonu was eager to accept American plans for a peaceful settlement of the Cyprus crisis.

Inonu also believed that it was too early to contemplate a military intervention in Cyprus, because, in his words, the "world public opinion" had not yet realized the justness of Turkey's cause.[84] An

Inonu supporter, Abdi Ipekci wrote that unless Turkey secured at least the implicit acquiescence of the U.S., Turkey's landing force could be forced to withdraw:

> Such a landing attempt . . . would be met by the intervention of our allies, especially the U.S. and Britain. Faced with such an intervention, our withdrawal would deliver a [tremendous] . . . blow to Turkey's prestige and would leave our kinsmen in Cyprus completely alone.[85]

Another factor which weighed heavily in Inonu's calculations was the Soviet support of Makarios, and the continuation of the Cold War atmosphere in the relations between Turkey and the U.S.S.R. The Soviets feared that Turkey's intervention would result in the partition of Cyprus between Greece and Turkey, two NATO powers. The preservation of Cypriot independence, however, would perpetuate the conflict between Greece and Turkey, thus destabilizing NATO. The Soviets supported Makarios because they believed he was the only person who could assure the independence of Cyprus. The partition of Cyprus would also eliminate the possibility of the establishment of a communist regime by AKEL, the pro-Soviet communist party which had large electoral support.[86]

Hence, the Soviets criticized Turkey's "warning flights" conducted on 25 December 1963 over Cyprus and its interference "in the domestic affairs of Cyprus for the purpose of its 'pacification.'"[87] After the December 1963 violence Soviet Ambassador to Cyprus Pavel Yermosin, delivered a message to Makarios indicating the full support of Moscow "for the Greek Cypriots and the independence, sovereignty and territorial integrity of Cyprus,"[88] and U.N. Representative of the U.S.S.R. Nicolai Fedorenko denounced the "unequal" 1959 Treaties which served only "NATO interests."[89] Faced with these declarations of support for Makarios, it is understandable that Inonu, who was not yet ready to intervene, would be more apprehensive about the intervention. The Soviets did not clarify how they would support Makarios, but cautious Inonu had to assume that military support was not out of the question.

The third factor which affected Inonu's decision not to intervene was the fact that Turkey was ill-prepared to undertake a naval landing in Cyprus. When the December 1963 violence erupted the Turkish general staff was caught off guard. It had no contingency plan concerning a naval or aerial landing readily available. In January 1964, "opposition leaders asked Inonu at a private meeting what plans had been prepared for invading Cyprus, and the old man answered, with military bluntness, 'none.'"[90]

Turkey also did not possess a single landing craft. The armed forces decided to use military and civilian cargo ships to ferry the troops to Cyprus. When the ships reached the shores of Cyprus, the troops would be loaded on small boats to get ashore. According to estimates the landing force would need fifteen days to be assembled and shipped to Cyprus.[91] This further curtailed the Turkish Government's freedom of movement. Inonu often complained that Turkey's intervention might fail because an intervention could only be successful if Turkey moved quickly and established a bridgehead within a few days.

Inonu therefore believed in these initial months that even if no outside power interfered, Turkey's landing might not be successful. One member of Inonu's cabinet, Kemal Satir explained:

> Ismet Pasha [Inonu] considered all the information provided by the commanders and the general staff and decided that a military success was doubtful if Turkey landed troops on Cyprus. He told me that instead of risking a military failure we should try to solve the crisis through

political means. Inonu said that even if we lost diplomatically this would not be as dangerous as a military defeat.[92]

The Cyprus State Crumbles

When Makarios rejected the NATO force plan on 4 February 1964, the state of Cyprus had already lost its bicommunal nature and come under the control of Greek Cypriots. Turkish civil servants, including cabinet members, did not return to their posts because they felt that their lives would be in danger if they entered the Greek sectors of the island.

At the outset the Turkish Cypriot leadership encouraged this development with the expectation that a new political settlement, territorial federation or partition, would soon be negotiated. The Greek Cypriot leadership was also pleased because the exclusion of Turkish Cypriots from the state apparatus, which was one of its main goals, was easily achieved.[93] Hence, when the Turkish Cypriots wanted to return to their jobs in mid-1964, Makarios refused. He explained his refusal to U.N. Secretary General U-Thant by arguing that ". . . the matter is considered by the government to be highly political and closely linked with the final settlement of the Cyprus question . . ."[94]

During the intercommunal violence of 1963-1964, Turkish Cypriots abandoned 98 of their 233 settlements and fled to the Turkish-controlled enclaves. Of the remaining 135 settlements 20 were under "government" control. These 20 settlements accounted for 8,000 Turkish Cypriots. The remaining 100,000 lived in Turkish-controlled enclaves which covered five percent of the island's territory. A Turkish Cypriot administration, established in the Turkish sector of Nicosia, overtook the functions of the central government in the Turkish enclaves all over the island.[95]

Turkish Cypriots' main loss was in the economic sector. As a result of intercommunal violence, 4,000 Turks lost their jobs in the public and Greek private sectors. An additional 25,000 fled their homes and lived in refugee camps. Many of those refugees had to abandon their lands. In 1964 the government discontinued its subsidy of 400,000 pounds, set aside for Turkish Cypriots. According to U.N. figures, the number of Turks receiving some kind of assistance from the Turkish Red Crescent was almost 56,000, or half the Turkish population.[96]

The Ball Mission

Upon learning of Makarios' rejection of the NATO force on 4 February 1964, the U.S. Administration decided to send Undersecretary of State George Ball to the area to convince Makarios that some kind of a peacekeeping force was necessary in Cyprus to prevent Turkey's intervention. Ball would also go to Turkey to convince Inonu that the U.S. was doing its best to end the crisis.[97]

Inonu accepted Ball's proposal of a peacekeeping force without U.S. participation on 10 February 1964.[98] Ball's negotiations with Makarios were not so successful. On 12 February 1964, Makarios told Ball that he could accept a U.N. peacekeeping force composed of troops from Commonwealth countries. Makarios added, however, that a U.N. Security Council resolution "guarantee[ing] the political independence and territorial integrity of Cyprus should precede the establishment of such a force."[99] In other words, Makarios wanted the U.N. to annul the Treaty of Guarantee and support the "unfettered" independence of Cyprus. As Ball put it, "Makarios' central interest was to block off Turkish intervention so that he and his Greek Cypriots could go on happily massacring Turkish Cypriots. Obviously we would never permit that."[100]

On 12 February 1964, while Ball was still in Cyprus, another Greek Cypriot attack against Turkish Cypriots took place in the southern city of Limassol. In Ball's words,

> [t]he situation of civil order here has deteriorated markedly overnight. [ ] has just advised me that there are 150 casualties at Limassol where the Greek Cypriot police are now firing heavy explosives into the Turkish quarter. It appears they have launched an all out attack.[101]

Upon learning of Makarios' rejection of the U.S. plan and the Limassol violence, Secretary of State Rusk directed Ball to return to Turkey. He stated that the "first objective in Ankara must be to keep Turks at home" and added that the "ball game is by no means over . . . Note that after Greek elections on Sunday, GOG [the Government of Greece] should be in a position to exert more positive influence on Makarios."[102] In Ankara, Ball also told Inonu that the U.S. would veto any U.N. Security Council resolution which ignored Turkey's right of intervention.[103] When Inonu once more told Ball that Turkey "might have to intervene at any time," Ball repeated his assurance by saying that "Makarios would get at the United Nations a severe lesson."[104]

Ball returned from Ankara with the impression that Turkey's military intervention was imminent. He told the President that "[t]aking a prudent view, we can count on only a few days. Even that time could be foreshortened by a major incident in Cyprus. The Turks are not bluffing."[105] Ball recommended "the joint action of the three guarantor powers to exercise their rights of intervention under Article 4 of the Treaty of Guarantee."[106] President Johnson accepted Ball's suggestion and asked the British government to convene a summit conference to make plans for a tripartite intervention.[107]

The tripartite intervention did not take place, because the U.N. Security Council had already started to discuss the Cyprus crisis. The deliberations of the Council ended on 4 March 1964 when it adopted a resolution calling for the creation of a U.N. peacekeeping force in Cyprus.[108] This was a resolution supported by all parties. Makarios was pleased that, for the moment at least, Turkey's intervention was prevented. Inonu welcomed the U.N. force because, given the fact that he did not intend to intervene, a U.N. force was better than nothing.[109]

Turkey's acceptance of the U.N. force did not abrogate its right of intervention under Article 4 of the Treaty of Guarantee, but Turkey's assertion that the constitutional order in Cyprus no longer existed lost some of its credibility. The U.N. force was not entrusted with the restoration of the constitutional order. On the contrary, it was to be sent to Cyprus only if Makarios' government accepted it. By accepting a U.N. role in Cyprus, Turkey was in a sense recognizing the Makarios regime and abandoning its role as the guarantor of the 1959 Agreements.[110]

The U.N. Force Fails to End Violence

Despite the 4 March 1964 resolution of the U.N. Security Council to send a U.N. peacekeeping force to Cyprus, the establishment of the force was delayed because the arrival of the troops could not take place as scheduled. This was probably the reason for the intensification of violence on the island. On 8 March Greek Cypriots attacked Turkish positions in Paphos (Baf), Nicosia (Lefkosa) and Kyrenia (Girne). This attack was perceived by the Turkish public as a last minute effort by Makarios to "finish off" Turkish Cypriots before the U.N. force arrived.[111]

During the following four days, the Inonu Government issued public warnings calling for an immediate cease-fire. Thousands of troops were loaded on ships, the bulk of which were anchored at the Iskenderun harbor opposite of Cyprus. On 12 and 13 March 1964, demonstrators in major towns of Turkey called for intervention. Even the pro-Government press, which earlier had supported Inonu's cautious policy, started calling for a hard-line approach against Makarios.[112] The main opposition party, the Justice Party (JP), was again in the forefront of those stressing the need for invasion. JP spokesman Faruk Sukan predicted, however, that the Government would not intervene and accused Inonu of ignoring Turkey's national interests.[113]

On 12 March Inonu took another step in his crisis diplomacy by convening the National Security Council (NSC). The NSC, which included the ministers of defense, domestic affairs and foreign affairs and top commanders of the armed forces, functioned as a crisis government. It decided to deliver an ultimatum to Makarios threatening a military intervention if the attacks did not stop.[114] The same day, Foreign Minister Erkin called in U.S. Ambassador Hare and showed him a copy of Turkey's note before it was sent to Makarios. Hare asked for a twenty-four hour delay in Turkey's action in order to inform Washington.[115] Within hours, Secretary of State Rusk started to make telephone calls to government officials of Canada, Sweden, Finland and Ireland to ask for the acceleration of the departure of their contingents of the U.N. force. The next day Rusk informed Hare that the "logjam regarding the establishment of the U.N. peacekeeping force [is] broken" and added that Hare should immediately see Inonu and use "all appropriate arguments to advise restraint."[116]

On 14 March 1964 the first U.N. contingent, forty-two Canadian troops, arrived in Cyprus. The Turkish government considered this a big diplomatic success. Dr. Ali Ihsan Gogus, the cabinet spokesman told the National Assembly that Turkey's diplomatic efforts had "provided for a quick arrival of the U.N. peacekeeping force and precluded a massacre."[117]

Actually, with the arrival of the U.N. force, violence on the island subsided for several weeks.

Inonu's motives for using his brinkmanship were several. First, he still thought that peaceful alternatives were not yet exhausted. As he confided to one of his advisors, the diplomatic maneuvers "stopped the attacks on Turks. We achieved this goal without the Turkish army suffering a single casualty."[118] Second, Inonu doubted that a military intervention would settle the Cyprus dispute. He feared that Turkey might end up fighting Greece, and given the Soviet threat, he could not afford a war with Greece or alienation of the U.S.[119]

The Johnson Letter

During the last two weeks of May 1964 the situation of Turkish Cypriots deteriorated markedly. Dozens of Turks were abducted by Greek-Cypriot gangs. Thirty-five of those abducted were later found murdered.[120] Moreover, the Greek dominated parliament, which excluded its Turkish members, enacted a conscription law on 1 June 1964 authorizing the "Government" to form an army. The Turkish papers also reported that Makarios was importing "heavy" arms for the newly established army.

The Turkish Government publicly protested these latest actions of Greek Cypriots as illegal acts of an illegal government.[121] The formation of a Greek-Cypriot army was, however, the last straw. On 2 June 1964, the National Security Council convened and decided to intervene in Cyprus to establish "a political and military beachhead." It was hoped that the intervention would enable Turkey to negotiate a satisfactory settlement within a short time.[122]

Those who at that time were close to Inonu suggested that for the first time in months Inonu seemed to be determined that Turkey had to intervene militarily.[123] Yet Inonu insisted on consulting with the U.S. before initiating the intervention, overruling

Foreign Minister Erkin who did not want even to inform the U.S.[124] The whole cabinet, the Cyprus specialists of the Foreign Ministry, and the commanders of the armed forces were pro-intervention.[125] Needless to say, the press, which had begun calling for an intervention since March 1964, shared the same view.

On 4 June 1964, Inonu called in U.S. Ambassador Raymond Hare to inform him of the Government's decision to intervene in Cyprus. Inonu said that despite all American assurances, attacks against Turkish Cypriots did not stop and that the situation was becoming worse every minute. Inonu added that the U.N. peacekeeping force had proven useless. Inonu concluded by saying that

> all GOT [Government of Turkey] has in mind is [to] occupy part of [the] island and stop there. Greeks could [also] occupy part [of it] and [the U.N.] peace force could remain between them. From that position one could get down to meaningful discussion.[126]

Hare asked why Inonu did not want to consult with the other two guarantor powers, Britain and Greece. Inonu replied that "most constructive talks could take place following [the] intervention when [the] Turks could discuss from [a position] of strength . . ." Then Hare asked for a twenty-four hour delay to consult the U.S. Administration, and Inonu accepted.[127]

Inonu's insistence on consulting the U.S. and his willingness to wait for a U.S. response may suggest that he was not serious about intervention. He actually may not have wanted to intervene, but could not stand up to the pro-intervention pressures of the public and the armed forces. In this case, the best way to avoid intervention was to consult the U.S. which would almost certainly oppose the proposed action. Inonu would then cancel the operation, blaming the U.S. for his own passivity.

Another explanation of Inonu's behavior—which seems more logical—is Inonu's belief in the necessity of consulting the U.S. as a matter of principle and expediency. Inonu often stated that on important issues allies should consult each other before executing their decisions. Second, Inonu was aware that the Soviet Union repeatedly expressed support for Makarios. Furthermore, at the beginning of June 1964, Soviet Ambassador to Turkey Nikita Rijov explicitly told Erkin that "the Soviets were absolutely against [a military intervention] in Cyprus."[128] Without at least implicit American acquiescence in Turkey's military intervention, the U.S.S.R. could be tempted to aid Makarios.

As a result, Turkey's operation might not only fail, but Turkey's own security could be endangered. It is hence possible that Inonu believed that there was a chance that the U.S. would implicitly approve Turkey's limited intervention in Cyprus. Informing the U.S. might also result in the abandonment of the invasion, Inonu thought, but the risk was worthwhile given the fact that the Soviet support to Makarios could end in a Turkish defeat in Cyprus. Inonu also believed that the U.S. was the only country that could prevent a war between Greece and Turkey. If the U.S. were to approve the operation, it could use its leverage with Greece to prevent a possible Greek attack on Turkey.

The U.S. response to the news of an impending Turkish invasion was abrupt and harsh. Within hours President Johnson directed SACEUR Lemnitzer "to proceed immediately to Ankara" to meet with Turkish military leaders and "make presentations as SACEUR, stressing harmful damage to NATO interests that would result from contemplated military intervention in Cyprus by Turkey."[129] The U.S. Administration also ordered a "Carrier Task Force consisting of one . . . carrier, one . . . cruiser, four . . . destroyers" to position itself eight hours from Cyprus.[130] This last action was perhaps a precautionary move, but it was later considered by the Turkish public as gunboat diplomacy and had harmful consequences for the U.S.[131]

The most important part of the American response was President Johnson's letter delivered to Inonu on 5 June 1964. The letter, written in a rather undiplomatic style, categorically rejected Inonu's suggestion that all peaceful means had been exhausted and stated that Turkey's "right to take unilateral action is not yet applicable."[132] In Inonu's words, this letter made use of all the "thunderbolts that could be assembled." Johnson stated that Turkey's intervention would lead to a war between Greece and Turkey.[133] As suggested earlier, this was one of the reasons why Inonu wanted to consult the U.S. By pointing to the possibility of a Greco-Turkish war, Johnson was in fact stating that the U.S. would not prevent Greece from attacking Turkey.

Furthermore, Johnson maintained that "a military intervention in Cyprus by Turkey could lead to a direct involvement by the Soviet Union." Johnson added:

> I hope you will understand that your NATO allies have not had a chance to consider whether they have an obligation to protect Turkey against the Soviet Union if Turkey takes a step which results in Soviet intervention without the full consent and understanding of its NATO allies.[134]

Johnson also stated that he had "no doubt that the general membership of the United Nations would react in the strongest terms to unilateral action by Turkey . . .," and added that "the United States cannot agree to the use of any United States supplied military equipment for a Turkish intervention in Cyprus under present circumstances."[135] Johnson concluded with the assurance that the U.S. would remain "deeply concerned about the interests of

Turkey and of the Turkish Cypriots" and invited Inonu to Washington for a discussion of the crisis.

It would have been a miracle had Johnson's letter been disregarded by Inonu. Johnson dwelt on the dangers Inonu feared most. He stressed that a Greek-Turkish war would be likely and failed to indicate what the U.S. would do to avert it. More significantly, Johnson insinuated that if Turkey's intervention led to a Soviet attack on Turkey, the U.S. might refrain from coming to its aid. The possibility of this contingency was bound to affect Inonu's decision to intervene, given the fact that only one month earlier Khrushchev had once more opposed Turkey's intervention in Cyprus.[136] Johnson also intimated that the U.S. might join other members of the U.N. in condemning Turkey and even imposing sanctions on it. Finally, Johnson reminded Inonu that he could not use American supplied military equipment. Inonu knew only too well that non-compliance could mean an American arms embargo.

Johnson had left Inonu a way out by proposing consultations in Washington. Inonu cancelled the intervention and accepted the offer of discussions by writing to Johnson that " . . . a settlement is likely to be reached if you lend your support and give effect with your supreme authority to the sense of justice inherent in the character of the American nation."[137] Inonu informed the public that Johnson had asked for the postponement of the intervention and had invited him to Washington to review the situation. He did not reveal, however, the full content of the Johnson Letter. Inonu probably feared that a full disclosure would create an instant public uproar and backlash which could harm Turkey's alliance relationship with the U.S.

Unaware of the extent of Johnson's censure, the criticism by the Turkish press was rather subdued. It blamed the U.S. for remaining indifferent to Turkey's problems but not for bullying Turkey. *Milliyet's* editor-in-chief wrote:

> There is no reason to believe that President Johnson has a special animosity towards Turkey . . . It is the State Department which is misleading Johnson . . . We don't doubt Johnson's goodwill toward Turkey. We doubt, however, the correctness of the facts and evaluations provided to him [by the State Department.][138]

The First Acheson Plan

Actually, the Johnson letter was not the result of "anti-Turkish" State Department officials misinforming the President. As President Johnson stressed in his letter, the U.S. "valued very highly [its] relations with Turkey. [The U.S.] ha[s] considered [Turkey] as a great ally with fundamental common interests."[139] Johnson also had to consider, however, America's relations with its other local ally Greece. Even at the outset of the crisis Johnson had stated that "we cannot be expected [to] impose one-sided solution[s] on either party, since this would mean taking sides between two good friends and allies and would obviously be unacceptable to one adversely affected . . ."[140]

Instead, the U.S. desired these two allies to seek ways to compromise and "not lose sight of [the] overriding need to maintain [the] NATO solidarity against [the] real enemy"[141] After forestalling Turkey's intervention, Johnson knew that he had to make an equally forceful presentation to Papandreou in order to induce him to be as forthcoming as Inonu. The President made several attempts to influence Greek officials. In one of them, Johnson told the ambassador of Greece, Alexander Matsas, that "Greece must avoid at all costs humiliating its ally Turkey" and should negotiate with it to reach a settlement. Johnson hinted that the next time he might not be as influential with Inonu by saying that negotiating with the Turks was difficult, "[b]ut it is more difficult to talk after an invasion."[142]

During Greek Premier George Papandreou's visit to Washington on 24 June 1964, Dean Rusk drove home this point once more when he told Papandreou that Johnson would not forestall a new Turkish attempt at landing, and even if he tried, the Turks would not heed his admonition a second time.[143] Hence, it was not surprising that Papandreou reversed his earlier stance and accepted Dean Acheson's mediation as proposed by Johnson.

Inonu's visit to Washington took place during the same week (22-23 June 1964) and was perceived by the Turks as a success. The joint communique issued afterwards upheld the Turkish thesis that the 1959 Agreements were still valid.[144] Inonu was also pleased to learn that former Secretary of State Dean Acheson would be appointed as a mediator by Johnson.[145]

Inonu's remarks after his return from Washington imply that he also discussed with Johnson the modes of solution of the Cyprus crisis. Whereas since January 1964 Inonu had called for a territorial federation in Cyprus, he began to make statements favoring quite a different settlement.[146] On 28 June 1964 Inonu stated that he would accept unification of Cyprus with Greece provided that Turkey received a large base area which could accommodate most Turkish Cypriots.[147]

Acheson's mediation started on 11 July 1964 in Geneva. On Papandreou's insistence, the Greek and Turkish delegations did not confer together, but Acheson met with them separately. On 14 July 1964 Acheson submitted his proposals to the delegations headed by Erim and Nicolareisis.[148] His plan provided for the union of Cyprus with Greece. Greece in return would make certain concessions to Turkey. These concessions included the cession to Turkey of "a portion of the island in perpetuity, that is in full sovereignty."[149] The plan also granted local autonomy to "one, two or three relatively small areas of the island in which Turkish Cypriots would be in the majority . . ." Turks who lived in other parts of the island would benefit from all human and minority rights granted by the Treaty of Lausanne (1923) to Turks remaining in Greece.[150]

The Turkish representative Nihat Erim told Acheson that Turkey was ready to accept his plan provided that the Turkish base area covered the whole Karpas peninsula. The Greek negotiator Nicolareisis replied that Greece not only considered the size of the Turkish base too large, but opposed the idea of cession of a base to Turkey. Instead, Greece offered to lease a small base on the Karpas peninsula for twenty-five years.[151] Before Erim considered the Greek proposal, the negotiations were interrupted by another burst of violence on Cyprus on 6 August 1964.

August 1964 Violence

While the Geneva negotiations were taking place, Makarios undertook several steps to bring the island further under the control of Greek Cypriots. On 17 July 1964 some 25 articles were considered as strategic materials, the purchase of which by Turkish Cypriots was forbidden without special authorization from the Ministry of the Interior . . . Secondly, [Makarios] imposed restrictions on the importation of [Turkish] Red Crescent supplies for the relief of the population."[152]

On 27 July 1964 several Turkish cargo ships carrying relief supplies were turned back by Greek officials.[153]

A second factor which further eroded the constitutionality of the Makarios regime was the introduction of mainland Greek troops on Cyprus. As Andreas Papandreou suggests, after the Makarios-Papandreou agreement in April 1964,

> [a] clandestine operation . . . began on a huge scale—of nightly shipments of arms

> and troops, of 'volunteers' who arrived in Cyprus in civilian clothes and then joined their 'Cypriot' units. This process was not completed until the middle of the summer. No less than twenty thousand officers and men, fully equipped, were shipped to Cyprus." [154]

The Makarios regime took another step on 6 August 1964 in bringing the island under its control. The "government" forces mounted an attack supported by mortars against the Turkish Cypriot positions in the Kokkina-Mansoura area in the northwestern part of Cyprus. This region was strategically important because the Turkish Cypriots were using it as a landing spot for military supplies from Turkey. On 7 August the attacks continued when "a Government patrol boat shelled the villages of Mansoura and Kokkina with 40 mm guns . . ."[155]

The same day the Turkish NSC met to consider Turkey's response to the attack. Throughout the meeting all cabinet members and commanders favored an aerial bombing to stop the attacks. Inonu refused to go along with the rest of the NSC and suggested calling for a cease-fire because U.S. Ambassador Hare had assured Turkey that Makarios was ready to stop the aggression. The Government decided to wait one more day.[156]

On 8 August the Greeks resumed their attack and overran all Turkish villages in the area except Kokkina (Erenkoy). While the Turkish NSC continued its deliberations, the Turkish positions in Kokkina "were subjected to a heavy bombardment, including fire from 25-pounder guns."[157] It was clear that the fall of Kokkina was only a matter of hours. By noon the NSC decided to "initiate [a] limited air action on access roads being used by Greeks in order [to] save Kokkina and its inhabitants. . . ." Foreign Minister Erkin informed U.S. Ambassador Hare that "Turkey's bombing would be a restricted action and [that] Turkey would make it clear to the Greeks." Erkin requested that the U.S. "use all [of] its influence with [the] GOC [Government of Cyprus] and GOG (Government of Greece] to prevent [the] spread of violence in Cyprus and [a] possible war with Greece."[158]

Inonu probably expected to receive a U.S. response by the next morning. Meanwhile, he ordered the air force to conduct reconnaissance flights over the Kokkina (Erenkoy) region. The commander in chief of the air force, Irfan Tansel, who like other commanders had insisted on bombings and even landing from the start, was not satisfied with the order. Instead, he ordered the pilots to bomb the positions of Makarios forces around Kokkina. The attack took place in the afternoon of 8 August 1964 with the participation of some 30 F-100 fighter aircraft.[159]

On 9 August 1964 the bombing continued. By then, however, the Government had already come to terms with the air force. Sixty-four aircraft participated in the second operation. Meanwhile, Inonu informed Makarios that the bombings would continue until the Greek forces withdrew to their pre-6 August 1964 positions. The crisis seemed to deepen when five fighter aircraft of the Greek air force arrived in Cyprus and bombed Kokkina.[160]

On 9 August 1964, two additional developments took place. First, the U.S. and Britain jointly sponsored a U.N. Security Council resolution calling for a cease-fire. Second, Khrushchev sent a note to Inonu calling on Turkey to end military operations against Cyprus and added that Turkey should be aware of "the responsibility which [it] is assuming in carrying out an armed attack on the Republic of Cyprus."[161]

These developments did not fail to have an effect on Inonu. As suggested earlier, it was the possibility of a Greek-Turkish war, of Soviet intervention, and of the desertion of Turkey by its allies that were the main reasons for Inonu's reluctance to intervene in Cyprus. The continuation of bombings could bring about additional Greek aircraft sorties in the area and a dangerous confrontation between the two countries. President Johnson had already asked for the cessation of hostilities and the U.S. had sponsored a U.N. cease-fire resolution. The U.S. had also convinced Makarios to announce on 9 August that he would abide by the cease-fire.[162] Inonu feared that Turkey's continuation of bombings would create the perception that it was the aggressor. As mentioned above, Khrushchev's 9 August message was unclear about Soviet intentions. Inonu had no reason, however, to believe that the Soviet Union would refrain from exploiting the opportunities arising out of a Greek-Turkish war.

At the Turkish NSC meeting on 10 August, Inonu's proposal for the cessation of aircraft sorties met with disapproval from all the commanders and several ministers. The commanders instead wanted to use the hostilities as a pretext to land forces on the island. The most heated exchange took place between Inonu and the air force chief, Irfan Tansel whom Inonu accused of being an adventurer. But Inonu ignored all objections and ordered a cessation of aircraft attacks.[163] Inonu's decision meant Turkey's acquiescence in the territorial gains of Greek Cypriots since 6 August 1964. As a matter of fact, when the bombings started, Turkey notified Makarios that it would end its operation only if the Greeks withdrew to their 6 August positions and lifted their economic blockade around all Turkish Cypriot enclaves. In his address to the National Assembly, Inonu admitted that these goals had not been achieved.[164]

Another reason for Inonu's reluctance to go on with air strikes was his belief that Acheson's mediation effort could still achieve a peaceful settlement of the crisis. The continuation of the bombings could further antagonize Greece which had 20,000 secretly infiltrated troops in Cyprus, and lead to a war between the two countries. Thus, it was not surprising that on 10 August 1964, the day Inonu rejected the commanders' calls for intervention, he sent a message to Greek Premier Papandreou urging the resumption of the Geneva negotiations. Inonu suggested that "it is possible to solve the Cyprus problem in one month if Greece would reciprocate Turkey's goodwill and compromises."[165]

Second Acheson Plan

The Greek, Turkish and American representatives returned to Geneva on 15 August 1964 for the second round of talks. The negotiations were interrupted on 6 August 1964 by the Greek Cypriot assault on Kokkina only hours after the Greek representative Nicolareisis had presented Greece's proposals. On 15 August Nicolareisis once more offered Turkey a temporary base on the tip of the Karpas peninsula for twenty-five to thirty-five years in return for *enosis*. Erim rejected the offer without even consulting Inonu.[166]

Turkey's objective, as Inonu formulated it, was to annex a part of Cyprus as large as the Karpas peninsula. In return Inonu was willing to accept Greece's union with the rest of the island provided that Turkish Cypriots were granted minority rights by Greece. Inonu calculated that a Turkish base on Cyprus would enable Turkey to deal with future contingencies including a Greek attack on southern Anatolia originating from Cyprus. A permanent base would also enable Turkey to ensure that the Turkish Cypriots, the bulk of whom would remain in the Greek sector, would not be attacked in the future. To be sure, a permanent base was far less than what the Turkish Cypriots and the mainland Turkish public desired. It was, however, a compromise solution for Inonu who wanted to settle the dispute as quickly as possible.[167]

On 22 August 1964 Acheson put forward the so-called "Second Acheson Plan" which was a result of an attempt to reconcile the Greek and Turkish positions. Whereas the "First Acheson Plan" granted

Turkey a permanent base on the Karpas peninsula, the compromise plan offered a smaller base to be *leased* to Turkey for fifty years. Second, Acheson withdrew his earlier proposal for several autonomous Turkish areas on the rest of the island. Likewise, the new plan eliminated the so-called "Central Turkish Cypriot Administration" to be established in Nicosia which was to deal with communal affairs such as educational, religious and judicial matters concerning the Turkish community.[168]

Despite pressures exerted by Ambassador Hare on Inonu in Ankara, and by Acheson on Erim in Geneva, Turkey promptly rejected the plan. Inonu once again told Hare that Turkey insisted on having full sovereignty over the base.[169] Even if Inonu had accepted the Second Acheson Plan, the U.S. would have a difficult time convincing Makarios if not Papandreou to go along with it. Whereas Papandreou had not yet made a decision, Makarios announced that even the Second Acheson Plan was unacceptable. He said: "I aspire to unite with Greece the entirety of Cyprus, not part of her. To succeed in doing so, I shall remain firm and unbent, prepared to sacrifice myself and die."[170]

Inonu Considers Inactivity A Realistic Policy

After the August battle in Kokkina, the Makarios regime blockaded all movements of people and supplies into the Turkish Cypriot enclaves of Nicosia, Lefka, Limnitis and Kokkina. On 5 September the Makarios forces also began blockading the Turkish quarters of Larnaca and Famagusta. The condition of Turkish Cypriots was so severe that the U.N. Secretary General commented:

> . . . [T]he conclusion seems warranted that the economic restrictions imposed against the Turkish communities in Cyprus, which in some instances have been so severe as to

> amount to a veritable seige, indicate that the Government of Cyprus seeks to force a potential solution by economic pressure as a substitute for military action.[171]

While the blockade of the Turkish enclaves was continuing, Inonu addressed the National Assembly to explain American mediation efforts and Turkey's Cyprus policy throughout 1964. Inonu stated that the reasons for Turkey's failure to solve the crisis were "the regional and international conditions which were unfavorable to Turkey." He maintained that "only an intervention which would last not more than one week could be successful" and added that "the [1959] Treaties require a consultation period and . . . other parties to the Treaty could prevent our intervention by footdragging."[172] Inonu also argued that despite these unfavorable conditions Turkey had attempted to intervene. Yet, "our attempts . . . have been frustrated by the U.N. and our allies." He added that the Soviet Union too objected to Turkey's landing and "as a result of [this] the issue acquired a special sensitivity. . . . It is not just to expect us to ignore all these factors and engage in adventures."[173]

Inonu's fear of a Soviet threat seemed to be justified. Khrushchev, in addition to his 9 August note to Inonu, often spoke of assisting Makarios against "external dangers." On 16 August 1964, six days after the cease-fire, he went one step further and committed the U.S.S.R. for the first time to the defense of the Makarios regime. He stated that:

> . . . if it comes to an invasion of Cypriot territory, the Soviet Union will not remain on the side-lines. In answer to the request of the Government of Cyprus and the personal request of President Makarios, the Soviet Government hereby states that if there is an armed foreign invasion of Cypriot territory, the Soviet Union will help the Republic of Cyprus to defend its

> freedom and independence against foreign intervention.[174]

Concerning the August air strikes, Inonu suggested that Turkey could afford "only two days of bombing because only this much was seen by the [world public opinion] as a retaliation for Greek attacks." He further argued that even this limited retaliation created a controversy in the U.S. concerning the use of American supplied arms in Cyprus. Inonu added:

> if we have to intervene we should make sure that our action is perceived as a legitimate self-defense. By doing so we can prevent many problems. We can never be sure what the U.S. and the U.S.S.R. would do in case of an intervention. . . . The Government is determined to save our . . . alliance relationships. . . .[175]

As we will see in the next chapter, Inonu's frustration at the failure of American efforts to mediate and settle the dispute contributed to his decision to try to improve Turkey's relations with the Soviet Union and Middle Eastern countries. In the meantime, Inonu further distanced himself from his earlier role of brinkmanship by playing down the importance of the economic blockade in Cyprus. Inonu's reaction to the presence of 20,000 mainland Greek troops in Cyprus was also subdued. He denounced their presence as provocative, but did not take any measures to remove them because he probably believed that another invasion threat would not be taken seriously by anybody.[176]

It should be stressed that the main opposition party, the conservative JP, did not dispute the fact that the U.S. had obviously not taken Turkey's side. The JP refused to blame the U.S., however, for the ongoing Cyprus stalemate. Instead, JP Secretary General Saadettin Bilgic held Inonu responsible for failing to demand U.S. support. He argued that Inonu's readiness to compromise at every phase of the crisis led the U.S. Administration to believe that in times of crisis U.S. pressure on Turkey would force Turkey to make concessions. Bilgic added that the U.S. could not be blamed since its goal was to prevent a Turco-Greek war. He maintained that "the U.S. has to put pressure on somebody who listens. In this crisis it was Turkey which heeded American advice . . ."[177] The conclusion the Turkish public drew from the arguments of both the JP and the RPP was that the U.S. did not support Turkey's "just cause." The efforts of the JP to blame America's "aloofness on Inonu's lack of assertiveness did not prevent the public from questioning—for the first time in decades—the wisdom of identifying Turkey's interests with those of NATO and the U.S. The demonstrations that took place at the end of August 1964 had one common theme: condemnation of the U.S. The speakers at these rallies "denounced the United States and President Johnson as false friends of Turkey and accused them of having betrayed this [country] over Cyprus."[178] Many uniformed officers and in one instance the commander in chief of the ground forces, Cemal Tural joined the demonstrators who shouted "Down with America" and "Army to Cyprus."[179]

The press not only accused the U.S. of forestalling Turkey's landing of troops in Cyprus, but also called for a revision of Turkey's foreign policy. Conservative columnist Ahmet Kabakli wrote that Turkey should not rely on the U.S. to protect its rights. Instead, urged Kabakli, Turkey should adopt a "dignified foreign policy" and join other Islamic states to stand up for its interests.[180] Socialist Cetin Altan suggested that criticizing the U.S. alone would not suffice to solve Turkey's problems and added that a policy of nonalignment was the best solution.[181] Liberal columnist Abdi Ipekci stressed that improved Turco-Soviet relations would benefit Turkish foreign policy. He cautioned, however, that Turkey should not make "any concessions" to the Soviets.[182]

The Greek Lobby

Throughout 1964 various Greek American associations, the Greek-Orthodox Church and many Greek Americans expressed their wish that the U.S. Administration support the Greek Cypriots' struggle to establish a Greek-dominated unitary state in Cyprus. The Greek Americans also demanded that the U.S. oppose Turkey's attempts to intervene on the island.

The Greek American efforts in 1964 were, however, less intense and less confrontational than the 1974 lobbying of Congress. In 1974 the Greek Americans organized a very effective lobby, pressuring the Congress to overrule the President and adopt an arms embargo against Turkey. In 1964, especially until the August 1964 Turkish air strikes, the Greek Americans focused their efforts on influencing the President, and devoted little time to lobbying Congress. The pressure exerted on the President took the form of letters and cables, and the content of the messages was much less confrontational than those in 1974.

It should be stressed that Congress as a whole showed few signs that it disapproved the President's handling of the crisis. The post-World War II consensus on foreign policy was still in effect and Congress considered the matter to lie within the President's prerogative as it did on other foreign policy issues. Hence, despite the fact that many Congressmen favored a pro-Greek resolution of the dispute, they took no action to force the President to "get tough" with the Turks. It should be added that neither the Congress nor the Greek Americans perceived the President's Cyprus policy as illegal or illegitimate as they did in 1974. This was another reason for their moderation in dealing with the President.

By the end of June 1964 the White House received a total of 2,598 letters and cables from Greek American organizations and individuals. Some of these organizations were the Greek American Progressive Association, the United Organizations of Greek Americans, the Cyprus Federation of America and the Justice for Cyprus Committee. There was only one pro-Turkish cable which was sent on 22 February 1964 by the Turkish Association of Colorado.[183]

A few legislators actively engaged the White House and the State Department. U.S. Senator Robert B. Keating (R-New York), protested several times the State Department's pro-Turkish "tilt" even in the early stages of the crisis.[184] On 22 July 1964 Senator Keating argued on the floor of the Senate that "[t]he 82 percent majority in Cyprus does not ask unreasonable ends; it asks merely that the old democratic principle of majority rule remain a reality in Cyprus."[185]

It was probably not a coincidence that Senator Keating was running for reelection in 1964 in a state where the Greek vote could play a decisive role. Keating's campaign manager was Eugene T. Rossides who in 1974 headed the American Hellenic Institute, one of the organizations of the Greek Lobby. Keating's opponent in the race was Robert F. Kennedy who did not want to look less pro-Greek than Senator Keating. Kennedy stated:

> The London-Zurich Agreements of 1960 which resulted in the present constitution of Cyprus must be amended. The people of Cyprus may decide that their future can best be assured through union with Greece.[186]

After the Turkish air attacks on 8-9 August 1964, the Greek Americans and pro-Greek legislators adopted a harder line. Archbishop Iakovos Primate of the Greek Orthodox Archdiocese of North and South

America, asked "all America's Hellenism to rise as one man" and protest Turkey's air attack with "American-built aircraft" to President Johnson and the Congress.[187] On 16 August 1964 more than 1,000 Greek Americans and Greeks demonstrated outside of the U.N. and sent a message to President Johnson arguing that Turkey's air strikes were a "clear violation of the Foreign Assistance Act of 1961" and asking for "the suspension of U.S. military assistance to Turkey."[188] AHEPA (American Hellenic Educational Progressive Association) went further than that and asked the President to suspend not only military but also economic aid to Turkey.[189] Several legislators agreed with AHEPA. Roman Pucinski (D-Illinois) who was known as an ardent philhellene, delivered a speech on 15 August 1964 on the House floor, maintaining that the U.S. should do whatever is necessary to stop Turkey's "aggression." He added that " . . . if necessary, I believe we should withdraw any further assistance to the Turks, both economic and military . . ."[190]

AHEPA also asked its members to write to their Senators and Representatives urging them to support the principle of self-determination. Many legislators responded to AHEPA members' appeals by stating that they would accept *enosis* if it were the outcome of self-determination.[191] It is interesting, however, that despite their pro-Greek tendencies these Congressmen referred to Turkey as a friend of the U.S., thus indicating that they still perceived events in the eastern Mediterranean in a Cold War context.[192] Therefore, although many Congressmen felt that Turkey's air strike in August 1964 violated U.S. laws, they took no action to cut assistance to Turkey.

Conclusion

By the time the 1964 crisis leveled off, Turkish foreign policy in general and Turco-American relations in particular had begun undergoing a transformation whose consequences would influence future Cyprus crises. This transformation, which we shall discuss in the next chapter, was preceded by the public examination of Turkey's post-World War II foreign policy. As we have seen, the public demonstrations and the criticism by journalists of various tendencies were initially directed against the alleged American interference which forestalled Turkey's intervention in Cyprus. Subsequently, these critics held Turkey's "unidirectional" foreign policy and Turkey's "self-imposed" isolation from the U.S.S.R. and the Third World responsible for the Cyprus debacle.

As suggested earlier, several factors influenced the outcome of the 1964 Cyprus crisis and shaped the American-Turkish influence relationship. Turkish domestic politics, and especially Inonu's decision-making were, however, the main determinants of the outcome. To be sure, the U.S. Administration continuously objected to Turkey's unilateral intervention in Cyprus. Yet in the last instance, it was up to Inonu to decide whether or not to abide by American suggestions.

Inonu took into account not only America's objections, but also the geopolitical and functional factors. He believed that the geopolitical circumstances were unfavorable. Turkey and the Soviet Union still had not normalized relations, and the U.S.S.R. publicly announced that it would assist Makarios if an intervention took place. Furthermore, Greece had made it known that it would aid Makarios. Inonu believed that Turco-Soviet or Turco-Greek confrontations could result if Turkey intervened in Cyprus, and that Turkey could not afford to deal with these contingencies. Inonu also took into account the fact that the armed forces were not prepared to undertake a landing on the island. With the arrival of 20,000 mainland Greek troops in Cyprus in the spring of 1964, the possibility grew that a Turkish intervention would lead to an all-out war between the two countries.

Several other factors tried to shape the outcome of the crisis. The Greek American lobby attempted to influence the President and the Congress, especially after the Turkish air strikes in August 1964. Yet there was no effective congressional activity to oppose Turkey's actions. There is also no evidence to link Johnson's Cyprus policy to the activity of the Greek lobby. Hence, it is difficult to determine the lobby's exact degree of influence on American policy in 1964.

American intelligence reports often referred to military pressures on Inonu. The most influential generals in the post-1960 coup era were often pro-interventionist and did, in fact, pressure Inonu. In one instance they even initiated the air strikes without Inonu's final order. We do not know, however, how much the military factored into Inonu's decision-making. It is likely that Inonu emphasized the military's dissatisfaction with his Cyprus policy in order to convince the U.S. to support his more moderate position. The press, especially the right-wing opposition press, also favored intervention. Yet we do not know just how much the press influenced Inonu.

Until the end of the spring of 1964, Inonu opposed intervention. Hence, his intervention threats in December 1963, and in January, February, and March 1964 were parts of his grand strategy to persuade the U.S. Administration to pressure Greece to accept a negotiated resolution of the dispute. Only once, in June 1964, did Inonu seem to be serious about intervention, but the Johnson Letter convinced him to give up the idea.

American opposition to Turkey's landing on Cyprus was very important for Inonu who feared that the U.S. might join other members of the U.N. Security Council in demanding Turkey's withdrawal from the island. Inonu also feared the possibility of dealing with a Soviet intervention in Cyprus on the side of Makarios, and did not want to face that contingency without U.S. support. Hence, Johnson's admonition that the U.S. might not stand by Turkey if its intervention in Cyprus led to a Turco-Soviet confrontation had the desired effect on Inonu. It should be added that Inonu's cautiousness contributed to the effectiveness of Johnson's reproof.

Several of the influence variables mentioned earlier proved to be relevant to the 1964 crisis. The proposition that the amount of influence a state wields over others can be related to the capabilities mobilized in support of specific foreign policy objectives has been verified.[193] American pressures on Inonu in June 1964 discouraged him from intervention. The U.S. was not as successful, however, in August 1964 when it tried to convince Inonu to accept the so-called Second Acheson Plan. The American capabilities mobilized in the first instance—threats of withdrawal of support if the Soviet Union attacked; prohibition of the use of American supplied weapons in Cyprus, etc.—were sufficient to deter Inonu. The same capabilities or resources were not used in support of the Acheson Plan in August 1964. In August 1964 these sources were neither relevant nor would they be taken seriously by Inonu.

This brings us to another proposition. The resources of influence are most effective when used negatively to veto or deny a specific outcome.[194] The same amount of power produces far less impressive results when it is applied to promoting an outcome. In June 1964 Inonu was deterred because the resources of U.S. influence were relevant and aimed at discouraging him. In August 1964 the American mediator Acheson had to deal not only with Inonu, but also with Makarios and Papandreou. The U.S. needed to use a much larger pool of resources to promote the Acheson Plan.

The 1964 crisis also bore out the so-called "rule of anticipated reactions."[195] Many times Inonu behaved in a way desired by the U.S. Administration even though the U.S. had not tried to make its wishes known. This was the case in December 1963 and

January 1964 when the U.S. avoided assuming responsibility and asked Britain to mediate the dispute. It is true that Inonu opposed intervention for the major part of the crisis, but his reluctance was based partly on his anticipation that the U.S. would oppose Turkey's landing. In one instance, in June 1964, Inonu decided to test the U.S. to see whether it would demand a reversal or whether he could get away with the intervention. The Johnson Letter showed that the U.S. still opposed Turkey's unilateral action.

The events of 1964 also demonstrated the validity of the proposition that states take into account two variables before making a decision to act: utility of actions and probability of reactions.[196] According to this thesis, if Inonu had estimated that the U.S. would very likely not punish Turkey then he almost certainly would have acted without taking the U.S. reaction into account. Yet even if Inonu expected that the U.S. would react hostilely, he might have adopted a bolder policy—including military intervention—if he had attached a high value to the outcome. The fact that Inonu failed to act assertively attests to his perception that the importance of American reactions outweighed the utility of assertiveness.

Earlier it was suggested that policymakers differ in the degree to which they stress either the probability or the preference element in their appraisal of an outcome. If the policymakers prefer a specific outcome, they tend to exaggerate its probability. Conversely, when a probability seems low, they tend to downgrade the attractiveness of the associated outcome.[197] Inonu was one of those who stressed the preference element. For a number of reasons he preferred an American-mediated settlement of the crisis. Thus, he believed that a solution could be achieved if only the U.S. Administration "learned the facts about Cyprus." Since, he did not consider the outcome of a Turkish intervention attractive, he downgraded the probability of success of the intervention.

There are three more propositions which are pertinent to the 1964 crisis: (1) there are variations in the skill or efficiency with which policymakers use the resources; (2) there are variations in the extent to which individuals stress influencing others; (3) influence is partly determined by the responsiveness of the influenced to the requests of the influencer.[198] In our case, the U.S. skillfully and extensively influenced Inonu whose responsiveness to the requests rendered the influence attempt successful. The U.S. did not enjoy comparable success in finding a peaceful solution to the crisis. The cause for its failure was that Greece did not respond as well to U.S. influence attempts and that the U.S. policymakers did not use their resources as skillfully and as extensively as they did to influence Turkey.

The U.S. Administration could have tried to pressure Inonu to accept *enosis* without any compensation for Turkey. Such an influence attempt would have been bound to fail, however, because Inonu almost certainly would have rejected any solution that the Turkish public would perceive as opposed to national interests. As suggested earlier, even client regimes that are highly dependent on a superpower would find it difficult to accept settlements which are considered by their people as contrary to national interests, and thus illegitimate. Inonu knew that if he were to accept *enosis*, his government would lose some of its legitimacy. Hence, no matter how responsive Inonu was to U.S. suggestions, he could not afford to comply with a humiliating settlement.

Toward the end of 1964, Inonu gave up his brinkmanship and seemed to have resigned himself to the stalemate in Cyprus. As a result, the U.S. Administration found it easier to delay its mediation role. The U.S. also seemed content with the *status quo* on the island and urged restraint on all the parties to the dispute. This development also verifies

Friedrich's proposition that influencers usually uphold the existing state of affairs and therefore object to a change in the *status quo* unless they are forced to such a change.[199]

NOTES

1. The Republican People's Party (RPP)—Justice Party (JP) coalition (Nov. 1961-June 1962); The RPP—New Turkey Party (NTP)—Republican Peasant and Nation Party (RPNP) coalition (June 1962-Dec. 1963); The RPP—Independents coalition (Dec. 1963-Feb. 1965); JP-NTP-RPNP coalition (Feb. 1965-Oct. 1965). See Feroz Ahmad, *The Turkish Experiment in Democracy: 1950-1975* (London: C. Hurst & Company, 1977), pp. 212-227.

2. Roger Nye, "The Military in Turkish Politics: 1960-1973" (Ph.D. dissertation, Washington University, St. Louis, 1974), p. 127.

3. *Ibid.*, p. 263.

4. *Ibid.*, p. 129; Kemal Karpat, "The Military and Politics in Turkey, 1960-1964: A Socio-Cultural Analysis of a Revolution," *The American Historical Review*, Vol. LXXV, No. 6 (Oct., 1970), p. 1680; Nurhan Ince, "Problems and Politics in Turkish Foreign Policy, 1960-1966" (Ph.D. dissertation, University of Kentucky, 1974), p. 66.

5. *Ulus* [Turkish daily], 20 July 1961.

6. See Turkish papers of 29 May 1960. See also: Haluk Ulman, R. H. Dekmejian, "Changing Patterns in Turkish Foreign Policy: 1959-1967," *Orbis*, Vol. XI, No. 3 (Fall 1967), p. 775.

7. Suat Bilge, "Turkiye-Sovyetler Birligi Munasebetleri" *Olaylarla Turk Dis Politikasi* (Ankara: Ankara Universitesi, 1977), pp. 435-436; Alvin Z. Rubinstein, *Soviet Policy Toward*

Turkey, Iran and Afghanistan (New York: Praeger, 1982), p. 17.

8. *The New York Times*, 17 June 1962; Mehmet Gonlubol, "27 Mayis 1960 Devrimi ve Sonrasi," *Olaylarla Turk Dis Politikasi* (Ankara: Ankara Universitesi, 1977), p. 336; Metin Toker, *Ismet Pasayla on Yil, 1961-1964* ([ ]: Burcak Yavinlari, 1969), p. 37.

9. Cuneyt Arcayurek, *Yeni Demokrasi, Yeni Arayislar, 1960-1965* (Ankara: Bilgi, 1984), pp. 262, 264.

10. *Millet Meclisi Tutanak Dergisi* ("Official Records of the National Assembly"), Vol. VIII (1962), p. 246 in Duygu Sezer, *Kamu Oyu ve Dis Politika* (Ankara: Ankara Universitesi, 1972), p. 123; Toker, *op. cit.*, p. 101.

11. Gonlubol, *op. cit.*, p. 338; See Turkish papers of 26 Oct. 1962.

12. Turkey had opposed the withdrawal of these missiles in 1961 and 1962. See: Ferenc A. Vali, *Bridge Across the Bosporus* (Baltimore: The John Hopkins Press, 1971), p. 128.

13. On October 1972, after receiving Khrushchev's message demanding the removal of Turkish missiles, the President asked Robert F. Kennedy to privately assure Soviet Ambassador Dobrynin that the U.S. would remove them within a short time. But publicly the U.S. refused to acknowledge that any deal was made. See: Robert F. Kennedy, *Thirteen Days* (New York: W.W. Norton, 1969), p. 108; George Harris, *Troubled Alliance* (Washington, D.C.: American Enterprise Institute, 1972), p. 93.

14. *Milliyet*, 19 February 1963.

15. M. Piri, "Fuzeler Meselesi" *Cumhuriyet*, 4 Jan. 1963.

16. Zenon Stavrinides, *The Cyprus Conflict: National Identity and Statehood* (Wakefield: Stavrinides, 1976), p. 40. See also Kyriacos C. Markides, *The Rise and Fall of the Cyprus Republic* (New Haven and London: Yale University Press, 1977), pp. 36-37.

17. Markides, *op. cit.*, pp. 36-37.

18. *Observer*, London, 2 April 1961, p. 4; Thomas Ehrlich, *Cyprus, 1958-1967* (New York: Oxford University Press, 1974), p. 43; Stanley Kyriakides, *Cyprus: Constitutionalism and Crisis Government* (Philadelphia: University of Pennsylvania Press, 1968), pp. 85-88.

19. Kyriakides, *op. cit.*, p. 92.

20. Stavrinides, *op. cit.*, p. 46.

21. Albert P. Blaustein, Gisbert H. Flanz, *Constitutions of the Countries of the World: Cyprus* (Dobbs Ferry, N.Y.: Oceana Publications, 1972), p. 51.

22. *The Times*, London, 23 Oct. 1961, p. 9. See also: Kyriakides, *op. cit.*, pp. 92-94; Ehrlich, *op. cit.*, p. 44.

23. Blaustein, *op. cit.*, p. 96.

24. Polyvios G. Polyviou, *Cyprus: Conflict and Negotiation, 1960-1980* (New York: Holmes & Meier, 1980), p. 34.

25. *Ibid.*

26. *The Times*, London, 3 Jan. 1963, p. 7.

27. *Elefteria*, Nicosia, 32 Dec. 1962 in Kyriakides, *op. cit.*, p. 98; *Milliyet*, Istanbul, 3 Jan. 1963.

28. *Reports of the Supreme Constitutional Court of Cyprus*, 25 April 1963, pp. 59, 74-77 in Ehrlich, *op. cit.*, p. 44.

29. Dimitri S. Bitsios, *Cyprus: The Vulnerable Republic* (Thessaloniki: Institute for Balkan Studies, 1975), p. 116.

30. Stavrinides, *op. cit.*, p. 62.

31. *Millet Meclisi Tutanak Dergisi*, Vol. XXX (1964), 5 May 1964, p. 207; Nihat Erim, *Bildigim ve Gordugum Olculer Icinde Kibris* (Ankara: Ajans Turk, 1975), p. 274.

32. *Keesings Contemporary Archives*, 1963, p. 19257.

33. "Memorandum for the President, 1 June 1962," *National Security Council History File: Cyprus Crisis* (hereafter: *NSCHF: Cyprus Crisis*], L. B. Johnson Library, Austin, Texas, p. 2.

34. "Memorandum for RWK", in *Ibid.*

35. "Memorandum for the President, 1 June 1962." in *Ibid.*

36. "Department of State Guidelines for Policy and Operations: Cyprus, Sept. 1962, "*NSCHF: Cyprus Crisis.*

37. "Tel. No. 4387 from State Dept. to American Embassy London, 15 Feb. 1963," *NSCHF: Cyprus Crisis.*

38. Archbishop Makarios, "Proposals to Amend the Cyprus Constitution," *International Relations* [Athens], No. 5 (April, 1964), pp. 8-25.

39. *Ibid.*, pp. 9, 13, 14, 20.

40. *Ibid.*, p. 10.

41. Fazil Kuchuk, *Cyprus: Turkish Reply to Archbishop Makarios' Proposals* (Nicosia: [ ], [1963], p. 21.

42. Stavrinides, *op. cit.*, p. 64.

43. See 21-30 Dec. 1963 issues of *The New York Times, The Washington Post, The Times* and other newspapers for different versions of what happened on 21 Dec. 1963.

44. *The Times*, London, 24 and 27 Dec. 1963. For more information see: Patrick, *op. cit.*, p. 50; Stengenga, *op. cit.*, p. 75; *Daily Telegraph*, London, 14 Jan. 1964; Vali, *op. cit.*, p. 253; Cristopher Hitchens, *Cyprus* (London and New York: Quartet Books, 1984), p. 55; Rauf R. Denktash, *The Cyprus Triangle* (Boston: Allen & Unwin, 1982), pp. 154-155.

45. See Richard A. Patrick, *Political Geography and the Cyprus Conflict* (Ontario, Canada: University of Waterloo, 1976), p. 42; James A. Stegenga, *The U.N. Force in Cyprus* (Columbus: Ohio State University Press, 1968), pp. 61-66.

46. See *Patris*, Nicosia, 21 April 1966 in Stavrinides, *op. cit.*, p. 59; Patrick, *op. cit.*, p. 42.

47. Stavrinides, *op. cit.*, p. 60.

48. *Aksam* [Turkish daily], Istanbul, 23 Dec. 1963. See also Metin Toker, *Ismet Pasayla On Yil* (Vol. IV, [ ]: Burcak Yayinlari, 1969), p. 107.

49. *Aksam*, Istanbul, 24 Dec. 1963.

50. Telegram Nos. 249, 543, 605 (23 Dec. 1963), in *NSCHF: Cyprus Crisis.*

51. Tel. Nos. 544, 606 (23 Dec. 1963) in *NSCHF: Cyprus Crisis.*

52. *Aksam*, 25 Dec. 1963; *Disisleri Bakanligi Belleteni* ("The Bulletin of the Turkish Foreign Ministry"), No. 1 (1964), p. 5; See also Toker, *op. cit.*, p. 106.

53. *Millet Meclisi Tutanak Dergisi*, Vol. XXIV (1963/64), 2 Jan. 1964, p. 126; *Disisleri Bakanligi Belleteni*, No. 1 (1964), p. 5; *Aksam*, 26 Dec. 1963.

54. *Aksam*, 27 Dec. 1963; *Disisleri Bakanligi Belleteni*, No. 1 (1964), p. 5.

55. *Aksam*, 27 Dec. 1963. See also: Erim, *op. cit.*, pp. 212-213.

56. Inonu's son-in-law and biographer Metin Toker wrote that Inonu wanted to intervene in June 1964. See Toker, *op. cit.*, p. 108.

57. Suat Bilge, "Kibris Uyusmazligi," *Olaylarla Turk Dis Politikasi* (Ankara: Ankara Universitesi, 1977), p. 391.

58. Erim, *op. cit.*, p. 218.

59. "Durum," *Milliyet*, 1 Jan. 1964.

60. Cetin Altan, "Akil ve Cizme," *Milliyet*, 1 Jan. 1964.

61. *Millet Meclisi Tutanak Dergisi* ("Official Records of the National Assembly"), Vol. XXIV (1963/64), 24 Dec. 1963 - 6 Jan. 1964.

62. Tel. No. 847 (25 Dec. 1963) in *NSCHF: Cyprus Crisis.*

63. Tel. No. 1777 (27 Dec. 1963) in *NSCHF: Cyprus Crisis.*

64. *Ibid.*

65. *Disisleri Bakanligi Belleteni* ("The Bulletin of the Foreign MInistry"), No. 1 (1964), p. 5.

66. Tel. No. 2822 (23 Jan. 1964) in *NSCHF: Cyprus Crisis*; *Milliyet*, Istanbul, 2 Feb. 1964.

67. *Ibid.*, See also *Cumhuriyet*, Istanbul, 17 Jan. 1964; *Milliyet*, Istanbul, 17 Jan. 1964 and 2 Feb. 1964.

68. Tel. No. 2822 (23 Jan. 1964) in *NSCHF: Cyprus Crisis.*

69. *Milliyet*, 22 Jan. 1964.

70. Tel. No. 653 (21 Jan. 1964) in *NSCHF: Cyprus Crisis.*

71. U.S., Department of State, "Memorandum of Conversation" (24 Jan. 1964), *NSCHF: Cyprus Crisis.*

72. Tel. No. 454 (25 Jan. 1964), *NSCHF: Cyprus Crisis.*

73. Tel. No. 670 (25 Jan. 1964), *NSCHF: Cyprus Crisis.*

74. *Cumhuriyet*, Istanbul, 26 Jan. 1964; *Ulus*, Ankara, 27 Jan. 1964.

75. Tel. No. 996 (26 Jan. 1964), *NSCHF: Cyprus Crisis*; See also: Ince, *op. cit.*, p. 151.

76. George Ball, *The Past Has Another Pattern* (New York: W. W. Norton, 1982), p. 341.

77. *Ibid.*, *The New York Times*, 3 Feb. 1964, pp. 1,8; *Disisleri Bakanligi Belleteni*, No. 1 (1964), p. 7.

78. *Milliyet*, Istanbul, 2 Feb. 1964; *The New York Times*, 1 Feb. 1964.

79. *Disisleri Bakanligi Belleteni*, No. 1 (1964), p. 8.

80. Tel. Nos. 759, 676, 350 (26 Jan. 1964), *NSCHF: Cyprus Crisis.*

81. See: The State Department, "History of the Johnson Administration: Cyprus Problem," *NSCHF: Cyprus Crisis.* See also: Toker, *op. cit.*, p. 114.

82. See *Milliyet*, 9 Sept. 1964.

83. Sevket Sureyya Aydemir, *Ikinci Adam* (Vol. I, Istanbul: Remzi Kitabevi, 1976), pp. 262-263.

84. Toker, *op. cit.*, p. 116; *Millet Meclisi Tutanak Dergisi*, Vol. XXXII (1964), 8 Sept. 1964, p. 387.

85. Abdi Ipekci, "Durum," *Milliyet*, 1 Jan. 1964, p. 1.

86. Thomas W. Adams and Alvin J. Cottrell, *Cyprus Between East and West* (Baltimore: The John Hopkins Press, 1968), p. 35.

87. *Izvestia*, 28 Dec. 1963 in *The Current Digest of the Soviet Press*, Vol. XV (1963), No. 52, p. 27.

88. *The New York Times*, 1 Jan. 1964.

89. U.N., Security Council, *Official Records*, 1096th Meeting, 19 Feb. 1964, Para. 18 and 21.

90. Stegenga, *op. cit.*, p. 48.

91. Cuneyt Arcayurek, *Yeni Demokrasi, Yeni Arayislar* (Ankara: Bilgi, 1984), p. 276; Erim, *op. cit.*, p. 218.

92. Alparslan Turkes, *Dis politikamiz ve Kibris* (Istanbul: Kutlug Yayinlari, 1974), p. 257.

93. See: United Nations, "Secretary General's Report No. S/5950," 10 Sept. 1964, Para. 108; For Turkish and Greek Cypriot positions see: Denktash, *op. cit.*, p. 34; Markides, *op. cit.*, p. 29.

94. U.N., Security Council Document, No. S/5950, p. 307.

95. *Ibid.*, See also: Patrick, *op. cit.*, pp. 80-84.

96. U.N., Security Council Document, No. S/5950.

97. Tel. No. 1184 from Ball to Rusk (9 Feb. 1964) in *NSCHF: Cyprus Crisis.*

98. Toker, *op. cit.*, p. 109.

99. Ball, *op. cit.*, p. 345; Tel. No. 725 from Ball to Rusk (12 Feb. 1964), *NSCHF: Cyprus Crisis.*

100. Ball, *op. cit.*, pp. 344-345.

101. Tel. No. 735 from Ball to Rusk and President Johnson, *NSCHFL: Cyprus Crisis.* See also: U.N., Security Council, *Official Records*, 1095th meeting, 18 Feb. 1964.

102. Tel. No. 512 from Rusk to Ball (13 Feb. 1964), *NSCHF: Cyprus Crisis.*

103. Toker, *op. cit.*, p. 111.

104. See Inonu's Letter to Johnson in *The Middle East Journal*, Vol. XX, No. 3 (Spring, 1966), p. 389.

105. Tel. No. 3961 from Ball to President Johnson and Dean Rusk (16 Feb. 1964), *NSCHF: Cyprus Crisis.*

106. *Ibid.*

107. Tel. No. 5223 from Ball to U.S. London Embassy (19 Feb. 1964), *NSCHF: Cyprus Crisis.*

108. U.N., Security Council, *Official Records*, Res. 186 in Document No. S/5575, 4 March 1964.

109. Toker, *op. cit.*, p. 111.

110. Philip Windsor, *NATO and the Cyprus Crisis* (London: The Institute for Strategic Studies, 1964), Adelphi Papers, No. 14, p. 15.

111. *Milliyet*, Istanbul, 9-14 March 1964.

112. See: *Milliyet* and *Cumhuriyet*, 8-15 March 1964.

113. *Millet Meclisi Tutanak Dergisi*, Vol. XXVIII (1964), 11 March 1964, pp. 548-552.

114. *Milliyet*, Istanbul, 13 March 1964; *Disisleri Bakanligi*, No. 1 (1964), p. 10.

115. Tel. No. 1159 from the U.S. Embassy in Ankara to the State Department (12 March 1964), *NSCHF: Cyprus Crisis.*

116. Tel. No. 950 from Dean Rusk to Raymond Hare (13 March 1964), *NSCHF: Cyprus Crisis.*

117. *Milliyet*, 16 March 1964.

118. Erim, *op. cit.*, p. 264.

119. *Ibid.*

120. *Cumhuriyet*, 12-30 May 1964.

121. *Cumhuriyet*, 1-5 June 1964; *Milliyet*, 5 June 1964.

122. Ball, *op. cit.*, p. 350.

123. Toker, *op. cit.*, p. 116; Erim, *op. cit.*, p. 300.

124. Cuneyt Arcayurek, *Yeni Democrasi, Yeni Arayislar*), p. 274.

125. Tel. No. 1616 from Ambassador Hare to the State Department (6 June 1964), *NSCHF: Cyprus Crisis.*

126. Tel. No. 1599 from U.S. Embassy in Ankara to the State Department (4 June 1964), *NSCHF: Cyprus Crisis.*

127. *Ibid.*

128. Aysel Aziz, "1964 Yilinda Kibris Buhrani ve Sovyetler Birligi," *Siyasal Bilgiler Fakultesi Dergisi*, Ankara, Vol. XXIV, No. 3, p. 188.

129. Tel. No. 1295 from Rusk to U.S. Embassy in Ankara (4 June 1964), *NSCHF: Cyprus Crisis.*

130. Tel. No. 904 from Rusk to U.S. Embassy in Nicosia (5 JUne 1964), *NSCHF: Cyprus Crisis.*

131. See: *Milliyet and Cumhuriyet*, 13 June 1964.

132. "President Johnson's Letter to Prime Minister Inonu," *The Middle East Journal*, Vol. XX, No. 3 (1964), p. 386.

133. *Ibid.*, p. 387; Ball, *op. cit.*, p. 354.

134. *Ibid.*

135. *Ibid.*

136. *Izvestia*, 5 May 1964 quoted in *The Current Digest of the Soviet Press*, Vol. XVI (1964), No. 18, p. 26.

137. "Prime Minister Inonu's Response to the President, 13 June 1964," *The Middle East Journal*, Vol. XX, No. 3 (1964), p. 386.

138. Abdi Ipekci, "Durum," *Milliyet*, 11 June 1964.

139. "President Johnson's Letter to Prime Minister Inonu," *op. cit.*

140. Tel. Nos. 759, 676, 350 to U.S. Embassies in Ankara, Athens, and Nicosia, *NSCHF: Cyprus Crisis.*

141. *Ibid.*

142. "Memorandum of Conversation: President's Meeting with the Greek Ambassador Matsas, 11 June 1964," *NSCHF: Cyprus Crisis.*

143. *Disisleri Bakanligi Belleteni*, No. 17 (28 Feb. 1966), p. 74; See also: Andreas Papandreou, *Democracy at Gunpoint: The Greek Front (Garden City, NY: Doubleday, 1970), p. 108.*

144. *The New York Times*, 24 June 1964.

145. *Milliyet*, 25 June 1964; 3 July 1964.

146. *Aksam*, 12 May 1964; *Milliyet*, 7 Feb. 1964.

147. *Milliyet*, 29 June 1964.

148. Erim, *op. cit.*, p. 350.

149. "Document No. 19: Acheson Plan I," *NSCHF: Cyprus Crisis.*

150. *Ibid.*

151. *Ibid.*, Erim, *op. cit.*, p. 376.

152. U.N., Security Council, "Report of the Secrctary General, S/5950," *Official Records*, Supplement for July, August and September 1964, p. 324.

153. *Vatan*, 28 July 1964.

154. Papandreou, *op. cit.*, p. 132; See also "Report of the Secretary General, S/5950," *op. cit.*, p. 288.

155. "Report of the Secretary General, S/5950, *op. cit.*, pp. 299-300.

156. Erim, *op. cit.*, p. 381.

157. "Report of the Secretary General, S/5950," *op. cit.*, p. 300.

158. Tel. No. 2 from the U.S. Embassy in Ankara to the State Department (8 August 1964), *NSCHF: Cyprus Crisis.*

159. Arcayurek, *Demirel Donemi, 21 Mart Darbesi*, pp. 204-205; *Cumhuriyet*, 9 August 1964.

160. *Ibid.*, *Cumhuriyet*, 10 August 1964.

161. *Keesings Contemporary Archives*, 1964, p. 20266.

162. Tel. No. 223 from the U.S. Embassy in Nicosia to the State Department (9 August 1964), *NSCHF: Cyprus Crisis.*

163. Toker, *op. cit.*, p. 122; *Milliyet*, 12 Aug. 1964; Erim, *op. cit.*, p. 393.

164. *Millet Meclisi Tutanak Dergisi*, Vol. XXXII (1964), 3 Sept. 1964, p. 276.

165. *Cumhuriyet*, 12 August 1964.

166. Erim, *op. cit.*, p. 398; *Milliyet*, 4 Sept. 1964.

167. See Inonu's speech: *Millet Meclisi Tutanak Dergisi*, Vol. XXXII (1964), 3 September 1964, p. 277.

168. "Acheson Plan II," *NSCHF: Cyprus Crisis.*

169. *Milliyet*, 4 September 1964.

170. *The National Herald* [Greek American], 30 August 1964, p. 9.

171. U.N., Security Council, "Document S/5950," p. 333; See also Patrick, *op. cit.*, p. 107.

172. *Millet Meclisi Tutanak Dergisi*, Vol. XXXII (1964), 8 Sept. 1964, p. 387.

173. *Ibid.*

174. U.N., Security Council, *Official Records*, 1153rd Meeting, 17 Sept. 1964, para. 91.

175. *Ibid.*, p. 389.

176. *Milliyet*, 4 Sept. 1964.

177. *Milliyet*, 7 and 8 Sept. 1964.

178. *The New York Times*, 2 Sept. 1964, p. 2; *Milliyet*, 2 Sept. 1964; *Cumhuriyet*, 28 and 29 August 1964.

179. *Ibid.*

180. Ahmet Kabakli, "Dayanisma," *Tercuman*, 1 June 1964.

181. Cetin Altan, "Tek Pusula Kibris mi," *Milliyet*, 11 July 1964, p. 2.

182. Abdi Ipekci, "Turk-Sovyet Munasebetleri," *Milliyet*, 5 August 1964.

183. Landau, *op. cit.*, pp. 12-13, 18.

184. *The New York Times*, 1 March 1964, p. 3.

185. *The National Herald*, 9 August 1964, p. 9; See also George Leber, *The History of the Order of Ahepa* (Washington, D.C.: The Order of Ahepa, 1972), p. 451.

186. *The National Herald*, 13 Sept. 1964, p. 9.

187. *Ibid.*, 30 August 1964, p. 9.

188. *The National Herald*, 23 Aug. 1964, p. 10.

189. Leber, *op. cit.*, p. 455.

190. *The National Herald*, 23 Aug. 1964, p. 10.

191. *The Ahepan*, November 1964, p. 7.

192. *Ibid.*

193. K. J. Holsti, *International Politics: A Framework for Analysis* (Englewood Cliffs, NJ: Prentice-Hall, 1983), p. 149.

194. Karl W. Deutsch, "On the Concepts of Politics and Power," *International Politics and Foreign Policy*, ed. by James N. Rosenau (New York: The Free Press, 1969), p. 260.

195. Carl Joachim Friedrich, *Man and His Government, An Empirical Theory of Politics* (New York: McGraw-Hill, 1963), p. 203.

196. David Singer, "Inter-Nation Influence: A Formal Model," *International Politics and Foreign Policy*, ed. by James N. Rosenau (New York: The Free Press, 1969), p. 386.

197. *Ibid*., p. 387.

198. Holsti, *op. cit*., p. 153; Robert Dahl, *Modern Political Analysis* (Englewood Cliffs, N.J.: Prentice-Hall, 1976), p. 33.

199. Friedrich, *op. cit*., p. 202.

III. 1967 Cyprus Crisis

Turkey Adopts A "Multi-Faceted" Foreign Policy

As indicated in the previous chapter, after the 1964 Cyprus crisis Turkish policymakers and the public began a thorough examination of the overall Turkish foreign policy in order to find the reasons for Turkey's failure to intervene. The consensus reached by most political parties and the public in general was that Turkey's political dependency on the U.S. and its isolation in the international community were the cause of the Cyprus debacle, and that Turkey needed to improve relations with the Soviet Union and the Third World.

Bulent Ecevit, then secretary general of Inonu's Republican People's Party (RPP), expressed a widely shared belief when he suggested that the Turkish people had discovered how unreliable Turkey's allies were. In an article published in *Milliyet* Ecevit argued that Turkey's NATO membership could be irrelevant in certain contingencies when Turkey's national interests were at stake. As a result, he said,

> we realized that our one-dimensional national security approach did not cover all contingencies. We began to discuss whether Turkey's membership in NATO contributed to Turkish security or actually increased dangers. We also realized that [NATO's commitment to our security] would be useless if our friends changed their minds

> [and did not stand up to their commitments] . . . We also realized how isolated we were. Because of the [international] isolation we faced enormous difficulties [in convincing other states] that our cause was just . . .[1]

Turkey's frustration would further increase on 11 October 1964 when the Conference of Nonaligned Countries in Cairo once more upheld the Greek Cypriot arguments. The final communique stated that Cypriots should enjoy "unrestricted and unfettered sovereignty" and that the independence of Cyprus should be respected.[2] This pro-Greek resolution passed despite the Turkish Foreign Ministry's eleventh hour efforts to dispatch bipartisan goodwill missions to Third World countries to propagate Turkey's Cyprus thesis.[3] Turkey was further humiliated when its delegates who wanted to attend the Conference as observers were denied the right to do so.[4]

Despite this initial failure in breaking Turkey's isolation, the Inonu Government went ahead with its "multi-faceted" foreign policy. For the first time in decades Turkey sent its foreign minister to Moscow on 30 October 1964 on an official visit. Erkin's visit is also important because it came only two weeks after the ouster of Khrushchev (15 October) who had repeatedly expressed his support for Makarios and only one month earlier, on 1 October 1964, had agreed to visiting "Foreign Minister of Cyprus" Kyprianou's suggestion to send arms to Cyprus.[5]

When Erkin arrived in Moscow on 30 October 1964, he found that the new Soviet leadership, in contrast to Khrushchev, was anxious to improve relations with Turkey. Perhaps more surprisingly, the Soviets told Erkin that they were ready to revise their Cyprus policy and recognize not only the existence of Turkish Cypriots as a national community, but also the fact that they possessed "legal rights." The joint communique issued at the end of the visit (6 November 1964) stated that both countries respected the independence of Cyprus and acknowledged "the legal rights of two national communities."[6] The use of "legal rights" implied but did not exactly spell out that the U.S.S.R. recognized the 1960 Cyprus constitution.

After his return from the Soviet Union, Foreign Minister Erkin told the National Assembly that Turkey welcomed the Soviet overtures and explained the newly adopted "multi-faceted" foreign policy:

> [Turkey] has decided to play an important role in world affairs. [Turkey] wants its national causes to be supported by as broad an [international community] as possible. Therefore, our government wants to create a peace ring around Turkey and establish good relations with its neighbors. We also want to intensify our relations with Afro-Asian countries."[7]

A broad spectrum of the Turkish population supported Inonu's opening to the Soviets and the Third World. The opposition JP party, and its speaker Yilmaz Akcal supported the new policy and suggested that Turkey should also establish relations with the People's Republic of China and improve Turco-Arab relations.[8]

During the following months the Soviets made additional overtures toward Turkey. Chairman of the Soviet Presidium Nikolai H. Podgorni visited Turkey from 4 to 13 January 1965 and apologized for Stalin's post-World War II claims on Turkey. Podgorni also promised not to sell "heavy arms" to Makarios.[9] Turkey reciprocated by informing the U.S. that it decided not to participate in the nuclear Multilateral Force (MLF) of NATO and withdrew its contingent from the "USS Claude Ricketts" destroyer where it served on a trial basis.[10] Turkish public opinion perceived this action as a response both to Soviet overtures and to America's "betrayal" of its "loyal ally." Deputy Foreign Minister Kemal Satir explained

Turkey's withdrawal from the MLF on 26 January 1965 by suggesting that

> our decision as regards the MLF is a normal development. It is also a consequence of changes in Turkish perspective caused by some events. If we assume that Turco-Soviet relations have improved, [we should be careful to note] that Turkey's withdrawal from the MLF is not as a result of this improvement. It is rather the other way around . . .[11]

Satir added that Turkey actually decided to withdraw in June 1964, or after the Johnson Letter, but "our friends had dissuaded us . . ."[12]

The Soviet Union's "tilt" toward Turkey was once more stressed on 21 January 1965 when Soviet Foreign Minister Gromyko stated that the two Cypriot "national communities . . . may choose a federal form of government."[13] As mentioned earlier, Inonu had advocated a federal solution for the Cyprus crisis since January 1963. Hence, the Soviet approval of Turkey's federation thesis as a possible outcome of negotiations was clearly a pro-Turkish gesture. It should be added, however, that the Soviets continued to consider Makarios as a legitimate ruler. In the U.S.S.R.-"Cyprus" joint communiques the Soviets went on denouncing "foreign" interference in Cypriot affairs.[14] The post-1964 Cyprus policy of the Soviets resembled a juggling act in which the Soviets did not want to offend any of the parties. Turkish policymakers, however, were clearly pleased with this evenhanded approach which they justifiably considered to be a development in their favor.

Conservative Suleyman Demirel whose Justice party had come to power in November 1964 with a comfortable majority in the National Assembly, continued the "multi-faceted" foreign policy. The program of the Demirel Government in 1965 stated:

> The bipolar system does not correspond to world realities. . . . Belonging to a particular alliance . . . does not preclude any state from improving its relations with members of another alliance or with Third World states.[15]

Demirel's version of the "multi-faceted" foreign policy was comprised of four factors: (1) Turkey's security should be strengthened by diplomatic initiatives; (2) Turkey needed additional economic resources for its development; (3) Turkey should have good relations with its neighbors irrespective of their political regimes; (4) Turkey should seek new friends in the international arena in order to acquire their support for Turkey's Cyprus policy.[16] Each of these four factors required improving relations with the Soviet Union. Known as an ardent anti-communist who accused Inonu's RPP of softness on communism, Demirel, nevertheless, seized the initiative to respond to Soviet gestures which intensified in 1965. On 28 December 1965, two months after coming to power, Demirel banned United States U-2 flights conducted in Turkey.[17]

As a result of both Turkish and Soviet willingness, economic relations between the two countries also experienced a thaw. In March 1967 "Turkey signed the most far-reaching industrial assistance agreement it had ever concluded with any country."[18] The Soviets agreed to build a number of industrial plants including a steel mill, an aluminum smelter and an oil refinery. By the end of the 1960s Turkey became the "recipient of more Soviet economic assistance than any other Third World country."[19] It must be stressed, however, that Demirel turned to the Soviets after the U.S. and other Western states refused to finance these ventures.[20] The economic cooperation and the normalization of state-to-state relations with the U.S.S.R. remained within certain bounds. On 22 December 1966, for instance, Demirel refused Soviet Premier Kosygin's offer to sign a non-aggression pact.[21]

Turkey Tries to Improve Turco-Arab Relations

The improvement of Turkey's relations with the Third World, and especially with its Middle Eastern neighbors, constituted an important part of the new "multi-faceted" foreign policy. Turkey's overtures toward its southern neighbors took the form of distancing itself from U.S. Middle East policy and slowly increasing its support for the Palestinians. Foreign Minister Erkin explained on 1 February 1965 that Turkey's interest in the plight of "refugees [would] eliminate the old disagreements between Turkey and the Arab World and lead to close and friendly relations with them . . ."[22]

The indications of Turkey's new attitude toward the Middle East could best be seen in diplomatic communiques issued jointly by Turkey and area states. In all of them the Demirel Government announced that "the establishment of peace in [the Middle East] could be possibly [only] after an equitable and just settlement of the Palestinian question. . . ."[23] The Arab states' response to Turkey's overtures was, however, far from being enthusiastic. Even traditionally friendly states hesitated to announce their full support for Turkey's Cyprus thesis. The usual statement in these communiques was that the Cyprus crisis should be solved through negotiations.[24] Only a few states such as Turkey's ex-Baghdad Pact ally Iraq or Jordan went as far as suggesting that "the legitimate rights of two national communities which are protected by the international treaties should be respected."[25]

Notwithstanding its initial failure to bring about a favorable response to its Cyprus policy, Turkey went ahead with courting the Arab states. During the June 1967 Arab-Israeli war the Demirel Government explicitly told the U.S. Administration that U.S. bases in Turkey could not be used to resupply the Israelis. The Arab states were informed about Turkey's decision even before the start of the hostilities.[26] After the war the Demirel Government consistently called on Israel to withdraw from territories occupied in the 1967 war. On 22 June 1967 Turkish Foreign Minister Caglayangil addressed the U.S. General Assembly, stating, "We have always stated that we cannot accept the use of force for the purpose of settling a conflict. . . . The Assembly must therefore call for the withdrawal of Israeli forces from the territories they occupied. . . .[27] Turkey also co-sponsored U.N. General Assembly Resolution 2253 calling on Israel "to rescind all measures already taken and to desist forthwith from taking any action which would alter the status of Jerusalem."[28]

Despite Turkey's pro-Arab tilt during and after the 1967 war, the "radical" Arab states such as Syria and Egypt continued their indifference toward Turkey's Cyprus thesis, even though they praised Turkey's behavior during the war.[29] These states probably considered Turkey's newly adopted policy as not sufficiently pro-Arab given the fact that Turkey maintained diplomatic relations with Israel. They considered Makarios on the other hand a "true friend" of Arabs. As in the case of Syria, bilateral problems prevented some of the Arab states from supporting Turkey's Cyprus thesis. Syria preserved its hostile attitude toward Turkey because it still could not accept the fact that Hatay (Alexandretta) remained within Turkish borders.

There were also few Third World states that chose to side with Turkey, and despite the adoption of the "multi-faceted" foreign policy, Turkey's actions toward the Third World were inconsistent. Turkey refused, for instance, to establish diplomatic relations with the People's Republic of China until 1971.[30] Turkey voted in the U.N. several times against the policies of the Republic of South Africa, but it failed to condemn Portugal's colonial policies.[31] It is not known to what degree this inconsistency affected the

Third World's perceptions of Turkey's Cyprus policy. It would be fair to assume, however, that the Third World states still would have opposed Turkey's Cyprus thesis even if Turkey had taken a stand against its NATO allies. Given the fact that many Third World countries were multinational, it would have been impossible for them to embrace the cause of a national community which was in the minority in its respective state.

It is thus no surprise that most Third World states consistently voted in favor of pro-Makarios resolutions at the U.N. One of the most celebrated or denounced U.N. resolutions was General Assembly Resolution 2077 (18 December 1965) which reaffirmed the sovereignty of Cyprus and the "illegality" of external interventions. Most of the forty-seven countries who voted in favor of it belonged to the Third World. The Soviet bloc countries and Western states were among those fifty-four who abstained. Only five states, Turkey, the U.S., Iran, Pakistan, and Albania, voted against the resolution.[32] The adoption of Resolution 2077 demonstrated that in spite of Turkey's efforts to break its international isolation it still had a long way to go. The vote also showed, however, that Turkey's efforts vis-a-vis the Soviet bloc, which abstained, were quite successful. Until the end of 1964 the Soviet bloc had been an ardent supporter of Makarios.

Relations with the U.S. (1965-1967)

In the second chapter we saw that the Turkish public blamed the U.S. Administration for Turkey's failure to intervene in Cyprus. Between 1965 and 1967 this feeling intensified, especially after the publication of the official version of the Johnson Letter in 1966. According to a public opinion poll conducted in Ankara and Istanbul in 1965, 84 percent of those questioned said that "the activities of the United States in regard to the Cyprus dispute" negatively affected their feelings toward that country. Only 18 percent of those surveyed still considered the U.S. as Turkey's best friend. The approval rating of Turkey's membership in NATO was, however, 78 percent which showed that despite the perceived lack of U.S. support for Turkey's Cyprus policy, Turkey's NATO membership still enjoyed popularity.[33] Another poll conducted among Ankara University students suggested that even 95 percent of the students mainly were interested in the Cyprus dispute and ignored its ramifications on larger foreign policy issues.[34]

It should be added that the Turkish public also blamed the U.S. for the unpreparedness of the Turkish armed forces to meet a contingency in Cyprus. As we have seen, the lack of suitable equipment to undertake a naval landing in Cyprus had influenced Inonu's decisions in 1964. The press reports that the U.S. intentionally neglected assistance to the Turkish navy were accepted by the public as undisputed facts. Yilmaz Cetiner wrote in *Cumhuriyet* on 30 April 1965 that whereas the U.S. had delivered forty-four landing craft to Greece, it ignored Turkey. Cetiner further argued that in the last decade the U.S. transferred to Greece six destroyers and two submarines while Turkey remained empty-handed. Cetiner, like most journalists, concluded that the U.S. was doing all this because it favored *enosis*.[35]

Following these reports, *Cumhuriyet* started a fund-raising campaign to strengthen the Turkish navy.[36] Within days the Government joined in the activity and announced on 4 May 1965 the establishment of the *Donanma Cemiyeti*, or the Navy Association, which would organize the official fund-raising efforts. Demirel, then Deputy Premier, stated that Turkey would invest $450 million in the manufacturing of landing craft.[37]

After 1965 the general public began losing interest in the Cyprus question and the U.S. role during the dispute. The student organizations, which eventually adopted socialist agendas, likewise relegated Cyprus to a secondary place in their discussions or demonstrations, even though it was the Cyprus dispute that had triggered the questioning of the merits of an alliance with the U.S.[38] Students began to demonstrate against the visits of the Sixth Fleet, "American imperialism," the Vietnam war and U.S. bases in Turkey.[39]

The conservative JP, which had blamed the 1964 Cyprus debacle on Inonu's inaptitude, did not want a deterioration in U.S.-Turkey relations. Demirel believed that Turkey's security needed an additional "collective assurance," and NATO provided that. He suggested that the lack of U.S. support for Turkey's Cyprus policy was regrettable but that Turkey's overall security interests required the continuation of its alliance ties.[40] The Demirel Government thus shunned any public criticism of the U.S. This is not to say, however, that Demirel opposed the "multi-faceted" foreign policy. As we have seen, it was Demirel who insisted that NATO would not hinder an assertive Turkish policy in Cyprus.

Demirel also insisted on reorganizing the status of U.S. bases and U.S. personnel in Turkey in order to reassert Turkish sovereignty over them. The misuse of privileges and installations had been major embarrassments which tarnished the Government's authority and legitimacy. Turkey started to informally review the Turco-U.S. bilateral agreements in August 1964 and asked the U.S. Administration on 7 April 1966 to conclude a new treaty.[41]

The negotiations ended on 3 July 1969 when the two countries signed the Joint Defense and Cooperation Treaty. Demirel cited the advantages of the new agreement by saying:

> The control of the Turkish Government over the joint defense installations and activities from them will be full and absolute. Turkey will inspect all these installations as she finds it necessary to ensure that they are used in accordance with the agreements. . . . The Turkish

> Government will allow the U.S. Government to engage in any of the joint defense activities in Turkey only after it has full and detailed knowledge of them.[42]

Conservative Demirel's action to reclaim Turkey's sovereignty over American installations was what Inonu's RPP had demanded since the 1964 Cyprus crisis. The RPP, which for the first time proclaimed itself as a "left-of-center" party in 1965, had insisted that the "multi-faceted" foreign policy also required "dignified and equal" relations with the U.S. Inonu insisted, however, that Turkey could not afford to withdraw from NATO.[43] Thus, despite the outward appearance of a difference of opinion on foreign policy between the right-wing JP and the left-wing RPP, both parties desired a similar revision in foreign policy. By the time the 1967 Cyprus crisis occurred, Turkish policymakers had largely carried out the measures they deemed necessary to cope with a new Cyprus crisis.

Developments in Cyprus Between 1964-1967

As noted in the second chapter, the "Cyprus Government" had imposed an economic blockade on the Turkish Cypriot enclaves after the August 1964 battle in Kokkina. At the end of 1964 it lifted the economic blockade in most Turkish sectors. The ban on "strategic" materials, including car tires, socks, gloves, leather jackets and building materials continued until 1968.[44]

After 1963 all Turkish government employees lost their jobs and became unemployed. Thirty to forty percent of Turkish farms could not be cultivated because their owners had fled to Turkish enclaves during the 1963-64 hostilities. About one-third of Turks lived in refugee camps "under conditions of abject misery and semi-starvation."[45] Rauk Denktash, then the strongman of the Turkish Cypriot administration, stated that

> [s]tarting with the events of 1963, all the economic resources of the island were utilized for the development of the Greek Cypriot community. By a 'Government' decree sale of land to the Turkish Cypriots was prohibited while licenses for building factories etc. were arbitrarily denied to them. The Turkish Cypriots were deprived of their freedom of movement and communication and lived in an economy of consumption in their enclaves at the mercy of the Greek Cypriot producers and importers.[46]

The Turkish Cypriots were quick to establish their own administration which resembled a small state but controlled only 5 percent of the island. The Turkish Administration possessed all the political, military, administrative, judicial and social institutions. It should be added that Turkey subsidized most of the functions of this administration by an annual grant of 10 million British pounds.[47]

After seizing the whole state apparatus, the Greek Cypriots passed laws in violation of the constitution and ran the country as if the Turkish Community did not exist. The Greek Cypriots considered the 1960 constitution as practically invalid though they did not formally abolish it.[48] Polyios G. Polyviou, a Greek Cypriot delegate at the 1974 Geneva Conference wrote:

> Throughout the 1963-74 period there seemed to have been a feeling on the Greek Cypriot side that it was for the Greek side to dictate terms and that eventually the Turkish Cypriot Community would be forced by its own self-segregation and the economic deprivation that entailed to come

> to the negotiating table. This was a monumental mistake of basic policy. Not only did we fail to grasp the emotional and psychological aspects of the Cyprus problem for Turkey . . . but we also identified 'majority' with 'power.'[49]

On 22 July 1965, after more than eighteen months, the Turkish members of the House of Representatives informed the U.N. peacekeeping force that they wanted to attend the House deliberations. When President of the House Glafkos Klerides learned the intention of Turkish representatives, he announced that

> certain provisions of the Constitution which conferred a special status on the Turkish Cypriot community could no longer be considered as being in effect, that by their prolonged absence from the sessions of the House and other actions the Turkish Cypriot members had allowed their mandates to lapse, and that in any case the Turkish Cypriot members would not be permitted to return to the House to participate in enactment of legislation . . .[50]

It was clear that the Greek Cypriots had no intention of going back to the pre-December 1963 order in Cyprus. Instead the Greek Cypriot leadership was determined to pursue its major aspiration, *enosis*, by whatever means necessary. On 26 June 1967, four months before the start of November 1967 hostilities, the House of Representatives, from which Turkish members were excluded, unanimously adopted the so-called *enosis* resolution. It stated:

> No matter what difficulties and hardships are encountered, the struggle being waged with the full support of the Hellenic world will not be terminated until its final goal is

> successfully achieved. By 'success' it is meant that the whole of the island will be integrated with Greece without any stop-overs.
>
> The House will contribute with all means at its disposal to the strengthening of the Cyprus-Greek cooperation, which it considers an inevitable condition for the success of the national struggle and the unity of the Greek and Greek Cypriot peoples.[sic][51]

Demirel's Cyprus Policy

As stated earlier, after the August 1964 air strikes in Cyprus, Inonu decided to adopt a low profile and abandoned the brinkmanship approach he had utilized since December 1963. His acceptance of failure was so strong that he ignored the continuing infiltration of mainland Greek troops onto the island. On 1 February 1965, Inonu's foreign minister Erkin told the senators in the National Assembly that "the Greek Government and the Makarios regime which infiltrated 10,000 Greek troops into Cyprus should know that we won't allow any more pressure attempts and that any aggression would be met with [Turkey's] response."[52]

As this statement shows, the Inonu Government had come to terms with the fact that Greece informally controlled Cyprus. Inonu, who once had decided to go to war over the establishment of the Greek Cypriot National Guard in June 1964, was now content with the preservation of the *status quo.* It should be added, however, that Inonu, like most Turks in 1964, saw the presence of the Greek troops as a possible deterrent to attacks by Greek Cypriot irregulars against Turkish Cypriots. Yet Inonu also knew that Greece's military presence on Cyprus was one more step in the direction of *enosis.*

It is interesting to note that Turkey, despite all of its denunciation of the Makarios regime, kept a *charge d'affaires* in Nicosia and accepted a Greek Cypriot Ambassador in Ankara. Hence, it was not surprising that Turkey did not ask third countries, including the U.S., to revoke their recognition of the illegal Makarios regime.[53]

Suleyman Demirel, who came to power in November 1965 in a landslide election victory, seemed intent on making a fresh start with the peaceful resolution of the conflict. In a press conference on 4 January 1966 he replied to a reporter's question of why Turkey did not react to Greece's invasion of Cyprus by saying that it was

> . . . a fact that Greece sent 10,000 troops to Cyprus. Yet, this doesn't mean *enosis.* As long as Turkey's treaty rights and its intention to use them exist, and as long as Turkish Cypriots' resistance lasts, *enosis* will be a pipe dream, and it will stay that way. At this stage, Turkey's dispatch of troops to Cyprus as a retaliation would mean an all-out war with Greece.[54]

Demirel's remarks demonstrate that in contrast to his earlier criticism of Inonu's lack of assertiveness, he exhibited the same caution once in power. According to the well-known Turkish political scientist, Haluk Ulman, Demirel believed that Cyprus was lost during Inonu's reign, and nothing could be done to recover it.[55] Demirel even continued Inonu's policy of reliance on the U.S. for peaceful settlement of the dispute. In an address to the Senate, he insisted that Turkey's allies would bear some of the responsibility for a "bad" outcome in Cyprus because "their concern or unconcern . . . will determine the solution of the crisis."[56]

The Demirel Government, like its predecessors, perceived the Cyprus crisis as a bilateral problem between Greece and Turkey and not one between

Turkey and the Makarios regime. The Foreign Minister of the JP cabinet, Ihsan Sabri Caglayangil, expounded this point in a National Assembly speech by saying that

> the Cyprus dispute is a problem between Turkey and Greece. Therefore it can be negotiated only between Greece and Turkey. We don't want to put our country through a disaster of war without first exhausting all peaceful possibilities of reconciliation. If, however, our community [in Cyprus] is attacked . . . we would not hesitate for one moment to use our right of intervention . . ."[57]

As this statement shows, the Demirel Administration believed that a Turkish intervention in Cyprus would almost certainly lead to a Greco-Turkish war and that this contingency should be avoided. Hence, as Demirel argued, "from the beginning, Turkey wanted to solve the Cyprus problem through bilateral negotiations with Greece."[58] Demirel's Cyprus policy, however, was more subdued than that of Inonu. Instead of blowing the intercommunal violence out of proportion in order to bring about a U.S. mediation, Demirel chose to deal quietly with it.

Demirel's behavior is actually not surprising because throughout his premiership he never clearly stated his desired solution to the Cyprus crisis. Although Inonu toyed with the idea of partition, he almost always favored territorial federation. Demirel opposed subscribing to a specific mode of settlement. He argued that

> to insist on a fixed and unchangeable formula would only complicate our attempts to arrive at a peaceful settlement. . . . To insist on only one solution would mean to dictate a solution. The opponent would

have no other alternative other than to accept or reject it."[59]

Instead, the Demirel Administration adopted a set of principles to indicate the parameters of a Cyprus settlement acceptable to Turkey. These principles were: (1) Cyprus should not be annexed unilaterally by either Greece or Turkey; (2) neither Cypriot community should dominate the other; (3) the balance of power established by the Lausanne Treaty (1923) in the Mediterranean between Greece and Turkey should be preserved; (4) 1959 Cyprus Treaties should not be revised unilaterally.[60]

These principles could be broadly interpreted. One could assume that as long as an action was not unilateral, even *enosis* would be a feasible objective. Since Demirel himself failed to clearly delineate Turkey's objectives, it is not surprising that Turkey failed to shore up international support for its ambiguous Cyprus policy. Turkey directed its diplomatic efforts at urging other states to recognize the validity of the 1959 Cyprus Treaties and that there were two national communities on Cyprus. Even these modest diplomatic goals enjoyed mixed success. Some of the countries that accepted the validity of the 1959 Treaties nevertheless considered Makarios' abrogation of the Turkish Cypriots' partnership status an internal matter of a sovereign state.

Turkish Cypriots did not appreciate Demirel's ambivalence. Rauf Denktash, president of the Turkish Cypriot Communal Chamber at that time, suggested that Makarios would again try to break the resistance of Turkish Cypriots and that the only way to prevent this was for Turkey to use its rights of intervention and establish a Turkish Cypriot state. He added that Makarios and Greece proved that *faits accomplis* could be used effectively and that Turkey should utilize the same method.[61] Demirel's response was surprisingly clear: "Turkey would preserve Turkish Cypriots' and Turkey's treaty rights until the end. Our government cannot subscribe to another idea."[62]

Demirel's refusal to adopt a specific mode of settlement in part was a result of his well-known pragmatism. Demirel disliked all kinds of rigidity. It is not surprising that the Turco-Soviet rapprochement took place mainly during the reign of Demirel who considered himself a staunch anti-communist. A social democrat, Sadun Tanju regards Demirel as a problem-solver who would not be restrained by the strict rules of either conservatism or capitalism.[63]

Demirel considered the Cyprus crisis a nuisance, however, which demanded the attention he might otherwise give to his development program. He often boasted that he came to power to create the "Great Turkey" not by territorial expansion, but by economic development. A Turkish military intervention in Cyprus would probably interrupt his economic program. In his Senate address on 8 January 1966, Demirel defended his moderation by saying, "we need to be common sensical . . . and consider our country's short and long term interests while trying to find a solution to this crisis. . . ."[64]

Demirel's intention to quietly settle the Cyprus dispute led him to initiate bilateral talks with Greece on 25 June 1966. The talks were initially conducted by low level specialists of the respective countries. When Turkish and Greek Foreign Ministers, Caglayangil and Toumbas, met in Paris for the first and last time, they agreed that Cyprus would be united with Greece in return for a base for Turkey. An agreement could not be reached, however, because Toumbas hesitated to grant Turkey full sovereignty over the base area.[65] Because of the political instability in Greece, which led to the 21 April 1967 coup, no further meeting took place with the constitutional governments of Greece to straighten out the differences.

After the coup on 21 April 1967, Demirel continued to ask for negotiations with Greece. His eagerness to negotiate is all the more interesting because the Greek junta, as its predecessor, persisted in calling for *enosis*. Both Greek Prime Minister

Kollias and the strongman of the junta Papadopoulos repeatedly stated that they favored *enosis* without any *quid pro quos* to Turkey.[66] When Demirel did not publicly react to these statements, Turkish Cypriot students demonstrated in Ankara to denounce Demirel's lack of support for the "Cyprus cause." The police not only forcefully dispersed them, but also detained some of the demonstrators.[67]

Turco-Greek negotiations resumed unexpectedly on 9 and 10 September 1967 when the Turkish and Greek Prime Ministers met in the Turkish and Greek border towns, Keshan and Dedeagatch. The talks ended in failure because while Greek Prime Minister Kollias demanded unconditional *enosis*, Demirel was ready to accept *enosis* only in return for a sovereign base.[68] Toward the end of the talks Kollias told Demirel: "Sooner or later, whether you want it or not, *enosis* will take place, so why not talk about it now?"[69]

1967 Attack and Demirel's Response

On 15 November 1967, a little more than one month after the Demirel-Kollias summit, a pre-planned attack took place against the Turkish Cypriots in the two Turkish villages in southern Cyprus. The Greek Cypriot National Guard and the Greek Cypriot police participated in the attack. Many observers alleged that Grivas directed the whole operation.[70] Some writers also argued that the Greek junta ordered the offensive without advising Makarios of it beforehand.[71]

Whether or not Makarios knew about the attack, it was his forces who participated in the operation. On 15 November 1967 these forces entered the Turkish Cypriot village of Theodhoros (Bogazici). The alleged motive for their entry was to inspect the Nicosia-Limassol road which passed through this village. Theodhoros (Bogazici) together with Kophinou (Gecitkale) constituted a Turkish enclave controlled by the forces of the Turkish Cypriot Administration. The Greek Cypriots apparently feared that the Turks would put the Nicosia-Limassol highway under their control as they had the Nicosia-Kyrenia road.[72]

The Greek convoy tried to enter Ayios Theodhoros without the U.N. escort which usually accompanied the forces of the "Government" within the Turkish controlled areas.[73] When this heavily armed force entered the village, the Greeks claimed, the Turks opened fire. In the ensuing eight-hour battle twenty-eight Turks and two Greeks died. By the evening of 15 November, Ayios Theodhoros was completely in the hands of Greek forces.[74]

At about the same time the Ayios Theodhoros attack started, some "armored cars and infantry moved against Turkish Cypriot fighter positions covering Kophinou, a village some two and a half miles away and unrelated to the patrol issue."[75] The coordination of the attacks in Kophinou and Ayios Theodhoros shows that they were pre-planned in order to break Turkish resistance in this area. U.N. Secretary General U-Thant suggested that

> [t]he magnitude of the Ayios Theodhoros operation and the speed with which it was carried out clearly indicate that the National Guard had planned in advance to carry out this operation in the event of any show of opposition by the Turkish Cypriots.[76]

The Turkish Government reacted slowly to the violence. Despite the fact that the clashes began at 2:00 P.M., the NSC did not convene until 9:30 P.M. that night. The chiefs of the army, navy, air force and the general staff were also present. Before the meeting, chief of the air force Irfan Tansel told reporters that Turkey was suffering as a result of its earlier mistakes of procrastinating about the intervention.[77] Throughout the NSC meeting the commanders demanded that Turkey intervene militarily on the island. The Cyprus experts of the Foreign Ministry also favored intervention.[78] By midnight the NSC had concluded that air strikes should take place in Cyprus if the Greek Cypriot forces did not withdraw from the two occupied villages by 6:00 A.M. on 16 November 1967. This decision was transmitted to Makarios in a note during the early hours of 16 November. Meanwhile, the commanders left the NSC meeting to go to the general staff headquarters to plan the military action.[79]

Later that night Demirel, Foreign Minister Caglayangil, and Defense Minister Topaloglu joined the commanders in the general staff headquarters to discuss the possibility of a naval landing. During the discussion concerning suitable landing spots, the chief of the navy, Necdet Uran was unable to find out the water level at Kyrenia.[80] Turkey was once more caught unprepared. Furthermore, chief of the army Refik Yilmaz said that a successful operation in Cyprus required at least fifty tanks and the fielding of a corps, but Turkey had only two landing craft, not enough to carry the troops ashore.[81] The air force fared no better. It had only six helicopters and 150 parachutes that could be used in Cyprus.[82] In sum, a landing on Cyprus would be precarious because the limited number of troops that could be landed would face a combined Greek Cypriot and Greek force of at least 30,000 well-armed troops. Nevertheless, Demirel ordered the preparation of a landing force which would take almost one week to assemble.[83] If necessary, this force would be shipped to Cyprus on ferryboats.

The limited air strikes planned against Greek Cypriot targets around Ayios Theodhoros and Kokkina were called off when the Greek forces began to evacuate the occupied villages at 4:00 A.M. on 16 November 1964. Demirel's decision to call off the air strikes was not surprising because Makarios had "blinked" and accepted Turkey's conditions.[84] Demirel knew, however, that the cancellation of Turkey's only response to Makarios's illegitimate actions during the last three years would be unpopular.

On 16 November various youth organizations held marches and meetings in Istanbul, Ankara and Erzurum and demanded Demirel's resignation. Some members of the National Assembly severely reprimanded the prime minister. The RPP representative Nihat Erim blamed Demirel for reacting slowly to the news of violence on 15 November 1964 and missing a good chance to teach Makarios a lesson.[85] The National Assembly debated the crisis for eighteen hours in executive session and once more empowered the Government to intervene by a vote of 432 to 1.[86]

Demirel was criticized not only by the opposition parties, but even by those within his own party. The conservative wing of the JP Government, the Bilgic-Sukan group, which controlled several ministries, continued to demand the partial occupation of the island.[87] There were also rallies and demonstrations calling for "decisive action" to end the plight of Cypriot Turks.[88] We do not know whether it was the pressures of the "hawks" within the Government, the armed forces, or the general public which led Demirel to adopt a harder line. On 17 November 1967 he decided to send a harsh note to Greece demanding the withdrawal of its illegally infiltrated troops from Cyprus. He also ordered the armed forces to continue their preparations for a landing on Cyprus within a week.[89] The Turkish note not only demanded the withdrawal of Greece's forces, but also called for the disbandment of the 20,000 strong National Guard.[90] The note was written in ambiguous language to give it the impact of an ultimatum. Hence, it was difficult from the first for the Greek Government to determine exactly what the Turks were demanding.[91]

After the necessary week's preparation by the armed forces, a landing could take place on 23 November or thereafter. In the meantime several external and internal factors influenced the Government which had announced that unless its conditions were met by Greece, it would intervene. One of the external factors was the pressure from U.S. Ambassador Parker Hart. Since the beginning of the crisis he maintained constant contact with Foreign Minister Caglayangil. Hart told Caglayangil that President Johnson opposed an intervention but chose not to send a written message because of the Turkish public's reaction to the Johnson Letter of 1964. Demirel in return sent a message to Johnson outlining Turkey's demands for a peaceful solution, i.e. the withdrawal of Greece's forces, and the disbandment of the National Guard.[92]

Another factor which might have restrained Demirel was the deployment of a task force of the Sixth Fleet close to the shores of Cyprus since 16 November 1967. It is clear that the Johnson Administration assumed that "fleet movements would be observed by the participants in the crisis and evaluated in light of previous U.S. behavior and current policy statements."[93] It is not so clear, however, whether the U.S. Sixth Fleet would have intercepted a Turkish landing force. We also do not know how much the presence of the Sixth Fleet in the area influenced Demirel's decisions.

We do know that Demirel confided to Inonu that he believed that Turkey's intervention would lead to a war between Turkey and Greece and that he "did not want a war at all." Demirel also said that he "would be satisfied to solve the crisis in a manner that would more or less save his and Turkey's prestige."[94] As mentioned earlier, Demirel accorded primary importance to his economic program and was reluctant to conduct a military operation in Cyprus.

Demirel's cautious policy was supported by the RPP leader Inonu, but not by other RPP members. Inonu reminded Demirel and Caglayangil that the Turkish army had had no overseas fighting experience and that a military defeat would mean disaster for Turkey.[95] Other RPP leaders resented Inonu's support of Demirel. They remembered that the JP had criticized Inonu's cautiousness in 1964 and had exploited the failure to intervene for reasons of domestic politics. To these leaders, Inonu emphasized that without convincing the U.S. and U.S.S.R. of the justness of Turkey's cause, the Government would not be able to achieve its goals in Cyprus.[96]

The Vance Mission

Despite the fact that Turkey delivered its note to Greece on 17 November 1967, Greece failed to respond until 22 November. In the meantime military preparations for a landing continued. The Turkish air force conducted daily reconnaissance flights over Cyprus, and a major portion of the Turkish fleet was sent to the Mersin harbor, the closest major harbor to Cyprus.[97] The major newspapers of the day indicated that the public mood was once again pro-intervention.

Demirel's public statements were, however, as subdued as before. In his message on 19 November to Fazil Kuchuk, the leader of Turkish Cypriots, Demirel tried to downplay the importance of the crisis. To be sure, he assured Kuchuk that Turkey would not hesitate to come to the aid of Turkish Cypriots if they faced another attack. He urged Kuchuk, however, "not to play into the hands [of Makarios forces] . . ." He added that Kuchuk " . . . should behave in a common sensical way that would not hurt our cause. . . ."[98]

Demirel's remarks indicate that he did not want to bring up the issue of the validity of the 1960 constitution. Neither did he suggest that a new constitutional settlement was necessary in Cyprus. In a way characteristic of Demirel, he thought that time would take care of the problems if everybody behaved in a common sensical way. Demirel apparently believed that if he did not accuse the Greek junta publicly, the immediate crisis would be solved without any bloodshed. Demirel based his optimism that Greece would withdraw its forces from Cyprus on his belief that the Greek junta could afford to ignore Greek public opinion and accept an accommodation with Turkey. He also took into account the fact that the junta desperately wanted to improve Greece's relations with the West. Therefore, he supposed that the junta would be ready to withdraw its troops from Cyprus.[99]

The appointment of Panayotis Pipinellis, who was known to be a "moderate," as Foreign Minister of Greece on 20 November 1967 was welcomed by the Turkish Government as the first sign of relaxation of tensions.[100] Yet the hopes of the Demirel Government proved to be short-lived. On 22 November 1967 Greece replied to Turkey's note of 17 November by rejecting Turkey's demands.

When the Greek note arrived, the Turkish armed forces had almost completed their preparations for an intervention. U.S. "intelligence reports indicated that Turkey would initiate military action within twenty-four hours."[101] The same day the State Department concluded that the U.S. had two alternatives to avert the invasion: (1) King Constantine and President Sunay could be invited to come to Washington to discuss the crisis with Johnson; (2) a presidential emissary could be dispatched to the area. Secretary of State Rusk believed that an emissary would be more beneficial and advised Johnson that he should send his former secretary of the army, Cyrus Vance to the region.[102]

Cyrus Vance "was told that Turkish troops were already at the embarkation port and were expected, according to [U.S.] intelligence, to invade Cyprus the next morning. This would mean war between Greece and Turkey."[103] President Johnson's instruction to Vance was clear and simple: "Do what you have to to stop the war. If you need anything, let me know. Good luck."[104]

The same day, on 22 November 1967, U.S. Ambassador Parker Hart informed Caglayangil that President Johnson was sending Cyrus Vance as his personal emissary to mediate between the parties. At the Cabinet meeting at 9:00 P.M. the Turkish Government decided to listen to Vance and give him a chance to convince the Greeks. Yet it was also decided that Turkey would ignore Vance's mission if he was carrying another "Johnson Letter."[105]

The Turkish public considered Vance's arrival in Ankara as another U.S. attempt to frustrate Turkey's "justified" intervention in Cyrus. In fact, the plane carrying Vance could not land at the civilian Esenboga airport because of anti-American demonstrations. The plane then landed at the nearby military Murted airport. The demonstrations continued, however, and the offices of the U.S. Information Agency and Pan-American Airways were attacked.[106]

After his meeting with Demirel the same day (23 November 1967), Vance left for Athens. By 25 November Vance had convinced the Greek junta to withdraw its forces from Cyprus. Greece insisted, however, on a stage by stage withdrawal to be completed within seven months. Demirel responded to the Greek demands by insisting on an unconditional and immediate withdrawal.[107]

On 28 November 1967 Makarios entered the picture, informing the U.S. that he would consent to the withdrawal of Greek troops provided that all foreign troops, including those of the legally introduced Greek and Turkish contingents, were withdrawn as well.[108] Despite Makarios' intransigence Vance was able to persuade the Greek junta to accept an accelerated withdrawal of mainland Greek troops on 30 November 1967.[109] Greece also agreed to Turkey's demand that the Greek Cypriot National Guard, which was established unconstitutionally on 1 June 1964, be disbanded, and its commander Grivas be recalled to Greece.[110] That same day, Vance arrived in Cyprus and further pressured Makarios. Makarios knew that once Greece decided to withdraw its forces he could not insist on keeping them. He also knew that the continued presence of Greek troops would justify a possible Turkish intervention. Hence,

Makarios retreated and consented to Vance's proposal. Makarios refused, however, to dismantle the National Guard and Vance was unable to convince him otherwise.[111]

Vance's mediation was completed on 3 December 1967 when both Greece and Turkey announced that they would abide by the appeal of the U.N. Secretary General who called for the withdrawal of foreign troops illegally introduced into Cyprus and the disbandment of paramilitary forces on the island.[112] The appeal of the U.N. Secretary General was part of the 30 November 1967 Agreement between Turkey and Greece. Greece had insisted on this face-saving formula so as not to be seen as letting down the Greek Cypriots.[113]

Demirel Settles For the Status Quo

Despite the Demirel Government's efforts to project the Turco-Greek Agreement of 30 November 1967 as a success, the Agreement was unpopular with Turkish Cypriots. The President of the Turkish Cypriot Administration, Dr. Kuchuk, told Vance this when he visited him in the Turkish quarter of Nicosia on 30 November 1967. Kuchuk told Vance that Turkish Cypriots desired a permanent solution which would eliminate the conditions of strife on the island. He asked Vance to make sure that the 1960 constitution was restored as a first step to a new constitutional settlement.[114] Kuchuk clarified his views on 6 December 1967 when he told a reporter that he preferred partition of the island. Yet Kuchuk added that "under today's conditions the only [realistic] solution is federation . . . of two autonomous communal administrations."[115]

The Turkish public and the Turkish political parties were not as frustrated as the Turkish Cypriot community, but neither were they engulfed by joy. Most believed that Turkey had missed another golden opportunity to intervene. Yet because the U.S. did not deliver a second Johnson Letter, the Turks felt little humiliation. There were reports that Vance told Demirel that Turkey could not use American supplied weapons in Cyprus, but these reports provoked little reaction from the public.[116] Perhaps the Turks had become accustomed to the idea that the U.S. would inevitably oppose an intervention in Cyprus.

Nevertheless, during the discussion of the crisis in the National Assembly, several small and extremist parties denounced Demirel's failure to disband the Greek Cypriot National Guard and achieve a new constitutional settlement. Alpaslan Turkes, an emigre from Cyprus who headed the right-wing Republican Peasants Nation Party (RPNP), stated that Makarios' refusal to dismantle the National Guard was a result of Demirel's lack of assertiveness.[117] He added that Turkey should not have been satisfied with Greek guarantees, and should have solved the whole Cyprus question if not all Greco-Turkish problems, such as the questions of minorities and the Dodecanese Islands.[118]

Turkes also called for a vote of confidence for the JP Government, and his motion was supported by the right-wing Nation Party and the left-wing Labor Party.[119] Inonu refused to support the motion. The RPP speaker Nihat Erim cautiously avoided taking issue with the Government's conduct during the crisis and stated that the RPP wanted to wait and see whether the Government's promise of success would come true.[120]

The RPP's refusal to criticize Demirel's lack of assertiveness was mainly due to Inonu's influence. Inonu apparently approved of Demirel's cautious conduct during the crisis, conduct which resembled his own style. He described the 1967 settlement as "the best that could be achieved." Inonu added that Turkey's military intervention in Cyprus would mean a war between Turkey and Greece, possibly ending in a Turkish defeat. He concluded that

> . . . political defeats are not important . . . New cabinets can always be installed. Yet military defeats leave a large mark in the history of nations. Hence, one should not be eager for adventures without taking into account all possible consequences.[121]

The Demirel Government did not, however, exhibit the same courtesy as did Inonu. In response to criticism of his failure to dismantle the National Guard, Demirel said that the National Guard "did not appear overnight," but was in place when he became Prime Minister.[122] Demirel's accusation was implicitly directed against Inonu during whose premiership the National Guard was established. Demirel added that he would try to settle this problem by first exhausting "all peaceful means" and by acting "with common sense."[123]

Demirel's Foreign Minister Caglayangil dwelt on the same point. He argued that the Demirel Government inherited an unsuccessful Cyprus policy and tried to make the best out of it. To accusations that Demirel missed an opportunity to finally settle the Cyprus dispute Caglayangil replied, "From the beginning of the crisis, our government wanted to solve the immediate problem [of the presence of Greek troops] and not the main [constitutional] problem. Therefore, we focused our attention on our immediate goals."[124]

In the same speech, Caglayangil suggested that Greece had promised the dismantlement of the National Guard and if this did not happen, then "the responsibility rest[ed] with Greece."[125] Caglayangil's and Demirel's arguments were not convincing, however, because they knew that once the crisis was over, Greece would be even less interested in pressuring Makarios to take a step which would be seen by all Greeks as "anti-Hellenic."

After almost two months the Demirel Government decided not to make the National Guard an issue in Turkey-Greece relations. On 20 February 1968,

Caglayangil told the National Assembly that "the pacification of irregular forces in Cyprus" was not realized because Makarios refused to dismantle the National Guard. Caglayangil argued that the question of "irregular forces" was now a matter to be settled between the U.N. and Makarios.[126]

As Caglayangil realized, the U.N. considered Makarios a legitimate head of state and was therefore in no position to dictate to him policies concerning the armed forces of the "Cyprus Government." Hence, the Demirel Government did not insist on U.N. intervention. The public's interest in the problem also waned after Demirel's announcement that on 16 January 1968 Greece informed Turkey that it had withdrawn all of its forces.[127] The Turkish Government later confirmed that all Greek troops had left the island, but informed sources alleged that at least 5,000 mainland Greek troops remained in Cyprus.[128]

Other Factors

As explained earlier, Khrushchev's opposition to Turkey's possible intervention in Cyprus in 1964 was a significant deterrent to Inonu's landing forces on the island. During the 1967 crisis, however, Soviet opposition to a Turkish military intervention in Cyprus was conspicuously absent. The change in Soviet behavior resulted in part from the post-1964 Turco-Soviet rapprochement. The 21 April 1967 coup in Greece also changed the Soviet attitude. After the seizure of power by the colonels, Soviet official statements assumed a clearly anti-Greek character. On 5 July 1967 TASS remarked:

> It is an open secret that the reactionary circles of Greece, supported by the United States and some other NATO members, have long been working on plans against the independence, sovereignty, territorial

> integrity of Cyprus . . . No one must interfere in the internal affairs of the Republic of Cyprus . . . Only the Cypriots themselves, both Greeks and Turks, have the right to decide their destinies.[129]

After the 15 November 1967 Greek and Greek Cypriot attack in Cyprus, the Soviet U.N. representative, Fedorenko immediately denounced "the reactionary circles in Greece, which, with the support of outside forces, have for a long time been working out plans for settling the problem of Cyprus . . . through what is called *enosis*. . . ."[130] Fedorenko carefully avoided any reference to Turkey's widely publicized military preparations for a landing.

On 23 November 1967, one day before the rumored landing of Turkish forces in Cyprus, Soviet Ambassador Smirnov met with Demirel. After the meeting Smirnov told reporters that he conferred with Demirel about the "policies of Greek fascists." Smirnov added that "it [was] the Greek junta's actions which caused Turkish Cypriot casualties."[131] A respected deputy of the National Assembly, Coskun Kirca later revealed that the Soviet Ambassador assured Turkey that the U.S.S.R. did not oppose a Turkish landing in Cyprus.[132]

Another factor that might have affected Demirel's evaluations was the absence of Greek lobby activity in the United States. In contrast to their activity during the 1974 and even the 1964 crises, the Greek American organizations preferred to remain inactive in 1967. Their inactivity was probably a consequence of Turkey's 1967 actions which were limited to an ultimatum delivered to Greece on 17 November 1967. In other words, the Greek Americans' failure to pressure Congress did not mean that they would not have exerted pressure had Turkey landed troops in Cyprus. One cannot be sure if the Greek Americans would have been as influential as they were in 1974, but the presence of several pro-Greek Congressmen in Congress would be reassuring enough for Greek Americans to mount a campaign similar to the one of 1964.

Demirel Is Not Against "Unitary" State

The November 1967 crisis had two important consequences for Turkish Cypriots. First, the Turkish Cypriot Administration was reorganized to be more effective. Second, Makarios apparently abandoned his pre-1968 policy of blockading the Turkish Cypriots. He lifted many of the restrictions placed on Turkish Cypriots and agreed to the so-called intercommunal negotiations which continued intermittently until 1974.

On 28 December 1967 the "Provisional Turkish Administration" was established in the Turkish part of Nicosia. Dr. Fazil Kuchuk was elected president and Rauf R. Denktash vice-president of the Administration. Zeki Kuneralp, a high-ranking Turkish Foreign Ministry official participated in the ceremonies, thus lending Turkey's official support to the Turkish Cypriot action. As before, Turkish Cypriots controlled 250 of the 9,251 square kilometers of the island's territory. The main Turkish enclave included Nicosia's Turkish sector and the area to the north of it which comprised about 100 square kilometers. It accounted for 40,000 Turks, or one-third of Cyprus' Turkish population.[133]

Whereas the establishment of a quasi-state Turkish Administration implied that the *de-facto* partition of the island would be permanent, Makarios's sudden adoption of a flexible policy changed those pessimistic expectations. In January 1968 Makarios stressed that a solution had to be sought "within the limits of what was feasible" and not what was desirable, i.e., *enosis*.[134] On 7 March 1968 Makarios lifted most restrictions placed upon the Turkish enclaves signaling that he no longer wanted a violent resolution of the conflict.[135] On 13 April 1968 Rauf Denktash, who since January 1964 had been barred from Cyprus on the pretext that he was a terrorist, was allowed to return.[136] As a result of these goodwill measures, the Turkish and Greek community representatives, Denktash and Klerides, opened the intercommunal negotiations in Beirut on 11 June 1968 and resumed them on 24 June 1968 in Nicosia.[137]

Demirel strongly supported the intercommunal negotiations. In a speech at the National Assembly on 7 November 1969, Demirel suggested that

> the Cyprus question is a problem which concerns many parties. Therefore, the crisis cannot be solved according to the wishes . . . of only one party. . . . The legitimate interests and rights of all parties have to be taken into account. . . . The only way to do this is through negotiations. . . .[138]

The Demirel Government offered no specific formula for settlement of the dispute. Unlike Inonu who was almost adamant in his preference for a federative solution, Demirel was ready to consent to a minority status for Turkish Cypriots. Foreign Minister Caglayangil argued that "Cyprus should continue to be independent and a *unitary* form of state could be adopted."[139] [Italics added] Demirel expressed his optimism when on 12 March 1970 he told the National Assembly that "today, everybody can go everywhere in Cyprus . . . [All Turks who were uprooted in 1964] have been resettled in Nicosia and other regions. . . ."[140]

Until 12 March 1971, the day Demirel stepped down as a result of a military ultimatum, Turkey made several concessions to the Makarios regime. Among others it was agreed that the Cyprus state should be unitary and not federal. The veto rights of Turkish Cypriots and the rule of separate majorities for the passage of laws in the parliament were to be abandoned. Turkish Cypriots also agreed to give up their 30 percent share of civil service jobs as stipulated in the 1960 constitution.[141]

The parties could not agree, however, on how much local autonomy the Turkish Cypriots should possess. Moreover, the talks stalemated on issues such as the organization of the police force, the army, and the judiciary.[142] Makarios' continuing agitation in favor of *enosis* further exacerbated the Demirel Government's frustration at the deadlock in intercommunal talks. In 1971 Foreign Minister Caglayangil criticized what he perceived as a hypocritical Greek Cypriot attitude. He stated that the intercommunal talks were based on the assumption that the Greek Cypriots "no longer insisted on *enosis*." Yet he added that Greek Cypriot "Government" officials continued to proclaim that their "national goal [had] not changed."[143]

Turkish Cypriot leader Denktash on the other hand had a more realistic perception of Greek aspirations. He argued:

> The [Greek Cypriot] proposals to be made to the Turks were worked out in detail with the Greek Government. If the Turks did not agree to these proposals nothing would be lost, because the Greek Cypriots were in control of the economy of Cyprus. The separate—and unconstitutional—Greek administration was still internationally recognized as the Government of Cyprus and the Greeks were making money on the continuation of the conflict, with all the U.N. money coming in, tourism booming and the budget of Cyprus being spent only on Greek sectors. The Greek side could afford to wait."[144]

Conclusion

By January 1968 the immediate cause of the November 1967 Cyprus crisis had been removed. The Demirel Government stopped the Greek and Greek

Cypriot combined attack against Kokkina and Ayios Theodhoros the day after it began by threatening retaliation. Makarios accepted the withdrawal of his forces from these two Turkish villages in order to prevent Turkish air strikes and a possible military landing. Makarios also had to accept the withdrawal of 10,000 to 20,000 mainland Greek troops after Greece decided that it could not afford to keep them there.

The underlying cause of not only the 1967 but also the 1964 crisis was, however, not eliminated. Even after Makarios' goodwill gestures, including the lifting of economic restrictions placed on Turkish enclaves and the start of the intercommunal talks in 1968, the illegal Makarios regime remained in power. Furthermore, Makarios and his supporters continued to proclaim their devotion to the struggle for *enosis* and argued that in the long run *enosis* would be inevitable. The Demirel Government tried to project the 1967 settlement as a great success for Turkey. Demirel suggested that as a result of his "assertive" policy Greece withdrew its forces and Makarios agreed to a peaceful resolution of the Cyprus problem through intercommunal negotiations. Demirel intentionally played down Makarios' refusal to disband the National Guard, acquiescing to the status quo when Makarios refused to abide by the original Greek-Turkish agreement.

Demirel's optimism was probably the most important factor in preventing the reign of a defeatist mood in Turkey. Demirel's assertion that he was responsible for the 1967 settlement and proud of it greatly influenced the Turkish public. Whereas Inonu had blamed his failure to intervene in 1964 on United States opposition, thus contributing to anti-Americanism, Demirel carefully avoided blaming the U.S. for any criticism leveled against him.

The U.S., which most Turks still perceived as the only major barrier to a military intervention in Cyprus, supported Demirel's handling of the crisis. In 1967 President Johnson avoided publicly humiliating the Turkish Government in the eyes of its own people as he had with the Johnson Letter in 1964. Instead, Johnson sent Cyrus Vance whose mediation effort succeeded in preventing a possible war between Greece and Turkey. The U.S.-mediated settlement between Greece and Turkey did not contain a long-lasting solution to the Cyprus problem, but its terms favored Turkey. Thus, Turks did not accuse the U.S. Administration of being pro-Greek as they had in 1964.

A second factor which had loomed large in Inonu's calculations in 1964 was the Soviet opposition to a Turkish military operation in Cyprus. In 1967 Soviet leaders carefully avoided criticizing Turkey's preparations for a landing. There were reports that the U.S.S.R. even consented to Turkey's use of force in Cyprus. Whether or not these reports were correct, it is fair to assume that Demirel had less reason than Inonu to be concerned about a hostile Soviet reaction.

Turkey also was less isolated internationally than it had been three years earlier. Turkey's Cyprus thesis still found few supporters, especially in the Third World, but several regional countries—including Iraq and Iran—would have been more supportive of Turkey had Turkey intervened. Egypt, which in 1964 had threatened to aid Makarios, remained conspicuously silent in November 1967. Perhaps Turkey's support of Egypt in the June 1967 Arab-Israeli war had embarrassed Nasser and forced him at least to be quiet. So Demirel also had less reason than Inonu to be concerned about a Third World, if not an Arab, reaction to an invasion.

During the discussion of the 1964 crisis, it was suggested that the armed forces' lack of readiness to undertake a landing operation on Cyprus contributed to Inonu's restraint. Despite private and official efforts to build a landing force in the previous three years, the armed forces in 1967 still did not have the necessary equipment to land troops and armored vehicles in Cyprus. The main barrier to military intervention in Cyprus was, however, Demirel's preconception that such an action was unnecessary and too costly. Demirel considered a Turco-Greek war, which would likely result from an intervention, too costly not only because it would interrupt his domestic programs, but also because he was afraid that Turkey might fail to capture a bridgehead in Cyprus if not lose the war to Greece.

Demirel was a statesman who shunned radical or hurried behavior. Instead of looking for ways to solve problems immediately, he would let them drag on until they became "solvable." Demirel believed that after the withdrawal of mainland Greek forces Makarios would realize the futility of achieving *enosis* through intercommunal fighting and opt for a negotiated settlement. Demirel calculated that once Makarios chose to negotiate, a peaceful resolution would be achieved easily. Demirel often stated that he would accept a *unitary* Cyprus state provided Turkish Cypriots were given local autonomy. Compared to Inonu's insistence on a federal settlement, Demirel's condition was more reasonable, and Demirel thought that Makarios would accept it immediately.

Several of the influence variables outlined earlier were proved relevant in the 1967 crisis. The proposition that "the amount of influence a state wields over others can be related to the capabilities *mobilized* in support of *specific* foreign policy objectives" has been verified.[145] In 1967, the U.S. Administration concentrated its capabilities on the prevention of war between Turkey and Greece. In order to accomplish this task, it sent Cyrus Vance as envoy to these two countries.

Vance was successful because the resources on which he relied were *relevant* to the issue at hand.[146] To prevent a Turkish military action he urged restraint on Demirel and promised that he would succeed in convincing the Greek junta to withdraw its troops from Cyprus. Vance could deliver on his promise, because, unlike in 1964, U.S. resources were pertinent to the Greek Colonels' needs. The junta was isolated internationally and thus could not afford to alienate the U.S. The Administration, on the other hand, clearly identified Greece as the instigator of the 1967 violence and put the necessary pressure on Greece. In other words, unlike in 1964, the U.S. not only urged restraint on Turkey, but it also effectively influenced Greece to compromise.

This point could also be related to the proposition that if A as influencer asks B to undertake a given action but fails to provide any other alternative, B would be inclined to reject A's "*diktat*." It was suggested that failing to provide alternatives "is to call for a probable showdown."[147] We could not test the reliability of this proposition because the U.S. offered a peaceful alternative in return for Turkey's postponement of its intervention. Yet the examination of not only the 1967 but also the 1964 crises shows that if A provides an alternative besides prohibiting B's proposed action, B would very likely try the alternative before ignoring A's advice. Demirel's decision to await the result of Vance's mediation effort confirms the validity of this point.

The 1967 crisis also enables us to test the validity of the proposition that influence is partly determined by the *responsiveness* of the influenced to the requests of the influencer.[148] Demirel's willingness to go along with Vance's mediation indicates that the success of the American influence attempt was partly due to the responsiveness or receptivity of the Turkish Government. Demirel's responsiveness is not, however, the whole reason for the fate of the Vance mediation. As suggested earlier, there are variations in the skill or efficiency with which statesmen use the resources.[149] In 1967, the Johnson Administration used its resources skillfully without alienating the influenced, Turkey, as it did in 1964 with its heavy-handed methods.

One should add that "[w]hat often seems to be influence turns out instead to be joint interests of the two parties."[150] Demirel conceded to an

American intervention in the crisis partly because he also believed that a peaceful resolution of the dispute was best for Turkey. This does not mean, however, that Demirel would have accepted any kind of solution Vance would offer. Vance needed to propose a settlement which could be accepted by Demirel without losing face.

Another influence variable we talked about earlier was that B's, the influenced state's expectation of A's, the influencer's, potential reaction to B's compliance or non-compliance affects B's decisions.[151] If B surmises that A would very likely not punish B, then it could act without considering A's desires. Even if B expects that A would actually carry out its threat, B may go ahead with its original plan if it attaches a high value to the outcome.[152] Whereas in 1967 the U.S. did not indicate what it would do if Turkey militarily intervened in Cyprus, Turks assumed that President Johnson's threats cited in his 1964 note to Inonu were still applicable in 1964. Demirel's preference for a peaceful resolution of the crisis was probably due to the fact that he did not attach a high value to the outcome of an invasion.

As suggested earlier, each nation and decisionmaker differs "in the degree to which they emphasize either the probability or the preference element in their appraisal of an outcome." Moreover, policymakers tend to exaggerate the probability of an outcome if they value it highly. "[C]onversely, when a probability looks very low, the tendency will be to downgrade the attractiveness of the associated outcome."[153] As stated earlier, Demirel's consultations with the military and Inonu led him to take a dim view of the prospects of a military action. Hence, he downgraded the attractiveness of a solution reached through a landing in Cyprus and opted for a mediated settlement.

The implications of the 1967 crisis seemed to contradict the proposition that the influencers would object to a change in the *status quo*.[154] The U.S.-mediated settlement changed the three-year-old *status quo* in Cyprus by causing the removal of some 10 to 20 thousand mainland Greek troops. Despite the appearance of an anti-*status quo* action by the U.S., the Turkey-Greece settlement actually preserved the overall *status quo*, in the eastern Mediterranean between those two countries. If the U.S. had not proposed the solution it did, Demirel would probably have been forced to intervene, and NATO's southeastern flank would be no more.

Lastly, one should stress the variable of the rule of anticipated reactions. Many times state B behaves in a way desired by state A even though A has not tried to make its wishes known. Often it is the case that B's policymakers anticipate the reactions of the influencer and behave in ways which would not evoke hostile reactions.[155] Sometimes, however, B's statesmen may decide to test state A to see "whether a reversal will be demanded. . . ."[156] Demirel's behavior fits into this pattern. His acquiescence in the armed forces' and the majority of his cabinet's demand for a military landing suggests that he was convinced that the U.S. would object to a Turkish military intervention in Cyprus. When he gave the order to prepare a landing force on 17 November 1967, Demirel expected that due to American opposition his order would not be executed. As anticipated by Demirel, the preparations for a landing provoked a U.S. intervention and enabled him to opt for a peaceful settlement without negatively affecting his political career.

NOTES

1. Bulent Ecevit, "Donum Noktasi," *Milliyet*, 26 April 1965.

2. *Milliyet*, Istanbul, 12 Oct. 1964; See also Deniz Atiye Erden, "Turkish Foreign Policy Through the United Nations" (Ph.D. dissertation, University of Massachusetts, 1974), pp. 105-106.

3. *Milliyet*, 5 Oct. 1964.

4. *Milliyet*, 12 Oct. 1964.

5. *Keesings Contemporary Archives*, 1964, p. 20371.

6. *Disisleri Bakanligi Belleteni*, ("The Bulletin of the Foreign Ministry"), 1964, No. 3, p. 19.

7. *Millet Meclisi Tutanak Dergisi* ("Official Records of the National Assembly"), Vol. XXXIII (1964), 24 Nov. 1964, p. 533.

8. *Ibid.*, Vol. XL (1965), 25 May 1965, p. 554.

9. *Disisleri Bakanligi Belleteni*, 1964, No. 3, p. 19.

10. *Milliyet*, 10 Jan. 1965. For Turkey's decision to participate see: *Cumhuriyet*, 25 Apr. 1963.

11. Mehmet Gonlubol, Omer Kurkcuoglu, "1965-1973 Donemi Turk Dis Politikasi," *Olaylarla Turk Dis Politikasi* (Ankara: Ankara Universitesi, 1977), p. 523.

12. *Disisleri Bakanligi Belleteni*, No. 4 (Jan. 1965), p. 77.

13. *Disisleri Bakanligi Belleteni*, No. 4 (Jan. 1965), p. 57. See also *Facts on File*, Vol. XXV, No. 1266 (Jan. 28-Feb. 3, 1965), p. 43.

14. Alvin Z. Rubinstein, *Soviet Policy Toward Iran, Turkey and Afghanistan* (New York: Prager, 1982), p. 32.

15. Duygu Sezer, *Kamu Oyu ve Dis Politika* (Ankara: Ankara Universitesi, 1972), p. 512.

16. Cuneyt Arcayurek, *Yeni Demokrasi, Yeni Arayislar, 1960-1965* (Ankara: Bilgi, 1984), p. 307.

17. *Ibid.*, p. 309.

18. Rubinstein, *op. cit.*, p. 26.

19. *Ibid.*, p. 27; See also: U.S. Congress, Senate, *Turkey's Problems and Prospects: Implications for U.S. Interests*, Report prepared by the Congressional Research Service of the Library of Congress for the Subcommittee on Europe and the Middle East of the Committee on Foreign Affairs, 3 March 1980, p. 45.

20. Arcayurek *op. cit.*, p. 303.

21. Cuneyt Arcayurek, *Demirel Donemi, 12 Mart Darbesi, 1965-71* (Ankara: Bilgi, 1985), p. 144.

22. *Disisleri Bakanligi Belleteni*, No. 5 (Feb., 1965), p. 61.

23. See Turkey-Saudi Arabia Joint Communique in *Disisleri Bakanligi Belleteni*, No. 24 (30 Sept., 1966), p. 47.

24. See Turkey-Tunisia Joint Communique in *Disisleri Bakanligi Belleteni*, No. 6 (March, 1965), pp. 81-82.

25. See Turkey-Iraq Joint Communique in *Disisleri Bakanligi Belleteni*, No. 17 (Feb., 1966), p. 70.

26. *Cumhuriyet*, Istanbul, 1 June 1967, p. 1; *Disisleri Bakanligi Belleteni*, No. XXXIII (June 1967), p. 40.

27. U.N., General Assembly, *Official Records*, 1532nd Plenary Meeting, 22 June 1967, p. 1.

28. Adopted on 4 July 1967: *U.N. Resolutions*, Series No. I, Vol. XI (1966-1967), p. 234.

29. *Cumhuriyet*, 1 July 1967, pp. 1,7; See also: Gonlubol, et. al., *op. cit.*, pp. 558-559.

30. *Disisleri Bakanligi Belleteni*, No. 7 (Apr., 1965), pp. 103-104.

31. Erden, *op. cit.*, p. 128.

32. See: United Nations Doc. A/5552/ADD.I.

33. "The Omnibus Study, Turkey", conducted by PEVA Company of Istanbul, mimeographed, Ankara, 1965, cited in Ferenc A. Vali, *Bridge Across the Bosporus* (Baltimore: The John Hopkins Press, 1971), pp. 107-114.

34. Ozer Ozankaya, *Universite Ogrencilerinin Siyasal Yonelimleri* (Ankara: Ankara Universitesi, 1966), pp. 32-39, in Sezer, *op. cit.*, p. 350.

35. Yilmaz Cetiner, "American Askeri Yardimi ve Gercekler," *Cumhuriyet*, 30 April 1965.

36. *Cumhuriyet*, 2 May 1965.

37. *Cumhuriyet*, 5 May 1965.

38. Sezer, *op. cit.*, p. 350.

39. *Cumhuriyet*, Istanbul, 8 Oct. 1967, p. 1.

40. *Disisleri Bakanligi Belleteni*, No. XXXI (April, 1967), p. 83.

41. *Disisleri Bakanligi Belleteni*, No. 27 (Dec., 1966), p. 110.

42. George Harris, *Troubled Triangle* (Washington, D.C.: American Enterprise Institute, 1972), p. 233.

43. *Milliyet*, Istanbul, 14 Apr. 1968 in Sezer *op. cit.*, pp. 338-341; *Cumhuriyet*, 9 Dec. 1967, p. 7.

44. Richard A. Patrick, *Political Geography and the Cyprus Conflict* (Ontario: University of Waterloo, 1976), p. 107; Necati M. Ertegun, *The Cyprus Dispute* (Oxford: The University Press, 1981), p. 189.

45. Patrick, *op. cit.*, pp. 80-81.

46. Rauf R. Denktash, *The Cyprus Triangle* (London and Boston: Allen & Unwin, 1982), p. 201.

47. Zenon Stavrinides, *The Cyprus Conflict: National Identity and Statehood* (Wakefield: Stavrinides, 1976), pp. 89-81.

48. See: Stanley Kyriakides, *Cyprus: Constitutionalism and Crisis Government* (Philadelphia: University of Pennsylvania Press, 1968), p. 114.

49. Polyvios G. Polyviou, *Cyprus: Conflict and Negotiation: 1960-1980* (New York: Holmes & Meier, 1980), p. 53.

50. U.N., Security Council, "Report of the Secretary General," *Document, No. S/6569*, 29 July 1965, para. 14.

51. Ertekun, *op. cit.*, p. 180.

52. *Disisleri Bakanligi Belleteni*, No. 5 (Feb., 1965), p. 56.

53. Vali, *op. cit.*, p. 254.

54. *Disisleri Bakanligi Belleteni*, No. 16 (Jan., 1966), p. 87.

55. Haluk Ulman, "Acik Konusalim," *Cumhuriyet*, 8 Dec. 1967, p. 2.

56. *Disisleri Bakanligi Belleteni*, No. 16 (Jan., 1966), p. 92.

57. *Disisleri Bakanligi Belleteni*, No. 29 (Feb., 1967), p. 40.

58. Disisleri Bakanligi Belleteni, No. 31 (Apr., 1967), p. 68.

59. *Disisleri Bakanligi Belleteni*, No. 36 (Sept., 1967), p. 43.

60. *Cumhuriyet*, Istanbul, 11 July 1967: *Disisleri Bakanligi Belleteni*, No. 28 (Jan., 1967), p. 46.

61. *Disisleri Bakanligi Belleteni*, No. 15 (Dec., 1965), p. 105.

62. *Disisleri Bakanligi Belleteni*, No. 16 (Jan., 1966), p. 87.

63. Sadun Tanju, *Tepedeki Dort Adam* (Istanbul: Gelisim, 1978), p. 143.

64. *Disisleri Bakanligi Belleteni*, No. 16 (Jan., 1966), p. 92.

65. *Disisleri Bakanligi Belleteni*, No. 27 (Dec., 1966), p. 116; Michael A. Attalides, *Cyprus: Nationalism and International Politics* (New York: St. Martin's Press, 1979), p. 71.

66. See *Cumhuriyet*, Istanbul, 13 and 17 August 1967.

67. *Cumhuriyet*, 24 August 1967.

68. *Cumhuriyet*, 9-12 Sept. 1967; *The New York Times*, 11 Sept. 1967; See also: Andreas Papandreou, *Democracy at Gunpoint* (New York: Doubleday & Co., 1970), p. 241.

69. Sharon A. Wiener, "Turkish Foreign Policy Decision Making on the Cyprus Issue" (Ph.D. dissertation, Duke University, 1980), p. 152.

70. Adams and Cottrell, *op. cit.*, pp. 70-71; Nancy Crawshaw, *The Cyprus Revolt* (London: George Allen & Unwin, 1978), pp. 376-377; Markides, *op. cit.*, p. 2; "History of the Johnson Administration: Cyprus Problem," p. 15, *National Security Council History File: Cyprus Crisis* [Hereafter: *NSCHF: Cyprus Crisis*], L.B. Johnson Library, Austin, Texas.

71. Papandreou, *op. cit.*, p. 242; Markides, *op. cit.*, p. 134.

72. Markides, *op. cit.*, p. 133; Crawshaw, *op. cit.*, p. 376.

73. U.N., Security Council, "Report of the Secretary General," *Document, No. S/8248*, 1967.

74. *Ibid.*; *Cumhuriyet*, 16 and 17 Nov. 1967.

75. U.N., Security Council, *Document, No. 8248*, 1967.

76. *Ibid.*

77. *Cumhuriyet*, 16 Nov. 1967; *Ulus*, 20 Nov. 1967.

78. *Cumhuriyet*, 20 Nov. 1967.

79. *Ibid.*; *Disisleri Bakanligi Belleteni*, No. 39 (Dec., 1967) pp. 45-47; *Ulus*, Ankara, 9 Dec. 1967.

80. Arcayurek, *Demirel Donemi, 12 Mart Darbesi*, p. 118.

81. *Ibid.*, p. 119.

82. Cuneyt Arcayurek, *Yeni Demokrasi, Yeni Arayislar*, p. 282.

83. Arcayurek, *Demirel Donemi, 12 Mart Darbesi*, p. 119; *Cumhuriyet*, 17 Nov. 1967.

84. *Cumhuriyet*, 17 Nov. 1967; *Disisleri Bakanligi Belleteni*, No. 39 (Dec., 1967), p. 47.

85. *Cumhuriyet*, 17 Nov. 1964.

86. *Ibid.*, *Disisleri Bakanligi Belleteni*, No. 39 (Dec., 1967), p. 47.

87. Wiener, *op. cit.*, p. 186.

88. *Cumhuriyet*, 20 Nov. 1967.

89. Wiener, *op. cit.*, p. 186.

90. Adams and Cottrell, *op. cit.*, p. 71.

91. Wiener, *op. cit.*, p. 189.

92. *Hurriyet*, 11 Jan. 1968; Wiener, *op. cit.*, p. 189.

93. Barry M. Belchman, Stephen S. Kaplan, et. al., *Force Without War* (Washington, D.C.: The Brookings Institution, 1978), p. 73; *Ulus*, Ankara,

19 Nov. 1967; *Cumhuriyet*, Istanbul, 18 Nov. 1967.

94. "Kibris Olaylari," *Akis*, 9 Dec. 1967, p. 4 in Wiener, *op. cit.*, p. 208.

95. Arcayurek, *Yeni Democrasi, Yeni Arayislar*, p. 282.

96. *Cumhuriyet*, 19 Nov. 1967.

97. *Cumhuriyet*, 20 Nov. 1967.

98. *Cumhuriyet*, 20 Nov. 1967.

99. Thomas Ehrlich, *Cyprus: 1958-1967* (New York and London: Oxford University Press, 1974), p. 100.

100. *Cumhuriyet*, 21 Nov. 1967.

101. "Document No. 27: History of the Johnson Administration," *NSCHF: Cyprus Crisis.*

102. "Memorandum for the Record: Vance Mission," 23 Nov. 1967, *NSCHF: Cyprus Crisis.*

103. Cyrus Vance, *Hard Choices* (New York: Simon and Schuster, 1983), p. 144.

104. *Ibid.*

105. Wiener, *op. cit.*, p. 192.

106. *Keesings Contemporary Archives*, 1967, p. 22436; *Cumhuriyet*, 24 Nov. 1967.

107. *Cumhuriyet*, 26 Nov. 1967.

108. *Cumhuriyet*, 29 Nov. 1967.

109. *Cumhuriyet*, 1 Dec. 1967; *The New York Times*, 1 Dec. 1967, p. 1.

110. *Cumhuriyet*, 1 Dec. 1967; Ehrlich, *op. cit.*, p. 114; *Disisleri Bakanligi Belleteni*, No. 39 (Dec., 1967), p. 47.

111. *Cumhuriyet*, 1 Dec. 1967; *The New York Times*, 5 Dec. 1967, p. 2.

112. *Cumhuriyet*, 5 Dec. 1967.

113. *Ibid.*

114. *Cumhuriyet*, 1 Dec. 1967.

115. *Disisleri Bakanligi Belleteni*, No. 39 (Dec., 1967), p. 43.

116. *Cumhuriyet*, 26 Nov. 1967.

117. *Millet Meclisi Tutanak Dergisi*, Vol. XXII (1968), 4 Dec. 1967, p. 318.

118. *Disisleri Bakanligi Belleteni*, No. 39 (Dec., 1967), p. 39.

119. *Cumhuriyet*, 5 Dec. 1967.

120. *Millet Meclisi Tutanak Dergisi*, Vol. XXII (1968), 4 Dec. 1967, p. 332.

121. *Cumhuriyet*, 9 Dec. 1967, p. 7.

122. *Cumhuriyet*, 6 Dec. 1967.

123. *Ibid.*

124. *Disisleri Bakanligi Belleteni*, No. 39 (December, 1967), p. 40.

125. *Millet Meclisi Tutanak Dergisi*, Vol. XXII (1968), 4 Dec. 1967, p. 347.

126. *Disisleri Bakanligi Belleteni*, No. 41 (Feb., 1968), p. 44.

127. *Disisleri Bakanligi Belleteni*, No. 40 (Jan., 1968), p. 55.

128. Murat Sarica, et. al., *Kibris Sorunu* (Istanbul: Fakulteler Matbaasi, 1975), p. 161.

129. *Pravda*, 5 July 1967 in Adams and Cottrell, *op. cit.*, p. 51.

130. U.N., Security Council, *Official Records*, 1383rd Meeting, 24-25 Nov. 1964, para. 77-78.

131. *Cumhuriyet*, 24 Nov. 1967.

132. Sarica, *op. cit.*, p. 156.

133. *Cumhuriyet*, Istanbul, 30 Dec. 1967.

134. Polyviou, *op. cit.*, p. 59.

135. *Ibid.*; *Disisleri Bakanligi Belleteni*, No. 52 (January 1969), p. 69.

136. *Disisleri Bakanligi Belleteni*, No. 43 (Apr., 1968), p. 74.

137. Polyviou, *op. cit.*, p. 62.

138. *Disisleri Bakanligi Belleteni*, No. 62 (Nov., 1969), p. 75.

139. *Disisleri Bakanligi Belleteni*, No. 63 (Dec., 1969), p. 83. For Inonu's views see: *Cumhuriyet*, 23 Jan. 1969.

140. *Millet Meclisi Tutanak Dergisi*, Vol. III (1970), 12 March 1970, p. 477.

141. Polyviou, *op. cit.*, pp. 265-315; Attalides, *op. cit.*, p. 103; Stavrinides, *op. cit.*, p. 112; Sarica, *op. cit.*, p. 163.

142. Stavrinides, *op. cit.*, p. 112; Attalides, *op. cit.*, p. 103.

143. *Disisleri Bakanligi Belleteni*, No. 77 (Feb., 1971), p. 94.

144. Ertekun, *op. cit.*, p. 28.

145. K.J. Holsti, *International Politics: A Framework for Analysis* (Englewood Cliffs, N.J.: Prentice-Hall, 1983), p. 149.

146. *Ibid.*, p. 151.

147. David Singer, "Inter-Nation Influence: A Formal Model," in James N. Rosenau, ed., *International Politics and Foreign Policy* (New York: The Free Press, 1969), p. 391.

148. Holsti, *op. cit.*, p. 153.

149. Robert Dahl, *Modern Political Analysis* (Englewood Cliffs: N.J.: Prentice-Hall, 1979), p. 33.

150. Alvin Z. Rubinstein, *Red Star on the Nile: The Soviet Egyptian Influence Relationship Since the June War* (Princeton, N.J.: Princeton University Press, 1977), p. xvii.

151. Singer, *op. cit.*, p. 386.

152. *Ibid.*

153. *Ibid.*, p. 387.

154. Carl Joachim Friedrich, *Man and His Government: An Empirical Theory of Politics* (New York: McGraw-Hill, 1963), p. 202.

155. Carl J. Friedrich, *Constitutional Government and Democracy* (New York: Harper and Brothers, 1937), pp. 16-18.

156. Friedrich, *Man and His Government*, p. 204.

IV. 1974 Cyprus Crisis

Developments in Cyprus after 1967

Despite the relaxation of tensions in Cyprus after 1967, the *de facto* division of the island continued. Makarios' lifting of the blockade around Turkish enclaves and the commencement of intercommunal negotiations suggested that normalcy was returning to the island. Makarios continued, however, stressing his allegiance to the goal of *enosis*. On 14 March 1971 he stated:

> Cyprus is Greek. Cyprus has been Greek since the dawn of her history, and will remain Greek; Greek and undivided we have taken her over; Greek and undivided we shall preserve her; Greek and undivided we shall deliver her to Greece . . .[1]

Makarios also caused the prolongation of the intercommunal negotiations by refusing greater local autonomy for Turkish Cypriots.[2] Later, Makarios regretted his inflexibility. In September 1974, several weeks after the Turkish intervention, Makarios admitted that he could have prevented Turkey's action if he had been more accommodating towards Turkish Cypriots. In an interview,

> Makarios conceded that he may have been mistaken in not having worked more effectively over the years for an agreement

> between the Greek and Turkish Cypriots. But had he done so, he [said], the Greek junta in Athens would have moved against him sooner than it did, and so he figured that . . . he could stave off the inevitable attack by prolonging the talks between the Island's two ethnic communities.[3]

In spite of his non-compromising attitude toward the Turkish Cypriots, Makarios preferred to avoid a confrontationist posture. While he matched the rhetoric of his hard-line rivals in calling for *enosis*, he failed to live up to his promises. The social democrat EDEK and communist AKEL parties, who feared that after *enosis* the Greek junta would not tolerate their existence, supported Makarios' hesitation.[4]

After Makarios' 1968 landslide reelection victory, his right-wing opponents established several terrorist organizations to overthrow him and strive for *enosis*. These included the *National Front, the Organization Akritas, the Enosist Youth Phoenix* and several others.[5] The officers of the Greek Junta who commanded the Greek Cypriot National Guard actively supported these groups. These officers, whose presence was illegal according to the 1960 constitution numbered between 1,500 and 2.000.[6] The mainland Greek officers also turned the Greek Cypriot National Guard into an anti-Makarios and pro-junta force by indoctrinating the new recruits.[7] The first major action of the pro-junta opposition took place on 8 March 1970 when Makarios' helicopter was shut down after it lifted off from the roof of the Presidential Palace. As in 1974, Makarios escaped unhurt. The culprits of the attack, which was later named *Operation Hermes*, were not apprehended, but it was widely assumed that the junta was behind them.[8]

In September 1971, Grivas, the leader of EOKA during the 1950s, "escaped" from his "house arrest" in Athens and assumed the leadership of the newly established EOKA-B to resume the struggle for *enosis.*[9] In February and July of 1972 two more coup attempts of the EOKA-B were foiled by the police.[10] Although Grivas shared the junta's view that the *enosis* struggle should be accelerated, he opposed an all-out war to achieve the unification of Cyprus with Greece. Especially after Makarios' establishment in March 1973 of the so-called Tactical Reserve Force, there were reports that Grivas disagreed with the Colonels' plan to overthrow Makarios because he was afraid that a *putsch* would lead to a civil war among Greeks.[11]

Two important developments altered the course of events in Cyprus. In November 1973 Ioannides, the chief of the military police of Greece, replaced Papadopoulos as the head of the junta. The new head, Dimitrios Ioannides was known as an extremist even within the Greek junta. In 1964 while serving in Cyprus, he and Nicos Sampson the leader of the 1974 coup visited Makarios and told him: "Your Beatitude, here is [our] project. To attack the Turkish Cypriots suddenly, everywhere on the island, and eliminate them to the last one."[12] The second development was the death of Grivas in January 1974. Within two months Grivas' hand-picked successor George Karousos, who was perceived by Ioannides as "too moderate," was kidnapped and sent back to Greece. Now Greece completely controlled the Greek Cypriot National Guard and EOKA-B.[13]

The final confrontation between Makarios and the junta came in July 1974 over the issue of Greek Cypriots' recruitment for the National Guard's officer corps. Until Makarios decided to make an issue out of it, the mainland Greek commanders of the National Guard chose anti-Makarios and pro-junta candidates for officer training. At the beginning of 1974 Makarios urged the mainland Greek commanders to submit the list of officer candidates for approval by the Cypriot "Minister of Interior." They ignored his suggestion and continued the old practice.[14] For Makarios, this was the last straw. He decided to go public about his ongoing friction with the junta. On

2 July 1974 he wrote a letter to General Phaedon Ghizikis, the figurehead President of Greece, and leaked it to the Greek Cypriot press which published it on 5 July 1974. In his letter Makarios argued that

> [t]he National Guard, staffed and controlled by Greek officers, was from the beginning the chief provider of men and materials for EOKA-B, the members and supporters of which were euphemistically self-styled the 'Unionist Group' [*Enosist* Group]. . . .
>
> [O]fficers of the Greek Military Regime support and direct the actions of the terrorist organization EOKA-B . . . The culpability of the circles of the military regime is proven by documents recently found in the possession of high ranking members of EOKA-B. From the National Center large sums of money have been sent for the support of the organization and after the death of Grivas . . . all important commands came from Athens.[15]

Makarios knew that his letter would further antagonize the junta, but he felt that it would overthrow him anyway unless he did something. Makarios believed that he could force the junta to abandon its plans once its role became known. Makarios also counted on the U.S. with which he had established a quiet understanding since the mid-1960s. In 1970 he had allowed the U.S. to base U-2 reconnaissance planes at Britain's Akrotiri sovereign base in Cyprus. He also permitted the CIA's Foreign Broadcast Information Service to eavesdrop on the Middle East and the Soviet Union.[16] The U.S. had informed Makarios about the 1970 assassination attempt, thereby demonstrating its interest in his survival.[17] Hence, Makarios expected that the U.S. once more would urge caution on the Greek junta.

Makarios' hopes were dashed, however, because the U.S. either could not or would not influence

Ioannides to give up the coup. It is also possible that for a number of reasons Ioannides ignored Washington's urgings for restraint. As a result, Makarios received the response to his letter of 2 July 1974 in the form of a coup engineered and partly executed by mainland Greek troops.

Turkish Politics, 1970-1974

As noted earlier, after the withdrawal of Greek troops from Cyprus in 1967, the Demirel Government announced that normalcy had returned to Cyprus. This announcement indicated that Demirel was eager to devote his attention to domestic problems and had no intention of striving for further Greek and Greek Cypriot concessions. Especially after Makarios' lifting of the blockade around Turkish enclaves and the commencement of intercommunal talks in 1968, not only Demirel, but also Turkish public opinion accorded a secondary significance to the developments in Cyprus.

Between 1969 and 1971 Demirel dealt with economic problems and the ever worsening problem of domestic terrorism. The latter led to domestic turmoil provoking several groups of low-ranking officers to devise military coup plots. In order to prevent the accession of a radical junta to power, the chief of the general staff and the three top commanders of the armed forces demanded Demirel's resignation on 12 March 1971. Needless to say, these commanders believed that a new government controlled by the armed forces stood a better chance of dealing with domestic terrorism.[18]

Demirel resigned on 12 March 1971. Three civilian "above-parties" governments which consisted mainly of technocrats and bureaucrats consecutively succeeded the Demirel Government. These governments, led by Nihat Erim, Ferit Melen and Naim Talu, were heavily influenced by the armed forces which chose to remain on the sidelines and allow the civilians to handle the everyday concerns of the country. The military concentrated on the problem of domestic terrorism by curtailing civil rights from 1971 to 1973.[19]

Before his resignation Demirel had continued to stress the importance of a "multi-faceted" foreign policy. Turkey participated in the first Islamic summit conference in Rabat, Morocco (22-25 September 1969) and joined other Islamic states in condemning Israel's occupation of Jerusalem and other Palestinian territories in the June 1967 war.[20] The participation of Turkey, which had earlier refused to attend meetings motivated by religious zeal, was by itself revolutionary in importance. Pragmatist Demirel had realized that currying favor with Middle Eastern states required not only separating Turkish foreign policy from U.S. foreign policy in the area, but also making the necessary sacrifices from Turkey's secular state outlook.

Demirel's pragmatism paid off handsomely. At the Summit Conference of Nonaligned States in Lusaka, Zambia in September 1970, the Greek Cypriot delegates pushed for the adoption of a pro-Makarios resolution. For the first time in decades the Arab states opposed these efforts. The Iraqi delegate told the conference that Iraq did not recognize the Greek Cypriot thesis and added that "at least twenty-six other states think similarly."[21] The resolution was not adopted. It should be stressed, however, that a pro-Turkish resolution was not even drafted, let alone adopted. Despite considerable progress, Turkey still had a long way to go to acquire the unqualified support of the Middle Eastern and Third World states.

The interval of 1971-1973 was characterized mainly by the lack of foreign policy initiatives. The bureaucrats who occupied government posts without much authority and with a limited popular basis of support were in no position to undertake courageous steps in foreign policy and especially in Cyprus policy. The major event of this period was the so-called *Lisbon Consensus* reached between Turkish and Greek

Foreign Ministers Olcay and Palamas in 1971. Both ministers agreed that the Cyprus crisis should be solved only through negotiations. During the talks Palamas seemed more enthusiastic than Makarios towards the autonomy demands of Turkish Cypriots, but the negotiations did not continue beyond Lisbon.[22]

The Opium Question

The most important factor affecting Turco-American relations between 1966 and 1974 was the cultivation of opium poppies in Turkey and the U.S. reaction to it. American pressures, which caused the Erim Administration to ban poppy cultivation in 1971, contributed to anti-Americanism and to a decrease in American prestige in Turkey.

In 1968 the U.S. Bureau of Narcotics and Dangerous Drugs (BNDD) established that "80 percent of the heroin illicitly consumed in the United States was derived from Turkish opium."[23] Following this report the Johnson Administration began pressuring Turkey to adopt more stringent control measures to prevent the illegal opium traffic in Turkey.[24] In 1969 the U.S. started to urge Demirel to terminate the poppy cultivation. As a result of these pressures, Demirel limited the regions of poppy cultivation from twenty-one in 1967 to seven in 1970, but refused to impose a total ban.[25] He stated on 1 August 1970 that "Turkey cannot ignore [the fact] that humanity . . . is being [destroyed] by drugs." Demirel added that Turkey was unable to stop the smugglers and had no option other than replacing the opium poppy with substitute crops in the long run.[26]

In 1971, both the U.S. Administration and the U.S. Congress increased their pressure on Turkey to totally ban the opium poppy. Congress included in the 1971 Foreign Assistance Act a clause which required the President "to suspend all military sales and aid [and] economic assistance" to governments that failed to prevent narcotics produced in their countries from reaching the U.S.[27] Between June 1970 and June 1971 there were approximately sixty bills introduced in Congress specifically calling for an end to American assistance to Turkey.[28]

In 1971 criticism against Turkey grew. There were indications that Congress, which had considered Turkey an ally against Soviet expansionism until the late 1960s, was having second thoughts about Turkey's utility to the U.S. Senator Walter F. Mondale (D-Minnesota) argued on 1 February 1974 that it was difficult to show that "any imaginable defense contribution by Turkey to our security could outweigh the damage done the United States each year by the Turkish opium crop."[29]

U.S. pressures, which had failed to influence Demirel, did have the desired impact on Nihat Erim, the prime minister selected by the armed forces in March 1971. On June 30 1971 Erim announced that opium posed a big problem to "humanity" and that he had no other choice but to ban poppy cultivation.[30] To sweeten the deal, President Nixon authorized Ambassador William Handley to offer Erim $35 million to compensate for Turkey's losses. Erim accepted the money, but the deal was kept secret from the public.[31]

The ban remained active until the Republican People's Party-National Salvation Party (NSP) coalition government led by RPP chairman Ecevit revoked it on 1 July 1974. The ban had been quite unpopular. In impoverished mountain villages "the poppy was the only crop that made a subsistence existence possible." To major poppy growing regions, "the poppy meant at least as much as tobacco to Kentucky."[32] Furthermore, the U.S. aid was too little to facilitate the farmers' transition to another crop.

Turks were outraged in August 1972 when they learned that the U.S. had decided to ask India to increase its opium production to meet the worldwide shortage estimated by the International Narcotics Board.[33] Most importantly, however, the economic plight of the former poppy growers led to enormous electoral pressure on political parties, which could not resist the temptation of promising the resumption of poppy cultivation. During the electoral campaign in October 1973 all political parties, including the JP, spoke out against the ban. RPP leader Ecevit, the most outspoken critic, considered the ban as having compromised Turkey's sovereignty.[34]

Ecevit Adopts An Assertive Foreign Policy

Bulent Ecevit, who replaced Inonu as RPP chairman in May 1972, believed that Turkey could afford to adopt an assertive foreign policy. In contrast to Inonu's policies of caution *vis-a-vis* the superpowers, Ecevit maintained in 1972 that

> . . . small and weak states can successfully challenge the strongest states. The Turkish nation [proved this in 1920s] . . . when it had lost all of its economic power, and when its state apparatus was in shambles, and its territories were partitioned.
>
> Especially in today's conditions [smaller states] stand more favorable chances. Because, . . . under certain conditions superpowers realize that their extraordinary powers prove to be a liability for them.
>
> Turkey could continue its alliance relations with stronger states without losing its freedom of action . . . if it kept the conditions of our age in perspective . . .[35]

Ecevit's argument that smaller allies did not need to correlate all of their foreign policy actions with the U.S. reflected the widely shared belief within the RPP, and to a lesser extent in Turkey proper, that more equality should exist in U.S.-Turkey relations.

In a sense, the RPP's insistence on equality and freedom of action was a natural extension of the "multi-faceted" foreign policy concept adopted in 1964 by Inonu and later by Demirel. In 1968, the RPP stated that Turkey "should not solely rely on the security provided by NATO, and a national defense strategy should be adopted."[36] The RPP further suggested that Turkey should not only improve relations with the U.S.S.R. as Demirel was doing, but also "should try not to be provocative" against it.[37] In other words, the RPP suggested that Turkey should disassociate itself from the Cold War rhetoric of NATO.

Ecevit also criticized Turkey's assumption of a role in the Middle East on behalf of the U.S. He consistently maintained that Turkey's participation in the 1950s in schemes like the Baghdad Pact was harmful to Turkey's national security interests.[38] Despite all of his criticism of the U.S., Ecevit did not consider nonalignment a viable alternative for Turkey. The Foreign Minister of the Ecevit Cabinet, Turan Gunes told the National Assembly on 22 May 1974 that "the RPP has never considered withdrawing from NATO" and added that Turkey's relations with NATO were "being conducted in a way that is compatible with our national interests and in a way that inspires confidence in our [regional] friends."[39]

Ecevit's insistence on more independence within NATO distinguished him from his predecessor who only half-heartedly supported this goal. Ecevit's assertiveness in Turco-Greek relations was, however, the major characteristic of his Administration which set it apart from previous governments. Foreign Minister Gunes told the National Assembly on 22 May 1974 that Turkey wanted to live in peace with Greece, but that "just because this is so, Greece will certainly not be allowed to gnaw away at Turkish interests in any manner whatsoever or to upset the balance between the two countries."[40]

After coming to power in January 1974, Ecevit told the Defense and Foreign Ministry officials that in order to assert its rights Turkey needed to create precedents in the Aegean and Cyprus.[41] This approach, characterized by Ecevit's foreign policy adviser Haluk Ulman as "going ahead of the developments," suggested that Turkey would create *fait accomplis* whenever there emerged an ambiguity regarding the rights of Turkey. Ulman maintained that this policy was superior to previous governments' "wait and see" approach.[42]

Ecevit tested this new policy in the Aegean Sea in May 1974, two months before the crisis in Cyprus. The Aegean dispute emerged in February 1974 when "the Greek Government announced oil and natural gas discoveries in the area, and went on to claim all mineral rights on Greece's continental shelf."[43] Since Greece claimed that the Greek islands also had their own continental shelves, the seabed of most of the Aegean Sea would belong to Greece. Upon learning of Greece's preparations for oil explorations in the area, Ecevit proposed negotiations to delineate the respective spheres of the Greek and Turkish continental shelves. Greece did not respond to the offer.[44]

Ecevit reacted to Greece's indifference more strongly than would have previous Turkish governments. On 29 May Turkey sent naval survey ship *Candarli* to the disputed areas accompanied by a navy squadron. It announced that *Candarli* would conduct "seismic explorations in the Turkish continental shelf" and that oil drillings would start soon.[45] *Candarli's* mission ended on 5 June without incident even though a number of Greek warships followed it closely in the disputed area.

Ecevit's behavior concerning *Candarli's* mission indicates not only that he was a proponent of assertive foreign policy, but also that he was a risk taker. Ecevit was aware that the unpredictable Greek junta and its more unpredictable new leader, Ioannides, could decide to challenge Turkey's show of force and that this might lead to a Turco-Greek war. Yet he felt the stakes were high enough to take that risk. It should be added that as a member of Inonu's cabinet in 1964, Ecevit had witnessed how Inonu's cautiousness had failed to achieve a favorable settlement in Cyprus. This experience gave him greater incentive to behave in a less cautious way in 1974.[46]

Ecevit continued, however, to offer Greece the option of bilateral negotiations to settle the Aegean dispute. After Foreign Minister Gunes's preliminary talks with Greek Foreign Minister Tetenes during the NATO Foreign Ministers Summit in Ottowa (18-20 June 1974), Ecevit asked Greek Prime Minister Androutsopoulos on 26 June in Brussels to establish a joint committee to examine the Turco-Greek disputes. Throughout the Brussels meeting, Androutsopoulos remained intransigent, refusing even to issue a joint declaration, let alone accept Ecevit's proposal.[47] Androutsopoulos' refusal once more convinced Ecevit that the Greek junta was not interested in negotiated settlements.

Ecevit's assertiveness was also manifest in his policy toward Cyprus. Unlike the Demirel Government's position which would have accepted a Greek-dominated unitary state, the Government program of the Ecevit-Erbakan coalition government stated that only a federal solution was acceptable to Turkey.[48] Foreign Minister Turan Gunes asserted that

> the Cyprus talks will be conducted on the basis that two communities exist on Cyprus, that both communities have rights over Cyprus, that they would be subject to different legislation in the fields [where] they differ from each other, and that there would be no unilateral amendment of legislation. This means that our government will not accept the idea of [a] unitary state, that is to say, changing the status of the Turkish Cypriot community into a minority.[49]

Ecevit's foreign policy adviser Haluk Ulman later explained that the Government desired a "functional" federation in Cyprus which would provide the Turkish Cypriots with a fair share in the administration of the state. Ecevit was ready, however, to scale down this "fair share" to 20 percent as opposed to the 30 percent of the 1960 constitution. Unlike the post-intervention Turkish demands, Ecevit's demands did not call for a territorial separation of two communities, yet they required autonomy for Turkish enclaves.[50]

Ecevit's perception of America's Cyprus policy also shaped his response to the 1974 crisis. According to an article he wrote in 1965, Ecevit believed that U.S. policy toward Cyprus was as follows:

> 1. Cyprus should not remain independent. If it remained independent it could become a communist base in the Mediterranean.
> 2. Cyprus should not be divided because a partition would . . . only worsen the crisis.
> 3. [Even if its interests required Turkey to intervene] . . . Turkey should refrain from doing so because this would lead to a Greco-Turkish war and to the dismemberment of NATO.
> 4. Cyprus should be united with Greece. This option would eliminate all the above mentioned problems and Cyprus would come under NATO's influence.[51]

As we will see, the absence of a U.S. reaction to the 1974 coup in Cyprus further convinced Ecevit that unless he acted without delay the U.S. would welcome *enosis*.

The Last Turco-American Friction

Before the Cyprus Intervention

As stated earlier, Ecevit's RPP/NSP coalition government lifted the ban on poppy cultivation on 1 July 1974. Ecevit later justified this popular decision by arguing that "no independent nation could negotiate with another state on which plants it should grow and which plants it should not."[52] The leader of the major opposition party, Demirel supported the lifting of the ban, maintaining that the original ban in 1971 was "wrong." Demirel cautioned, however, that in the long run Turkey might regret the lifting of the ban because of hostile reactions from its allies.[53]

Demirel's fear proved to be justified. On 7 July 1974, the Nixon Administration signaled its displeasure by recalling Ambassador Robert Macomber to Washington for "consultations."[54] The U.S. had earlier ignored Ecevit's efforts to sound out America's response to a mutually agreed cancellation of the 1971 verbal accord on banning poppy cultivation.[55] Ecevit's assurance that Turkey would adopt a new method of opium production that would curb illegal trafficking also fell on deaf ears in Washington.[56]

Congress reacted more harshly than did the Executive. Members of the House and Senate proposed a number of draft resolutions asking for the imposition of embargoes. One of them, House Concurrent Resolution 507, was co-authored by Lester L. Wolff (D-New York) and Edward Derwinski (R-Illinois) who represented states where the opium issue occupied the minds of the electorate.[57] Resolution 507 urged the President to:

> (1) immediately initiate negotiations at the highest level of the Turkish Government to prevent the resumption of opium production; and (2) if such negotiations prove

> unfruitful, exercise the authority provided by the Congress under the Foreign Assistance Act [of 1971], to terminate all assistance to the Government of Turkey.

It should be added that New York and Illinois contained formidable numbers of Greek and other ethnic voters. It is thus not surprising that both Wolff and Derwinski became ardent supporters of the arms embargo imposed on Turkey after its Cyprus intervention.

Resolution 507, cosponsored by 239 members of the House, indicated that Congress as a whole considered the issue a national emergency. On 5 August 1974 the House passed Res. 507 which was subsequently approved by the Senate.[58] Congress did not, however, pressure the President to implement the resolution because after the second Turkish intervention in Cyprus on 14 August 1974, congressional opponents of the poppy cultivation, including the Black caucus, chose to support the arms embargo favored by the Greed Lobby and "the rule of law" proponents.

The Turkish Government and the Turkish public were outraged at Congress' eagerness to adopt coercive measures against a loyal ally. More importantly, the congressional opponents of the poppy cultivation made use of an offensive rhetoric that was considered humiliating by the Turkish people. Lester Wolff (D-New York) told the House on 16 July 1974, one day after the Sampson coup in Cyprus, that the Congressmen had a more important commitment to their constituents than they had to Turkey's security. He continued by quoting approvingly from a newspaper commentary which urged the U.S. Administration to bomb the Turkish poppy fields if Turkey did not change its policy.[59]

This and similar statements by many Congressmen were judged by the Ecevit Government as indications of, at the least, insensitivity toward Turkish national interests. Thus, when the 1974

Cyprus crisis broke out after the Sampson coup on 15 July 1974, Ecevit had one more reason to reject U.S. mediation to solve the crisis. The fact that when the coup took place, U.S. Ambassador to Turkey Robert Macomber had already been recalled to Washington and Congress was discussing ways to penalize Turkey symbolically illustrates the lack of trust between the two countries.

The U.S. Fails to Prevent the Sampson Coup

Since March 1974 the U.S. State Department had been swamped by reports of an imminent coup against Makarios. The Ambassador of Cyprus, Nikos Dimitriou had also told Assistant Secretary of State for Near Eastern Affairs Rodger Davies and Cyprus Country Director Thomas Boyatt that there would shortly be an assassination attempt against Makarios.[60] For a while the State Department chose to pay no attention to these warnings because in recent years such reports had become commonplace for Cyprus.

In June 1974 additional and more reliable reports began to pour in. On 20 June 1974 the head of the Greek junta, Ioannides informed a CIA operative in Athens that Greece had decided to remove Makarios from power.[61] After receiving the report concerning Ioannides' coup preparations, Cyprus Country Director Boyatt sent a message to U.S. Ambassador in Athens Henry Tasca urging him to see Ioannides and inform him that the U.S. disapproved of his plan.[62] Boyatt's directive contradicted the earlier U.S. stance of quasi-indifference concerning the coup reports. Ambassador Tasca had not been informed about the details of intelligence reports and he asked Boyatt to review the order once more.[63] Meanwhile Tasca went to see figurehead Prime Minister Androutsopoulos who assured him that the coup rumors were inaccurate.[64]

In Washington Boyatt brought the intelligence reports to the attention of Undersecretary of State Joseph Sisco who decided that there was no need to send a message to Ioannides. A subsequent CIA report from Athens in early July reassured Sisco that a coup was not imminent. This report maintained that Ioannides "had now decided not to move against Makarios, at least for the time being."[65] Even after the Greek Cypriot press published the letter written by Makarios to figurehead President Ghizikis, the CIA reports from Athens persisted in advising Washington that Ioannides had no intention of toppling Makarios.[66]

Despite Boyatt's continuing pleas, the State Department and Secretary of State Kissinger disregarded the possibility of a coup. Even after the resignation of Greek Foreign Minister Tetenes and two other high level officials of the Greek Foreign Ministry for "health" reasons on 8 July 1974, State Department officials, with the exception of Boyatt, felt no urgency for action.[67] Later it became clear that the Greek officials had resigned because they opposed the planned coup in Cyprus.

Another reason for U.S. failure to prevent the coup in Cyprus was the fact that Ambassador Tasca did not talk to Ioannides and warn him that the U.S. disapproved of his plan. Tasca did not want to meet with Ioannides because he felt it was unnecessary. According to his own account, in 1972 he had "raised hell" with the former junta leader Papadopoulos when he learned about Papadopoulos' similar plans to engineer a coup in Cyprus. Tasca added that if he had had "a *reliable* report that Ioannides seemed about to move [he] would have turned the place upside down."[68] In 1974 the CIA did not adequately inform Tasca about Ioannides' intentions, and the State Department did not order him to see Ioannides.

Secretary of State Kissinger was also negligent in dealing with the coup reports. In early June 1974 Senator William Fulbright, then chairman of the Senate Foreign Relations Committee, visited Kissinger and told him that he had received information that Ioannides was preparing for a Cyprus coup. Kissinger rejected Fulbright's suggestion that he should avert the coup by arguing that the U.S. should not interfere in the internal affairs of the Greeks.[69]

Kissinger refused Fulbright's suggestion because he was unable to grasp the seriousness of the situation. He later admitted that if he "had ever had twelve hours and been able to pick out an intelligence report [he] would have seen that the situation needed attention."[70] Kissinger's excuse was understandable because as one observer suggested,

> [t]he Yom Kippur war which erupted in the Middle East in October [1973] and the peace-making efforts that ensued, absorbed most of his diplomatic energies . . . Kissinger was under personal attack for his alleged role in the wiretapping of government officials and journalists . . . Even for a man of Kissinger's resourcefulness and stamina, Cyprus and Portugal in 1974 were two sorrows too many."[71]

There is no evidence that Kissinger ever admonished the Greek Ambassador to Washington Constantine Panayotakos about the dangers of a move against Makarios.[72] Ioannides also knew that Kissinger did not approve of Makarios' friendly relations with the Soviets. Hence, he might have assumed that Kissinger was not opposed to a coup against Makarios, and Ambassador Tasca's warnings to formal Greek Government officials were just window dressing.

There have been several allegations concerning the CIA's role in the Cyprus coup. The Greek Cypriot "Government," for instance, argued before the coup that the CIA was financing the EOKA-B forces in Cyprus.[73] Some observers also claimed that the coup resulted from Ioannides' cooperation with the Israeli Secret Service, Mossad, and the CIA. According to this version, the CIA and Mossad knew very well that Turkey would oppose the putschists and that partition would take place, but they assured Ioannides that Turkey would not react.[74]

Since these allegations are not supported by facts, they are not reliable. It should be added, however, that many CIA operatives in Greece were Greek Americans who possibly shared Ioannides' goal of unifying Cyprus with Greece. One of them, Peter Koromilas, met several times with Ioannides shortly before the coup and assured him that if Makarios were to be removed, the U.S. would keep quiet.[75] If Greek American members of the CIA were responsible for misleading Ioannides, they might also have tried to misinform the U.S. Administration. Actually, twice, on 3 and 14 July 1974, the CIA reported that Ioannides had abandoned the idea of a coup.[76] It is thus not surprising that on the day of the coup, 15 July 1974, Ioannides assured the chiefs of the navy and air force, Arapakis and Papanicolau, that he had assurances from the Americans that Turkey would not intervene in Cyprus.[77]

Makarios Is Overthrown

On 15 July 1974 the units of the Greek-officered Greek Cypriot National Guard attacked and destroyed the Presidential Palace. Makarios survived the attack and fled the island on a British military aircraft.[78] At first the Greek junta's hand-picked leader of the coup Nicos Sampson promised general elections within a year and the continuation of intercommunal talks.[79] Yet Sampson had a reputation as "a sadistic killer of Turks and Britons. . . . In the Turkish enclaves, his name was a household synonym for terror . . ."[80] Therefore, his consolation of Turkish Cypriots was not convincing.

The circumstances of the coup and Sampson's relations with Ioannides have been documented elsewhere.[81] Therefore, we will not deal with them. It should be stressed, however, that Sampson later admitted that his goal was *enosis* and that had the

Turkish intervention not taken place, he would have declared the unification of Cyprus with Greece.[82] Makarios' speech before the U.N. Security Council on 19 July 1974, one day before the Turkish intervention, suffices to demonstrate Sampson's and Ioannides' intentions. Makarios stated:

> The coup did not come about under such circumstances as to be considered an internal matter of the Greek Cypriots. It is clearly an invasion from outside, in flagrant violation of the independence and sovereignty of the Republic of Cyprus. The so-called coup was the work of the Greek officers staffing and commanding the National Guard . . . It was an invasion which violated the independence and the sovereignty of the Republic.[83]

Concerning the Cyprus Turks, Makarios suggested that "[i]n the circumstances that have now been created in Cyprus, I cannot foresee the prospects of the [intercommunal] talks. I would rather say that there are no prospects at all. . . The Turks of Cyprus are also affected . . ."[84]

The Sampson coup, during which hundreds of Greek Cypriots, but also some Turkish Cypriots, lost their lives,[85] created only a low-key reaction in Washington. In a detached manner State Department spokesman Robert Anderson stated that the U.S. policy remained that of "supporting the independence and territorial integrity of Cyprus and its constitutional agreements . . ."[86] On 17 July 1974 Anderson maintained that "in our view, there has not been outside intervention in [Cyprus]."[87]

Secretary of State Kissinger, it seemed, ignored the fact that Greece had militarily intervened in Cyprus. The day the coup took place Kissinger met with Makarios' Ambassador in the U.S., Dimitriou, and told him that the U.S. usually recognizes *de-facto* governments, but he added that in this case the U.S.

would "wait and see."[88] The next day Kissinger chaired a meeting of the Washington Special Action Group (WSAG) which was composed of top officials of the State and Defense Departments. At the meeting Kissinger reportedly stressed that "the U.S. would do nothing to jeopardize the air and sea bases in Greece."[89]

Other Administration officials criticized the indifference of Kissinger, who did not hesitate to refer to Makarios as "the Castro of the Mediterranean."[90] Many State Department bureaucrats and Secretary of Defense Schlesinger urged Kissinger to confront the Greek junta and ask for Sampson's removal.[91] Kissinger chose not to do that because, as he suggested, he believed that "[e]xplicit condemnation of the Greek junta by the United States" would have been seen by Turkey as an approval of its intervention. Since Turkey's intervention was almost certain, it was necessary "that the United States not be seen in Greece as the agent of its humiliation."[92]

Kissinger later suggested that the U.S. "could not avoid diplomatic engagement in a NATO crisis, but in the last three weeks of Nixon's presidency we were in no position to make credible threats or credible promises the instrumentalities of diplomacy." Kissinger also blamed his rivalry with Schlesinger for his failure to peacefully solve the crisis. He argued that "the bureaucratic struggle reduced my dominance only to create a deadlock; for it could not be resolved by a president *in extremis* three thousand miles away . . ."[93]

Ecevit Decides to Intervene

The Sampson coup of 15 July 1974 caught the Ecevit Government by surprise. The latest intelligence report received from Cyprus dealt with intra-Turkish rivalries. Only the Cyprus Coordination Committee of the Foreign Ministry suspected a move against Makarios but could not alert the Government in advance.[94] On 15 July Foreign Minister Turan Gunes was on an official visit in China, and Turkey's Ambassador to Greece, Kamuran Gurun was on a yacht trip in the Mediterranean accompanied by a Greek friend. The chief of staff of the armed forces was in Istanbul and the commander of the navy on an inspection tour in the Mediterranean.[95]

Ecevit received the news of the coup as he was about to board a plane to Afyon, where he was scheduled to address poppy farmers to explain the Government's decision to lift the ban on poppy cultivation. Ecevit still went to Afyon but decided during the trip that Turkey should intervene militarily if a peaceful solution could not be found within a reasonable period.[96] Ecevit also admitted that he was not hopeful about a peaceful solution and added that his "biggest worry was to lose time unnecessarily" with negotiations.[97]

That same day, Ecevit returned to Ankara and attended the National Security Council's emergency session. During the meeting Finance Minister Deniz Baykal, in a speech that closely adhered to Ecevit's world view, suggested that a military intervention in Cyprus had become inevitable. Baykal said that as a result of detente the superpowers' reaction to regional crises had changed. Instead of interfering, he maintained, the superpowers had begun to appease the parties in regional conflicts. He argued that states which took the initiative and created *fait accomplis* were now in more favorable positions and added that Turkey

> has two alternatives. Either we could deliver tough notes to Greece and try to find a solution through diplomatic means. We know that this would not work. Or, we could reply [to the crisis] with a crisis of our own. The most important aspect of today's coup is not the installation [to power] of Sampson, the murderer of Turks and the British, but the inevitability that

> Greece would soon be our southern neighbor. Greece is about to take this last step. This should be prevented.[98]

Ecevit supported Baykal's remarks and argued that as a result of the coup, central and southern Anatolia were within the range of the Greek air force. Ecevit further maintained that world public opinion condemned the coup and opposed the Greek junta. Nobody doubted, said Ecevit, that the coup was engineered by Greece. He concluded that if Turkey did not do something in a short time, it would face grave problems later.[99]

Some ministers raised questions about the readiness of the armed forces to undertake military intervention in Cyprus. Chief of Staff Semih Sancar assured them by saying: "We are ready, but I wonder if you [the government] are ready?" The commander of the navy, Kemal Kayacan, added that if a decision was made, he would land troops on Cyprus by using even fishing boats if necessary.[100] Actually, Turkey was ready this time to meet the challenge. Whereas in 1967 it had only 6 helicopters, 2 landing craft and 150 parachutes, in 1974 it had 100 landing craft built at Turkish ship yards and 15,000 parachutes. Turkey had also bought 100 helicopters from France and Italy.[101]

Then the Council discussed several contingency plans. Two of these plans calling for bombing raids within twenty-four and forty-eight yours were easily discarded. The NSC adopted the third plan which required a two-stage landing and invasion. The commanders assured the Government that a landing force would be ready by the 20th of July.[102] Even though some ministers talked about the disadvantages of a military intervention, the National Security Council decided unanimously to land forces on Cyprus.[103] The chief of the Greece Desk of the Foreign Ministry, Ecmel Barutcu, played a significant role in convincing the Government that a landing was necessary. Vice-Premier Necmettin Erbakan, who was the leader of the religionist National Salvation Party (NSP), insisted on an immediate invasion, but the final consensus was to first consult with Britain. As a result, Turkey delivered a diplomatic note requesting bilateral negotiations regarding a joint military intervention to the British charge d'affaires on 16 July 1974 and asked for a reply within twenty-four hours.[104]

Despite his conviction that an invasion would be necessary if consultations with Britain did not work, Ecevit was unsure of the eventual goal of a Cyprus landing. During their meetings with leaders of political parties on 16 and 18 July, neither Ecevit nor the other ministers could state clearly what an intervention would accomplish if it took place. In one of the meetings, JP leader Demirel asked whether Turkey's goal was to revive the 1960 constitution and bring back Makarios from exile or if the Government had something else in mind. Upon receiving no satisfactory answer, Demirel argued that without a political goal Turkey's landing of forces in Cyprus was an adventure.[105]

Ecevit's eagerness for an invasion was partly provoked by Secretary of State Kissinger's failure to condemn the Sampson coup. Despite Kissinger's call to Ecevit assuring him that Sampson was unacceptable to the U.S., publicly the U.S. Administration seemed indifferent to the events in Cyprus.[106] Ecevit's foreign policy adviser Haluk Ulman suggested that Kissinger's indifference stemmed from his pro-*enosis* inclinations.[107] Even Ecevit had maintained as early as 1965 that the U.S. favored *enosis*.[108]

The press agreed with Ecevit that unless Turkey intervened, *enosis* would be inevitable. After a hesitation period of two days, both the right- and left-wing press began suggesting that Turkey should not miss this last opportunity.[109] It was, however, the pro-RPP press which maintained that the Greek junta accomplished its coup with U.S. collaboration and that the United States' failure to denounce Sampson or the Greek junta proved its guilt.[110]

The Sisco Mission

On the afternoon of 16 July 1974, the British government replied to Turkey's note delivered earlier the same day. The British informed Ecevit that they were ready for bilateral consultations as proposed by Ecevit. Ecevit had insisted on consulting Britain because, as he later admitted, he wanted to comply with Article IV of the Treaty of Guarantee of 1959 which entitled Turkey to intervene in the affairs of Cyprus.[111] Ecevit believed that the British would refuse to join Turkey in a joint military operation in Cyprus, but he felt that he had to comply with the stipulations of the Treaty of Guarantee "in order to convince the world public opinion that Turkey's cause was just."[112]

In London, Ecevit met with Prime Minister Harold Wilson and Foreign Minister James Callaghan on 17 July 1974. Wilson rejected Ecevit's offer of a joint military intervention by suggesting that peaceful alternatives had not been exhausted.[113] During the meeting Ecevit learned that Kissinger was sending Undersecretary of State for Political Affairs Joseph J. Sisco to London to join the Turco-British talks. Ecevit rejected the offer of trilateral talks by arguing that the U.S. was not a guarantor power. He suggested, however, that he was ready to meet separately with Sisco to discuss the crisis. Ecevit later acknowledged that he refused a trilateral meeting because he did not want the Soviets to think that a NATO-plan was being hatched.[114]

Kissinger later maintained that he sent Sisco to London "to help Britain start a negotiating process that might delay a Turkish invasion and enable the structure under Sampson in Cyprus to fall of its own weight."[115] The Ecevit-Sisco meeting took place on 18 July 1974 in Turkey's London Embassy. Kissinger told Sisco that he should do whatever he could to stop an intervention. Sisco knew, however, that he "didn't have very many cards to play with."[116]

Nevertheless, Sisco did his best to dissuade Ecevit from landing troops in Cyprus. Before mentioning the disadvantages of a landing, Sisco promised Ecevit that U.S. deliveries of military assistance which had slowed down during the last weeks would start flowing normally. The U.S. had slackened the pace of the deliveries to protest Turkey's resumption of poppy cultivation.[117] Sisco further told Ecevit that a Turkish intervention would lead to a war between Greece and Turkey and that Turkey-U.S. relations could be damaged as well. Sisco also stressed that the Soviet Union would oppose such an operation and might try to take advantage of a Turco-Greek war. Sisco did not forget to add that U.S. assistance to Turkey could be cut if Turkey went ahead with its plans.[118]

Ecevit seemed undeterred by Sisco's gloomy predictions if not threats. He told Sisco that he could cancel the intervention provided that: (1) Sampson and putschist Greek officers were withdrawn by Greece; (2) Turkey sent as large an armed force to Cyprus as Greece currently had; (3) Turkish Cypriots were given control of a coastal region; and (4) negotiations to create a federal system of government started immediately between the two Cypriot communities.[119]

Sisco promised that he would try to convince the Greek junta to accept these conditions but asked Ecevit not to move until he returned from Athens.[120] In Athens Sisco spent precious time finding Ioannides. Only after thirty-six hours of waiting did he succeed in arranging a meeting with Ioannides, Chief of Staff Bonanos, and Prime Minister Androutsopoulos. The Greeks refused Turkey's conditions and told Sisco that the most they could do was to replace those Greek officers who took part in the coup.[121]

Sisco then went to Ankara to tell Ecevit about the Greek "concession." Ecevit insisted on his demands. Sisco once more flew to Athens but came back empty-handed. In the meantime Kissinger had conducted eleven phone conversations with Ecevit who "advised Kissinger against the kind of pressure Lyndon Johnson had exerted in 1964 and warned him that such a tactic would mean the permanent 'loss' of Turkey to the Western Alliance."[122] Kissinger continued to oppose the intervention, but as Ecevit acknowledged, he never tried to intimidate Ecevit. Moreover, Kissinger created the impression that he believed Turkey's grievances concerning Cyprus were justified.[123]

At 3:00 A.M. on 20 July 1974, only two and a half hours before the Turkish operation started, Sisco returned from Athens and asked Ecevit for another forth-eight hour delay in the Turkish operation. Ecevit replied that "ten years ago both Turkey and the U.S. made mistakes. The U.S. prevented Turkey's military action, and Turkey acquiesced." Ecevit added that as a result of the 1964 Johnson Letter, Turkey-U.S. relations were harmed and that Turco-Greek relations further deteriorated. He concluded that "this time Turkey will not repeat its mistake. I hope that you would not either."[124]

Before discussing the landing operation and its aftermath, some of the factors which affected Ecevit's decision for an immediate action should be examined. Earlier it was noted that Ecevit believed that the Cyprus question, like other Turco-Greek problems, could be solved in Turkey's favor if Turkey acted assertively. Ecevit also thought that U.S. omnipotence belonged to an earlier era, and smaller allies of the U.S. could therefore ignore American preferences, creating *fait accomplis* with reasonable prospects for a favorable outcome.

Ecevit also found encouragement in the fact that as a result of the Sampson coup, the unpopular Greek junta was further isolated internationally. Ecevit calculated that world public opinion could not be any more favorable for a Turkish intervention, and that if executed carefully, Turkey's landing could be projected as a rescue operation of both Turkish and Greek Cypriots. Ecevit realized, however, that any change in conditions might remove the cover of legitimacy from the Turkish intervention and the West might fall back on its traditional identification of Turks as barbaric invaders. In fact, some high-ranking military leaders believed from the outset that "[t]he world would have hated us even if we had fired roses instead of bullets."[125]

Ecevit's pro-invasion stance seemed to be further justified when Greece continued to send reinforcements even after the coup of 15 July 1974. The Greeks undertook their build-up in daylight and Turkish reconnaissance planes discovered dozens of Greek transport aircraft and ferryboats carrying troops to Cyprus.[126] The Greek build-up lent an additional urgency to the situation causing Ecevit, who was not known for his patience, to become increasingly restless.

A major factor that contributed to Ecevit's assertiveness was the Soviet acquiescence in, if not support of a military intervention. The Soviet leaders knew that the Sampson coup not only would eliminate the Cypriot nonalignment, but that *enosis*, which they believed would follow shortly, would bring Cyprus under the firm control of Greece and thus NATO. Ecevit carefully exploited the Soviet opposition to *enosis*. Both he and Foreign Minister Gunes told Soviet Ambassador Grubyakov that Turkey "did not intend to annex or partition Cyprus and . . . will respect not only the independence of the [island], but also its nonalignment."[127]

Throughout the week following the 15 July 1974 coup, Turco-Soviet dialogue continued. The Soviets consistently indicated that they were ready to accept a limited Turkish action provided that Cyprus' international status was preserved.[128] The Soviet support can be seen in official Soviet announcements concerning the events in Cyprus. Even after the second Turkish operation (14 August 1974), the U.S.S.R. continued to blame the Greek junta, NATO and the U.S. for what had happened in Cyprus. The Soviet failure to hold Turkey accountable for its military invasion even angered British U.N.

Ambassador Richard who told Soviet Ambassador Malik that "not once did [you] . . . see fit to mention the present advance of the Turkish army in Cyprus . . . Once again, not for the first time, you have treated us to a diatribe against NATO . . ."[129]

First "Peace Operation"

At 5:30 A.M. on 20 July 1974, Turkey's naval and aerial landing on Cyprus started. According to the general staff's plans, Turkey would conduct the operation in two stages. During the first stage, which was to last for two days, Turkish forces would capture a bridgehead in northern Cyprus. After the completion of the first stage, officials would begin negotiations to conclude a new settlement in Cyprus. If the Greeks refused a new constitutional order, the Turks would launch the second operation and achieve their goals forcefully.

During the first so-called "Peace-Operation," Turkey used only 30 percent of its landing craft. The rest remained on the western shores of Turkey facing the Aegean islands. Both the Government and the commanders of the armed forces feared that the Greek junta would declare war on Turkey and that the main area of confrontation between Greece and Turkey would be Trace and the Aegean islands, not Cyprus. The stationing of 70 percent of Turkish landing craft in the Aegean further indicated that Ecevit expected to capture several of the Greek Aegean islands and settle most of the Turco-Greek problems in Turkey's favor.[130]

Since the armed forces used only 30 percent of the landing craft (31 landing craft) during the first day, they could land only 6,000 troops on Kyrenia (Girne) on the northern shore of Cyprus. Several hundred commandos parachuted into the main Turkish enclave surrounding the Kyrenia-Nicosia highway. Throughout the first operation which ended on 22 July 1974, this token force had to confront a well-armed

Greek force of 30,000 troops which included at least 3,000 mainland Greek troops.[131] Faced with this formidable force which far exceeded the Turkish general staff's expectations, the Turkish invasion force could expand only very slowly.

Ecevit ordered that aerial bombings be limited and that the troops not shoot unless shot at.[132] Ecevit had hoped that by restricting its fire power Turkey would escape being stigmatized as an invader. As a result, by the evening of 22 July 1974 Turkey had failed to capture its intended targets and Greek forces had overrun many Turkish enclaves around the island. On 22 July Turks controlled less territory than they did before the intervention.[133]

The Cyprus intervention was, nevertheless, very popular with the Turkish public. All political parties, trade unions and youth organizations declared their support for the intervention and the National Assembly unanimously approved the use of force in Cyprus.[134] The newspapers of 21 July 1974 genuinely reflected the emotions of the Turks when they filled their pages with stories of exaggerated victories and congratulated the assertiveness of the Ecevit Government.[135] The RPP probably owed most of the 24 percent increase in its electoral support in the 1977 elections to Ecevit's Cyprus intervention.[136]

It should be stressed that world public opinion initially sympathized with Turkey's intervention. It identified the Greek junta as the culprit in the fall of Makarios and thus perceived Turkey's landing as a legitimate attempt to prevent Greece's annexation of the island. *The Sunday Times* probably articulated the consensus on this issue when it suggested that "[t]he Turkish invasion of Cyprus is a justified exercise of national power to defend an interest and fulfill a treaty obligation."[137]

As stated earlier, Ecevit was determined to use the presence of Turkish troops on Cyprus as leverage in the Turco-Greek negotiations which he expected to soon follow. Ecevit was not as certain of the kind of settlement he should ask for at the negotiations.

Before the Sampson coup he favored a functional federation, the details of which have been discussed. On 20 July 1974 Ecevit suggested that "solutions acceptable to all sides could be sought . . . when a balance of power is established on the island . . ."[138] Neither Ecevit nor other ministers explained what Turkey's eventual goal was. It is possible that Ecevit considered the intervention more as an opportunity to strive for a more favorable Cyprus settlement than as a return to the 1960 constitution or even a functional federation, but could not decide what the new Turkish thesis should be. It is also possible that the Ecevit Government estimated that the U.S. and U.S.S.R. could raise objections to Turkey's intervention if they knew that Turkey intended to revise the 1960 Cyprus constitution and establish a territorial federation. Turkey's failure to make its goals known is important because it led the Greek Cypriots to underestimate Turkey's determination to impose its preferred settlement on Greek Cypriots, and caused the execution of the second phase of the Turkish intervention. This second intervention, in return, resulted in the failure of Kissinger's mediation effort.

The U.S. Efforts to Contain the Conflict

As recounted earlier, Kissinger had sent Sisco to London "to help Britain start a negotiating process that might delay a Turkish invasion. . . ."[139] Kissinger had hoped that if Sisco succeeded in postponing Turkey's intervention, the U.S. could apply pressure on the Greek junta and achieve the removal of Sampson from power. Kissinger had underestimated, however, the irrationality of the Greek junta. Sisco located Ioannides after three days of searching in Athens, yet could not convince him that reaching an agreement with Turkey was the least costly way for Greece to settle the Cyprus question.

Once the Greek junta had rejected Turkey's proposals it became clear that Ecevit would intervene.

At that point it was necessary for Kissinger to personally intervene in the crisis and ask the junta to accept a new settlement in Cyprus. Since Makarios was already off the island it would be easier for the Greek junta to come to terms with Turkey. However, since the U.S. limited its intervention to Sisco's clumsy mediation effort, Ioannides believed that it was not serious and that he could afford to ignore it. Kissinger also recognized the inadequacy of the Sisco mission, but maintained that the U.S. could not alienate Greece by taking a public stand against it because the loss of Greece would be detrimental to the NATO Alliance.[140]

The second way to prevent Turkey's intervention was to publicly oppose the action. Kissinger refused to do that arguing that the U.S. "could not without cost resist a Turkish invasion because that would be considered as objectively supporting the Greek junta."[141] Hence, when the U.S. Ambassador to Greece, Henry Tasca, suggested that the U.S. Sixth Fleet be deployed near Cyprus to indicate American dissatisfaction with Turkey's expected invasion, Kissinger refused to comply.[142] Thus, unlike its responses during the 1964 and 1967 crises, the U.S. kept the Sixth Fleet at a "safe" distance from Cyprus when the Turkish forces reached the shores of the island.[143]

Between 20 and 22 July 1974, the U.S. focused on preventing a war between Greece and Turkey and on achieving a cease-fire. When the Turkish operation started the leader of the Greek junta, Ioannides decided to attack Turkey on all fronts. On 21 July 1974 Ambassador Tasca met with the junta and, in his words, "took a very . . . strong stand against anything of this kind."[144] The U.S. pressure probably helped convince other members of the junta that Ioannides' proposal was irrational. As a result, not only did Greece not attack Turkey, but the Greek junta and its extension in Cyprus, the Sampson Government, disintegrated.

Kissinger also tried to arrange a cease-fire in Cyprus through telephone conversations with Ecevit and the mediation of Joseph Sisco in Athens. During the first day of the intervention, Ecevit told Kissinger that Turkey would accept a cease-fire as soon as it captured a viable bridgehead in northern Cyprus, but it needed some time to accomplish this. For the same reason, Foreign Minister Gunes refused Sisco's cease-fire offer on 21 July 1974.[145] During the night of 21 July 1974, the chief of the general staff told Ecevit that by the evening of 22 July, Turkey would be in a position to accept a cease-fire.[146] The same night, Ecevit accepted Kissinger's offer of a cease-fire effective the next day.

Kissinger later argued that "[d]uring the night of July 21-22 we forced a cease-fire by threatening Turkey that we would move nuclear weapons [in Turkey] from forward positions—especially where they might be involved in a war with Greece."[147] We don't know how much this "threat" affected Ecevit's decision to accept the cease-fire, but the fact that the cease-fire went into effect only after Turkey secured a bridgehead in Cyprus indicates that Kissinger's "threat" did not play a decisive role in the adoption of a cease-fire. During his phone conversations with Ecevit, Kissinger did not use the threat of a cut-off of American assistance as leverage to bring about a cease-fire. Throughout the following weeks, while Turco-Greek negotiations continued in Geneva, Kissinger carefully avoided mentioning the threat of sanctions as a means to induce peaceful behavior on the part of Turkey.[148] In practice, however, the U.S. slowed the delivery of arms and spare parts to Turkey.[149] The State Department also avoided signing any new arms contracts with Turkey for several months after the Turkish intervention.[150] Kissinger's use of the sanctions was thus a more subtle way of employing threats as a means of foreign policy. Turkish policymakers were aware of the *de facto* arms embargo, but they did not indicate publicly that they opposed it. There is also no indication that their behavior became more accommodative toward U.S. goals because of the *de facto* embargo.

The First Geneva Conference

On 22 July 1974 both Turkey and Greece announced that they would abide by the U.N. Security Council Resolution 353 (20 July 1974) calling for a cease-fire in Cyprus. The U.S. Administration facilitated the Turco-Greek agreement to adopt a cease-fire by providing a face-saving formula ensuring that both parties would announce their adoption of a truce at the same time (1400 GMT). The U.S. proposal that peace talks should begin as soon as possible played a significant role in convincing Greece and Turkey to come to an agreement to end the hostilities.[151]

Meanwhile, on 23 July 1974, the Greek junta stepped down and turned the political power over to a civilian cabinet to be formed under the leadership of Constantine Karamanlis. In Cyprus the Sampson junta also fell on 23 July 1974. Glafkos Klerides, the president of the Greek Cypriot House of Representatives was sworn in the same day as President of the Republic of Cyprus.[152]

The first Geneva Conference opened on 25 July 1974, only two days after the return of democratic rule to Greece. Turkey, Greece and Britain were represented by their Foreign Ministers, Turan Gunes, George Mavros, and James Callaghan. The U.S. had sent an observer, Assistant Secretary of State William Buffum, to the conference. Greece's first priority at the conference was to stop Turkey's expansion on Cyprus which continued on a low scale after the 22 July cease-fire.[153] Greek forces, on the other hand, went on occupying additional Turkish enclaves on other parts of the island. By the end of July, the "National Guard" occupied 198 Turkish villages containing 35,882 Turkish Cypriots and surrounded an additional 21,157 in 60 villages.[154] Turkish sectors in larger towns were also raided and thousands of Turkish males taken hostage.[155]

Mavros announced on 26 July 1974 that unless Turkey agreed to withdraw its forces to the 22 July cease-fire boundaries, Greece would abandon the conference. Turkish Foreign Minister Gunes responded by indicating that the Greek forces, too, had extended their occupation area and added that "unless the cease-fire is accepted by everybody in all parts of the island . . . I can assume no [responsibility] on behalf of the Turkish [forces] on Cyprus."[156]

On 27 July 1974 the negotiations reached an impasse over the issue of the violations of the 22 July cease-fire. At this stage Secretary of State Kissinger intervened, talking with Ecevit and Karamanlis by telephone. Within one day Kissinger succeeded in persuading both parties to adopt a new cease-fire line which acknowledged the respective expansions of both Greek and Turkish forces.[157] Kissinger also mediated between Turkish Premier Ecevit and Foreign Minister Gunes after Ecevit refused to approve Gunes's recognition of U.N. Security Council Resolution 353. Kissinger persuaded Ecevit that recognition of Resolution 353 did not mean that Turkey should immediately withdraw its forces from Cyprus.[158]

Except for its recognition of Resolution 353, Turkey made no compromises in Geneva. The same was not true for Greece. Greek Foreign Minister Mavros opposed some of the Turkish demands but eventually accepted most of them. The Geneva Declaration signed on 30 July 1974 by the Foreign Ministers of Greece, Turkey and Britain linked Turkey's withdrawal of its forces from Cyprus to the achievement of "a just and lasting solution acceptable to all parties concerned."[159] Britain and Greece thus lent their recognition to the military presence of Turkey on Cyprus. They also acknowledged that Turkey had a legitimate right to occupy part of the island until such time as a new constitutional order was established.

The Geneva Declaration also bestowed credence on Turkey's argument that the 1960 constitution no longer suited the peaceful coexistence of the two communities by calling for a "just and lasting solution acceptable to all parties concerned." The Declaration did not refer to the "Cypriot State" as much, but to the "representatives of the Greek Cypriot and Turkish Cypriot Communities." It also conferred legitimacy on the Turkish Cypriot Administration which had existed on the island since 1964 by noting "the existence in practice in the Republic of Cyprus of two autonomous administrations—that of the Greek Cypriot community and that of the Turkish Cypriot community."[160]

The Second Geneva Conference

After the first Geneva Conference, Turkey continued to reinforce its troops on the 7 percent of Cyprus it controlled. The Greek Cypriot National Guard still occupied Turkish enclaves on other parts of the island despite the fact that the Geneva Declaration required their immediate evacuation.[161] The National Guard, still dominated by the mainland Greek officers, believed that its control of Turkish enclaves was the only factor holding back the Turkish army from continuing its expansion.

Within a week after the Geneva Declaration, Prime Minister Ecevit began officially suggesting that he desired a territorial federation in Cyprus.[162] Ecevit's coalition partner, Necmettin Erbakan, the leader of the religionist NSP favored, however, the partition of the island and could be convinced only with difficulty by Ecevit that the preservation of Cyprus' independence was a more favorable solution for Turkey.[163] The opposition Justice Party (JP) and Democratic Party (DP), however, insisted that Turkey should partition the island. Suleyman Demirel, leader of the JP maintained that "federation is not and cannot be a solution to the security of the Turkish community. . . . The solution must in no way leave the safeguarding of the Turkish community and of its economic self-sufficiency to others."[164] Despite its disapproval of the federation thesis, the opposition quietly acquiesced in the Ecevit Government's position at the second Geneva Conference.

The Greek Cypriots were aware that Ecevit favored territorial federation at least one week before the start of the second Geneva Conference. Glafcos Klerides, the new "President of Cyprus," who replaced Sampson after the latter's resignation on 23 July 1974, stated that he did not believe that "the idea [of federation] is feasible, on the basis, in any case, of geographically homogenous territories, because this would imply the transfer of tens of thousands of people . . ." Instead, Klerides argued that a unitary state which granted "local autonomy" to Turkish Cypriots should be established.[165] As we shall see, the reluctance of Greek Cypriots to consider a settlement based on territorial federation led to Turkey's second operation.

One factor which contributed to the Greek Cypriots' intransigence was Makarios' opposition to negotiations with Turkey. Before the start of the second Geneva Conference, Makarios, who was in exile in London, maintained that since Greece was "incapable of imposing her will" the Greeks should not attend the conference. Makarios also suggested that "certain great powers" were trying to manipulate the conference to eliminate the independence of Cyprus.[166] Makarios' opposition to the conference restricted the maneuver room of Klerides who did not have a political following in Cyprus comparable to that of Makarios. Greek Foreign Minister Mavros, who had good relations with Makarios, also became uncompromising, largely due to Makarios' opposition to any concessions to Turkey.

Meanwhile the Ecevit Government had concluded that at the second Geneva Conference Turkey should insist on the negotiation of a new Cyprus settlement, preferably a bizonal federation. The Government also decided that if the Greeks refused to accept the principle of a federative solution and tried to procrastinate, the Turkish delegation should withdraw from the conference and Turkey should achieve its goal by resuming its offensive in Cyprus.[167]

The chances for a peaceful settlement looked very dim on 9 August 1974 when the Geneva Conference opened. Upon his arrival Turkish Foreign Minister Turan Gunes maintained that despite the clear stipulation of the Geneva Declaration, the Greek forces had not yet evacuated the Turkish enclaves. Greek Foreign Minister George Mavros replied that Turkey, too, violated the Geneva Declaration by extending its zone of occupation by thirty square kilometers.[168]

Perhaps more important than the alleged violations of the Geneva Declaration was Mavros' confrontational attitude at the second conference. Whereas the Turkish representatives at the first Geneva Conference perceived him as "reserved and undecided," at the second conference they saw him as "uncompromising."[169] There is no reason to doubt the correctness of this observation. Only one day after the first conference, Mavros stated that during the upcoming conference in Geneva, Greece and Turkey would "seek a solution to the Cyprus issue acceptable to both communities."[170] On 11 August he reversed himself and argued that "the guarantor powers do not have the right to impose a [new] constitution . . . on Cyprus."[171] Mavros added that revisions in the 1960 constitution could only be negotiated between the two Cypriot communities.

The petrification of the negotiating positions of the Turkish and Greek delegations was once more underlined on the second day of the conference when Klerides offered the position of vice-president to Denktash and a return to the 1960 constitution. Denktash replied, saying that

> for eleven years, the Greeks have tried, and did all they could, to destroy the 1960 constitution . . . [Now w]e are invited to

> go back to the 1960 constitution. This is impossible; that constitution did not save the Turks, did not save Cyprus, has given no protection.[172]

On 10 August 1974, the second day of the conference, Rauf Denktash submitted the Turkish-Turkish Cypriot settlement proposal to British Foreign Secretary Callaghan who transmitted it privately to the Greek and Greek Cypriot delegations.[173] The Turkish proposal offered the establishment of a bizonal federal state that would provide a great deal of autonomy to the Turkish Cypriots. The Greek delegations almost immediately rejected the proposal. Both the proposal and its rejection were informal and took place not in plenary sessions but in private meeting rooms.[174]

At this stage Kissinger intervened once more by calling Ecevit and suggesting to him that even though he understood that Turkish Cypriots needed more territory and more autonomy, he believed that these goals should be accomplished through negotiations. During the telephone conversation which took place on 12 August 1974, Kissinger maintained that he felt that Klerides would be more willing to accept a cantonal rather than a federal settlement on Cyprus.[175]

That same day, Ecevit discussed Kissinger's proposal at the National Security Council (NSC) meeting. The NSC decided to comply with Kissinger's suggestion and offer a cantonal solution to the Greeks. By evening, the Turks had delivered the new cantonal plan to the British and Greek delegations. The cantonal plan was not popular with Turkish Cypriots and Turkish Foreign Minister Gunes who believed that the six Turkish cantons around six major Cypriot towns would still leave Turkish Cypriots vulnerable to Greek attacks.[176]

Meanwhile, Callaghan told Klerides that he was in constant touch with Kissinger and that Kissinger had told him that he would not exert any further pressure on Turkey in order to prevent a second operation. Callaghan added that Britain was ready to use its forces in Cyprus to prevent Turkey's expansion, provided the U.S. and the U.N. favored such an action. Callaghan felt that since Kissinger would not approve a British intervention, Klerides would have no alternative but to accept Turkey's federation thesis. He concluded that if Klerides did so, then Kissinger and he could put pressure on Turkey to limit the Turkish Cypriot zone to 20 to 22 percent of Cyprus. Klerides adamantly refused a federative settlement.[177]

On 13 August the Turkish delegation decided that it was time to publicly propose its two different plans to Greece. At the plenary session on 13 August 1974 Turkish Foreign Minister Gunes repeated Turkey's proposals and urged Mavros and Klerides to give a final answer. Klerides replied that he could give a definite answer only if he had an additional forty-eight hours to consider the proposals. Gunes, who believed that the Greeks had no intention of accepting a negotiated solution and were only trying to gain time, refused a forty-eight hour recess.[178]

As Polyvios Polyviou, a Greek Cypriot delegate, admitted, Klerides actually believed that time was on the Greeks' side and that if the negotiations lasted long enough, international pressure on Turkey would make it increasingly difficult for Turkey to pursue a policy of "blackmail." Thus, Klerides hoped that even a forty-eight hour prolongation of the negotiations would help.[179] Polyviou said that Greek Cypriots had three objectives:

> first, to gain time, since the more time that elapsed the more difficult it would be for Turkey to attack again; secondly, to mobilize international opinion and try to sway Anglo-American policy towards firm acceptance of the view that since constitutional legitimacy had been restored hostilities had to end and meaningful

> negotiations be resumed; and thirdly, to try (if at all possible) to conduct any negotiations not on the basis of geographical separation but on the lines of integral and bicommunal state. [sic][180]

Another reason for Klerides' intransigence was his lack of a political base in Cyprus. He knew that if he accepted the federation proposal, neither the Sampson nor the Makarios supporters would stand by him. He also would be unable to assure that other Greek Cypriots would respect his agreement with Turkey.[181] Hence, Klerides chose to procrastinate on the negotiations with the belief that losing territory in a second Turkish operation would have fewer disadvantages than abandoning the same territory through an agreement. The resumption of Turkey's offensive, he expected, would isolate Turkey internationally and contribute to the Greek cause.

Greek Foreign Minister Mavros' closeness to Makarios was an additional element favoring an uncompromising Greek-Greek Cypriot attitude. Mavros communicated daily with Makarios and was thus open to his influence. Klerides realized quickly that it was not Mavros in Geneva or Karamanlis in Athens, but Makarios in London who was setting the tone of the Greek negotiating position.[182] Prime Minister Karamanlis, who always disliked Makarios, was usually less informed about the developments in Geneva. Karamanlis, for instance, learned about Turkey's cantonal plan only after the second Turkish offensive started on 14 August 1974.[183] Had there been better communication between Karamanlis and his foreign minister Mavros, the second phase of the Cyprus war could have been prevented.

By the end of 13 August 1974 the Turks became convinced that the continuation of the negotiations would bring no favorable results and that the second operation, which from the beginning had been considered an integral part of the Turkish strategy, would be rendered less probable. The Turks knew that international public opinion was slowly turning against them and that if they were going to do something, they must do it quickly. The Ecevit Government also feared that the Soviet and American stances might change in the long run and Turkish Cypriots could be forced to content themselves with the seven percent of the island that Turkey controlled.[184]

Before ordering the start of the second operation, Ecevit succumbed to Kissinger's last minute pressures and offered Greek Prime Minister Karamanlis another way out of the deadlock. According to this "last alternative," Ecevit wanted the Greeks to demilitarize the area around the Turkish forces who occupied seven percent of Cyprus' territory. After this evacuation Turkey would extend its control toward Famagusta on the eastern shore, thus seizing 17-18 percent of the island's territory.[185] The enlargement of the Turkish zone would free 10,000 Turkish Cypriots encircled by Greek troops in Serdarli (near Nicosia) and another 10,000 in the besieged Turkish quarter of Famagusta.[186] Ecevit told Kissinger that if the Greeks accepted this "interim" solution he would postpone the negotiations not only for forty-eight hours but for several weeks. Kissinger failed however, to persuade the Greeks and Greek Cypriots to accept this suggestion.[187]

By the end of 13 August 1974 Ecevit became convinced that Turkey would not be able to achieve a favorable settlement unless it once again acted "assertively." Ecevit suggested that

> once their prestige had been restored [after the fall of the junta], the Greeks thought that they could take advantage of the hopes concerning the new regime by mobilizing Western opinion against Turkey and establishing closer relations with the socialist countries in order to exert pressure on Turkey.

> The second Geneva Conference took place under very unfortunate circumstances. The Greeks felt so sure of support on the part of international opinion that they adopted an inflexible attitude. Unfortunately, the British encouraged them in this. We put our proposals on the table, including a solution of a multicantonal kind which was against our own interests and was not very logical because it would have led to friction on the island.[188]

Ecevit was also encouraged to act assertively by Kissinger's reluctance to use threats to prevent Turkey's resumption of its offensive. Unlike President Johnson who tried to intimidate Turkey with a number of undesirable eventualities, Kissinger only reasoned with Ecevit to discourage him. Even when it became clear that the Geneva Conference was doomed to failure, Kissinger chose not to bully Turkey. On 13 August Callaghan called Kissinger and told him that the Conference was about to break down. Kissinger replied: "Let's wait and see."[189]

Kissinger later defended his unwillingness to employ threats, and especially the threat of an arms embargo to restrain the Turks by suggesting that

> [t]he United States did not threaten the cutoff of military aid to Turkey, for these reasons: First, it was considered that such an action would be ineffective and would not prevent the threatening eventuality; secondly, as was pointed out in this statement, we are giving economic and military aid as a reflection of our common interest in the defense of the Eastern Mediterranean. Once such a decision is taken, it will have the most drastic consequences and not just over a period of time covering a few days but over an extended period of time . . . Short of this

> [embargo threat], however, we made the most repeated and urgent representations to Turkey in order to prevent the military action that happened. We have criticized the action, and we believe also that the inflexibility of all of the parties in Geneva contributed to it.[190]

Kissinger had realized that he was dealing with a Turkish Government that, unlike its predecessors, considered assertiveness a virtue in itself. Any threat, he thought, would be counterproductive and would probably accelerate Turkey's second operation. Kissinger knew that after having made the crucial decision to land forces on Cyprus, Ecevit was not likely to cut his losses and accept a return to the 1960 constitution as suggested by Greek Cypriots who had shelved the same constitution eleven years ago. The best way to prevent Turkey's expansion, Kissinger believed, was to continuously assure the Turks that the U.S. considered their demands legitimate and that negotiations would sooner or later bring favorable results. On 13 August 1974, one day before the second offensive, State Department Spokesman Robert Anderson explained Kissinger's policy, stating:

> We recognize the position of the Turkish community on Cyprus requires considerable improvement and protection. We have supported a greater degree of autonomy for them.
>
> The parties [in Geneva] are negotiating on one or more Turkish autonomous areas. The avenues of diplomacy have not been exhausted. And therefore the United States would consider a resort to military action unjustified.[191]

Another factor which led Ecevit to conclude that the second offensive would also be a low-risk operation was the continued Soviet silence concerning

Turkish demands. Ecevit was encouraged by the fact that despite several Greek Cypriot appeals for military assistance, the Soviets had refused to even give a response. The last Greek Cypriot appeal came on 9 August 1974 when Klerides told the Soviet observer at the Geneva Conference, Victor Menin, that the Greek Cypriots would welcome Soviet military assistance if Turkey resumed its offensive. Menin promised to inform his superiors in Moscow, but the Soviets once again failed to respond.[192]

On 14 August 1974 the second phase of Turkey's Cyprus operation started. Unlike the first offensive, Turkey had enough troops and tanks to successfully complete the intervention. By 16 August the Turkish forces had captured the northern 36 percent of the island. As a result of the three-day fighting, thousands of Cypriots had to abandon their homes and emigrate to the respective Turkish and Greek controlled parts of Cyprus. It should be stressed that the Greek losses far exceeded the Turkish ones. Yet most of the Greek casualties were military personnel, whereas Turkish casualties included hundreds of civilians who were massacred by the Greek forces.[193]

Turkish Prime Minister Ecevit's statements after the second offensive suggest that he believed that Greeks and Greek Cypriots would soon return to the negotiating table at Geneva, and that Turkey would exploit its improved position in Cyprus to achieve a favorable settlement.[194] The Greeks refused, however, to return to Geneva, and the probability of a negotiated settlement diminished rapidly. Ecevit later admitted that the intra-coalition rivalry between the RPP and Erbakan's NSP prevented the Government from offering concessions to Greece which could have facilitated the renewal of Turco-Greek dialogue.[195] Ecevit was ready to make several concessions to Greek Cypriots, but Erbakan's last minute refusal to approve them led to the petrification of the Turkish decision-making process and eventually to Ecevit's resignation on 7 November 1974.[196] Because of Ecevit's resignation Kissinger had to abandon his planned trip to the eastern Mediterranean, and an early resolution of the conflict became the victim of first, Turkish domestic political squabbles, and later, of the arms embargo imposed by the U.S. Congress on Turkey.[197]

The Arms Embargo

After Ecevit's resignation, the country was ruled by a caretaker government which did not have a parliamentary majority to support its policies. Sadi Irmak, an independent senator, presided over the "above-parties" government which failed even to receive a vote of confidence from the parliament. Nevertheless, Irmak remained in power until Demirel formed a right-wing coalition government on 31 March 1975.[198]

The Irmak era coincided with the congressional activity to impose an arms embargo on Turkey. Throughout this period the Irmak Government did not take the steps necessary to calm the U.S. Congress. It made no offers such as territorial concessions to Greek Cypriots. Congress was convinced that Kissinger's easygoing approach toward Turkey had caused the Turkish expansionism and that Congress had to take control of the U.S. policy towards Turkey. The congressional activity resulted in the imposition of an arms embargo on Turkey on 5 February 1975 while Turkey was still in the midst of a governmental crisis.[199]

The imposition of the arms embargo was partly a result of the Watergate crisis and the Nixon administration's loss of credibility. Aside from the effects of Watergate, the administration's authority was diminished by Kissinger's and Nixon's mishandling of U.S. foreign policy. When the Cyprus crisis broke out, Congress was already showing signs of disappointment with the administration's policies towards Vietnam, Cambodia, Chile, the U.S.S.R. and Pakistan. As a presidential observer wrote:

> The theory, so dominant and so persuasive in the years after the Second World War, that a foreign policy must be trusted to the executive, went down in flames in Vietnam. Who could say, for example, that the National Security Council had been all that much wiser in this melancholy period than the Senate Foreign Relations Committee? One after another the traditional arguments in favor of presidential supremacy-unity, secrecy, superior expertise, superior sources of information, decision, dispatch-turned out to be immensely overrated. Vietnam discredited executive control of foreign relations as profoundly as Versailles and mandatory neutrality had discredited congressional control.[200]

Congress' new assertiveness also resulted from the structural reforms of the early 1970s which were intended to decentralize and democratize Congress. These reforms led to the "explosion of personnel and information sources available to individual members."[201] Committee chairmen, the majority leader, the speaker and their aides lost most of their power.[202] Prior to the adoption of reforms, "the practice was for committee recommendations to be accepted almost automatically by the full membership."[203] After the reforms, however, especially in foreign affairs and defense policy areas, the Senate and House committees began to share their responsibilities with other committees and the full membership of the Congress. For instance, the annual foreign military and economic assistance bills could easily be amended by individual members on the floors of both houses.[204] Senators Rosenthal and DuPont, who headed the embargo effort in the Senate, often made use of this procedure to circumvent the more lengthy process of going through the appropriate committees. Another reason for the effectiveness of the pro-embargo effort was the fact that the party system had lost its former power. Interest groups—in this case the Greek Lobby—now gained easy access to individual Congressmen.[205]

The activity of the Greek Lobby in the U.S. also strengthened the hands of those who were promoting the embargo and convinced some other Congressmen to join the embargo bandwagon. The Greek Orthodox Church played a significant role in activating a Greek American population of three million. On 30 July 1974, a combined meeting of the Archdiocesan Council of the Greek Orthodox Archdiocese of North and South America and presidents of Greek associations was convened by Archbishop Iakovos. During the meeting it was decided that a "Public Relations Office" be established to ask Congress to cut all military and economic aid to Turkey.[206]

Throughout the congressional deliberations on the Turkish arms embargo, "Greek Orthodox priests read from the pulpit the names of the damned-congressmen who voted with the Administration against the 'Turkish ban,'" and urged Greek Americans to pressure their representatives to change their votes.[207] During church services petitions urging Congressmen to support the embargo were circulated among the congregation.[208] The Orthodox Church also organized "letter-writing and telegram/telephone campaigns" by using its front organization, the United Hellenic American Congress (UHAC).[209]

Another important lobbying group was the American Hellenic Educational Progressive Association (AHEPA) which had offices in every state and claimed 125,000 active members. AHEPA urged Greek Americans to write personal letters to those Congressmen and Senators who seemed to be "wavering" on the embargo issue.[210] Both AHEPA and the American Hellenic Institute (AHI), another lobbying organization, maintained voting records on individual Congressmen and Senators. Before congressional votes, AHEPA and AHI mounted massive telephone campaigns across the U.S. to apply additional pressure on those who were still undecided.[211]

Greek Americans also staged daily demonstrations in Washington and New York. Some of the rallies attracted up to 70,000 people. Thousands of Armenians and blacks who opposed Turkey's opium-poppy cultivation joined the Greeks.[212] Senator Eagleton, one of the major proponents of the embargo, described the role played by Greek Americans, saying:

> . . . Credit for our victory in the Senate must be given to many people who worked long and hard for the [embargo] amendment. Probably the greatest contribution, however, came from . . . the Hellenic Americans across the country.
>
> During the last few weeks the United States Senate and other branches of the Federal Government have become aware of a new political force in this country. Many of my colleagues in the Senate told me that they were surprised to find out how many Greek Americans lived in their state.[213]

Eagleton's argument is justified when one analyzes the voting patterns in some congressional districts in New York, Massachusetts, Indiana and Illinois where Greek Americans and other ethnic minorities constitute a body of electoral significance. The examination established that there were 16 districts in the above mentioned states where the existence of a linkage between congressional votes and the influence of ethnic voters could be discussed. Not surprisingly, none of the 16 Congressmen voted against the arms embargo in any of the five votes in the House.[214]

Other studies have also suggested that the pressure from Greek Americans affected the votes of many Congressmen. There is an especially significant correlation "between the size of the Greek American constituency and the way in which the Republican House member[s] voted."[215] Since, however, the Democrats usually tended to vote against the Administration, a comparison between districts with a significant ethnic vote and districts where the Greek vote is negligible was not conclusive. Yet anti-embargo votes of both Republicans and Democrats usually came from southern states with little or no Greek electorate.[216]

The Senate voting patterns also showed a correlation between "the number of Greek Americans in the individual states and the way in which Republican Senators from these states voted."[217] The Democratic Senate votes were again less indicative of any relationship because of the tendency of Democrats to vote against the Administration. It should be added that the Black caucus in Congress supported the embargo because of its opposition to Turkey's poppy cultivation.[218]

It would be wrong, however, to attribute to adoption of the Turkish arms embargo solely to the pressures of the Greek Lobby. Several rallying points were effectively used by the embargo proponents. The major argument was that the Administration had ignored the rule of law by continuing its assistance to Turkey which had used American arms outside of the borders of Turkey. The relevant laws, the Foreign Assistance Act of 1961 and the Foreign Military Sales Act of 1968, were often invoked to prove that Turkey should be ineligible for further assistance because it did not use U.S. arms for "internal security and . . . legitimate self-defense . . ."[219]

The embargo proponents also suggested that the embargo would force Turkey to make concessions to Greece and accelerate the peace process. Representative Benjamin Rosenthal (D-New York) argued:

> If we pass this resolution today, it is a twofold signal: It is a signal to the American people that we are going to obey

> the law, and that we are a responsible, law-abiding Congress and Government. It is [also] a signal to the Government of Turkey that they cannot have military equipment to continue and maintain this kind of aggressive action. It is, indeed, a signal to the Greek Government, which says, 'why don't you come on along in the negotiations because we are going to use all the effort and muscle we can vis-a-vis the Turkish Government.'[220]

The embargo advocates also intimidated their colleagues by emphasizing that Greece might adopt a hostile attitude toward the U.S. if the latter did not pressure Turkey to make concessions. Rosenthal argued:

> i[t] is, in my view, indispensable that Greece be able to enter negotiations on an improved basis. Otherwise, the risk is very great that the provisional Karamanlis Government will succumb to pressures from the right or the left. This, in turn, would make a Cyprus compromise extremely unlikely and the Greek drift away from the United States more acute.[221]

Several other arguments were also used to convince Congress that any association with Turkey was undesirable. The opium issue was a favorite theme of Turkey's critics. Representative Glenn Anderson (D-California) maintained that it was "self-defeating to provide assistance to any country which openly advocates the cultivation of opium poppies that wind up as deadly drugs inflicting our youth."[222] There were also those, like Cronin (R-Massachusetts), who argued that Turkey was no longer important to the geopolitical interests of the U.S. and thus did not deserve assistance. Cronin maintained that "[t]oday our new radars supercede anything that is in Turkey and give us improved capabilities."[223] Cronin even implied that Turkey was about to join the Warsaw Pact: "Russian ships currently sit in Turkish ports. There is no additional threat involved today; it is already a reality."[224]

Nevertheless, it was the emphasis placed upon the Administration's alleged violation of the law and the unceasing pressures of the Greek Lobby that were mainly responsible for the arms ban. Representative John Brademas (D-Indiana) stressed the combination of these two factors when he said:

> If we members [of Congress] had not been able to put together a compelling case, in terms of law, policy and morality, we would not have been effective. But on the other hand, without the kind of support we got from the Greek community, our case might not have been sufficient to win the day.[225]

Before ending the discussion on the arms embargo, the legality of it should be addressed. As a Library of Congress study revealed, the

> [u]se of articles and services for other than defensive purposes, i.e., for aggressive purposes, is barred by law. However, neither the Act [Foreign Assistance Act of 1961] nor its legislative history make clear what kinds of activities separate defensive from aggressive purposes.[226]

Thus, it could be argued that the best defense is offense or a preemptive strike, and Turkey's Cyprus intervention could be classified as a defensive operation. Moreover, Section 502 of the Foreign Assistance Act of 1961 allows recipient states "to participate in regional or collective arrangements or measures consistent with the charter of the United Nations."[227] Hence, Turkey's action could be regarded as a collective security operation aimed at preserving the independence of Cyprus, and therefore not in violation of U.S. laws. Representative Stephen Solarz (D-New York) drove home this point when he suggested that in many international conflicts, such as the India-Pakistan war in September 1965, or the six-day war in the Middle East in June 1967, American weapons were used "in a highly dubious fashion."[228] It is also a fact that the mainland Greek forces had used American arms when they overthrew Makarios.

The U.S. failure to universally apply its laws and impose arms embargoes on those states who used U.S. arms for apparently aggressive purposes proves that the Turkish arms embargo was not the result of a simple compliance with the law, but rather an exercise of a substantial normative judgment on the part of Congress.[229] It is interesting that when asked why the law did not apply to Israeli actions, an embargo proponent, Senator Eagleton (D-Missouri) replied:

> Israel should not be subject to an aid cutoff as a result of enactment of this legislation . . . I think that it should be made clear that in acting in its defense, and fighting for its survival, Israel was not the aggressor and would not be subject to a denial of U.S. aid.[230]

Conclusion

The outcome of the 1974 Cyprus crisis was determined by a combination of geopolitical, domestic, and functional factors. The geopolitical factor, or Turkey's sense of security *vis-a-vis* the Soviet Union and other regional states, enabled the Ecevit Government to ignore the usual American intimidations that a Turkish intervention in Cyprus would provoke a hostile Soviet reaction. As Ecevit expected, the Soviet Union did not oppose Turkey's Cyprus landing, and even continued its silence after the first offensive, thus fostering Ecevit's conviction that a second offensive would also be a low-risk venture.

Turkey's Cyprus intervention likewise did not arouse an antagonistic response on the part of the Third World states and regional countries. There were no hasty condemnations of Turkey either in the U.N. or in other international organizations. Moreover, some regional countries including Libya, Pakistan, Iran, and Iraq openly supported Turkey's action.[231] The fact that world public opinion clearly identified the Greek junta as the culprit in the Sampson coup further enabled Turkey, at least initially, to be seen as the savior of both Turkish and Greek Cypriots.

As discussed earlier, both during the 1964 and 1967 crises Turkey lacked the necessary military equipment to conduct a rapid aerial and naval landing on Cyprus. In 1974, however, Turkey possessed enough landing craft and helicopters to land forces not only on Cyprus, but also on the Aegean Islands if a war broke out between Turkey and Greece.

The 1974 crisis came one decade after the first Cyprus crisis. During this period, the Turkish public and the political parties repeatedly examined the factors which led to perceived Turkish failures in Cyprus. Ecevit, who determined Turkey's response to the 1974 crisis, had also drawn his conclusions. In 1974, Ecevit believed not only that Turkey had to act assertively, but that it could afford to act assertively. Ecevit was convinced that in the detente era the U.S. was in no position to interfere in the affairs of its smaller allies. Hence, he disregarded the possibility of a U.S. ultimatum demanding Turkey's withdrawal from Cyprus after a landing took place. As discussed earlier, this contingency was an important deterrent for Inonu in 1964.

Secretary of State Kissinger's failure to prevent and later to condemn the Sampson coup also played an important role in convincing the Turkish Government that the U.S. either did not care about Turkey's interests or that it was collaborating with the Greek junta. Kissinger's inability or unwillingness to restore Makarios to power served as additional testimony that the U.S. was no longer interested in its traditional role of mediation between Turkey and Greece. It should be added, however, that the uncompromising behavior of both the Greek junta and the Karamanlis Government rendered Kissinger's efforts ineffective. This was the case especially during the second Geneva Conference where the Greek delegation adamantly refused to consider a new Cyprus settlement.

The Watergate affair also contributed to the U.S. failure to solve the crisis peacefully. In the last three weeks of Nixon's presidency, the U.S. was not in a position to make credible threats or credible promises to either Turkey or Greece. Secretary of State Kissinger blamed the constitutional crisis for the Cyprus debacle:

> It was impossible to keep going through crises with the procedures we were . . . following; sooner or later something would get out of hand. The unspoken corollary was that our own constitutional crisis had to be brought to an end if the nation was to avoid catastrophe.[232]

Two other developments further rendered the Cyprus crisis insolvable. The first was the Turkish governmental crisis. The disagreement between Ecevit and his coalition partner Erbakan on how to settle the dispute prevented Turkey from offering concessions to Greek Cypriots and caused the break-up of the RPP-NSP coalition government. The Sadi Irmak caretaker government that followed did not have the power and authority to conduct negotiations with the U.S. or Greece. Thus, after Ecevit's resignation in November 1974, Turkey's negotiating position hardened.

The congressional interference in the Administration's handling of the crisis and the imposition of an arms embargo on Turkey further reduced the chances of an early settlement of the dispute. By linking the lifting of the embargo to the peaceful resolution of the Cyprus crisis, the U.S. Congress gave Greece leverage over U.S. policy. The Greeks were able to assure the continuation of the embargo by simply ignoring Turkey's proposals which started in the latter part of 1975.[233]

The arms embargo proved to be a failure and Congress lifted it in 1978. Congress had tried to influence Turkey by setting deadlines and formulating acceptable bargaining positions. Whereas in domestic politics these types of parliamentary maneuverings might work, in foreign policy they are not applicable because they curtail the flexibility of negotiators. As a political scientist observed, "[t]he skills of negotiation, the recognition of nuances, of the importance of timing and of symbolic considerations are not part of the congressional repertoire, at least in the realm of foreign affairs."[234]

Some of the influence variables discussed earlier were relevant to the 1974 crisis. The propositions that not all power is usable or convertible to influence and that "the amount of influence a state wields over others can be related to the capabilities *mobilized* in support of *specific* foreign policy objectives" were supported by the facts of our case.[235] The power of the U.S. proved to be unusable during the crisis because several factors prevented its successful application to the crisis. Let us discuss some of these factors.

Despite Kissinger's attempts the U.S. was unable to *mobilize* its capabilities in support of *specific* objectives. These objectives were, first, the prevention of the Sampson coup, and later, of the Turkish intervention. The U.S. failed in both of these goals because it did not effectively use its *resources*. Kissinger could not forestall the coup because Ambassador Tasca's warnings to the formal Greek Government officials who possessed no real power convinced the Greek junta that American protestations were insincere. The U.S. needed to strongly urge the head of the junta, Ioannides, that it would not tolerate a coup against Makarios and would do its best to reverse such a coup if it took place.

After the coup the U.S. had to mobilize its capabilities to mediate between Turkey and Greece and assure Turkey that its interests would not be harmed. Kissinger's decision not to confront Greece publicly implied that Washington accepted the Sampson regime. Ecevit's fears that the U.S. favored *enosis* seemed justified when U.S. envoy Sisco shuttled between Athens and Ankara as merely a message carrier instead of an initiator of action.

Kissinger's unsuccessful mediation also bears out Robert Dahl's proposition that there are variations in the skill or efficiency with which statesmen use resources. Second, as Dahl proposed, there are variations in the extent to which individuals stress influencing others.[236] Kissinger's conduct during the 1974 crisis seemed to justify the allegation that he intentionally chose to sit out the crisis, expecting that after Turkey's intervention he would be able to mediate more effectively. If this was the case, Congress preempted his intervention by imposing an arms embargo.

If Kissinger had in fact wanted to prevent Turkey's second or even first offensive, then his failure to do so rested partly on the fact that he proposed to Turkey few if any alternative ways to solve the crisis. Throughout the crisis, Kissinger was too accommodating toward the Greek junta and Turkey. A more effective mediator would have been tougher with the junta and would have offered Turkey a peaceful alternative that could prevent Greece's annexation of Cyprus.

Kissinger preferred not to publicly challenge the Greek junta's coup in Cyprus in part because he feared that Greece would see the U.S. "as the agent of its humiliation" and Turkey would consider a public protest as approval of its planned intervention.[237] Kissinger also believed that the U.S. "could not without cost resist a Turkish invasion because that would be considered as objectively supporting the Greek junta."[238] Kissinger thought that preventing Turkey's intervention or taking a public stand against Greece would alienate both of these countries. Kissinger's behavior suggests that he weighed the costs and benefits of challenging these two U.S. allies and chose not to do so because the costs would outweigh the benefits. This finding corroborates David Baldwin's argument that "A will continue to apply resources to influencing B only up to the point at which [its] estimated marginal return equals [its] estimated marginal cost."[239]

The proposition that influence is partly determined by the responsiveness of the influenced to the requests of the influencer is also relevant to the 1974 crisis. By 1974, not only the RPP, but most Turkish political parties had concluded that accepting a U.S.-mediated solution in Cyprus would eventually result in an unfavorable settlement for Turkey. Thus, Ecevit allowed Kissinger and U.S. envoy Joseph Sisco only forty-eight hours on 17 July 1974 to formulate an acceptable solution, and refused to extend this period. His actions show that Turkey no longer was responsive to U.S. demands concerning the Cyprus question, even though Turkey continued to be as responsive as before with regard to East-West issues, and other aspects of U.S.-Turkey relations.

Earlier, it was proposed that the influenced state B's expectation of the influencer A's potential reaction to B's compliance or non-compliance with A's wishes affects B's decisions. As David Singer maintained, A may succeed or fail depending on the importance of the issue for B and B's perception of the probability of A's carrying out the threatened punishment. If B estimates that A would very likely not punish B, then it would almost certainly act without considering A's desires. Even if B expects that A would actually carry out its threat, it may go ahead with its original plan if it attaches a high value to the outcome.[240]

Ecevit knew that the U.S. opposed a Turkish intervention, but he thought that the U.S. could not afford or would not be able to "punish" Turkey if he went ahead with the intervention plan. While Ecevit did not believe that the U.S. would acquiesce in a complete occupation of the island, he was convinced that a limited intervention would not provoke an angry American response. Ecevit also believed that unless Turkey intervened, Cyprus would be unified with Greece within a short time. He felt that landing forces on Cyprus was a necessary and low-risk operation.

Ecevit's decision can be more clearly understood by taking into account two additional dimensions: utility and probability. Decision-makers differ "in the degree to which they emphasize either the probability or the preference element in their appraisal of an outcome."[241] Moreover, policymakers tend to exaggerate the probability of an outcome if they value it highly. Ecevit's conviction that an intervention was necessary quite possibly led him to believe that Turkey's action would lead to nothing but a favorable outcome.

Turkey's Cyprus landing indicates Ecevit's assertiveness, but its' limited nature suggests that Ecevit operated within self-imposed limits. The first phase of the operation ended with Turkey controlling 7 percent of the island which it extended to 36 percent after its second offensive. Despite Deputy Premier Erbakan's insistence, the Government refused to occupy the entire island. Turkey's adoption of voluntary restrictions suggests that as an "influenced" state it was wary of the influencer's, the United States', reaction. Ecevit thought that the U.S. would be less likely to "punish" Turkey if the operation on Cyprus remained within reasonable bounds. Ecevit's behavior could be explained by Carl Friedrich's proposition of *anticipated reactions*. Friedrich maintained that even if A, the influencer, does not explicitly express its preference, B, the influenced state, might behave in a way which it believes is desired by A.[242]

Yet, as Friedrich suggested, sometimes the influenced states fail to anticipate the reactions of the influencers due to

> . . . possible errors in anticipation, . . . to oversight, lack of insight, and the like . . . It is possible to forget about the preference, though it be known; it is also quite possible that he who wishes to anticipate the reaction does not know what the preference of the influencer might be.[243]

As maintained above, Ecevit correctly anticipated the response of the U.S. Administration to Turkey's two-part intervention. He erred, however, in that he did not foresee the reaction of the U.S. Congress. Congress, motivated by a zeal to reinstitute the rule of law in the conduct of foreign policy, moved quickly to impose an arms embargo on Turkey, which was enthusiastically supported by the Greek Lobby.

Both the threat of the arms embargo and its actual imposition proved to be a failure. Sanctions usually fail because states refuse to respond to threats. Congress apparently failed to realize that even if it were highly dependent on A, B might still resist A's demands if it believed that they would harm its national interests. Even if the national interests were not involved, B "may be concerned that this compliance will set a precedent," and increase "A's propensity to believe in the efficacy of threat, and to utilize it again and again."[244] In Turkey's case, the Turkish Government chose to suffer the deprivations of the embargo rather than accept the humiliating conditions set by Congress which practically meant the adoption of Greek demands prior to negotiations.

NOTES

1. Zenon Stavrinides, *The Cyprus Conflict: National Identity and Statehood* (Wakefield: Stavrinides, 1976), pp. 71-72.

2. Nancy Crawshaw, *The Cyprus Revolt* (London: George Allen & Unwin, 1978), p. 383.

3. Stanley Karnow, "The Indispensible Man: An Interview with Makarios," *The New Republic*, 14 Sept. 1974.

4. Kyriacos C. Markides, *The Rise and Fall of the Cyprus Republic* (New Haven: Yale University Press, 1977), p. 67.

5. *Ibid*., p. 83.

6. *Disisleri Bakanligi Belleteni* ("The Bulletin of the Foreign Ministry"), No. 79 (Apr., 1971), p. 99.

7. Leslie Finer, "The Colonels' Bid for Cyprus," *New Statesman*, 10 March 1972.

8. *Der Spiegel*, Vol. XXIV, No. 12 (16 March 1970), p. 129, Laurence Stern, *The Wrong Horse: The Politics of Intervention and the Failure of American Diplomacy* (New York: Times Books, 1977), 0. 86.

9. Stern, *op. cit*., p. 88.

10. *Ibid*., pp. 89-90.

11. Markides, *op. cit*., p. 86; Crawshaw, *op. cit*., p. 386.

12. *The Washington Post*, 17 Nov. 1974, p. C3.

13. *The Times*, London, 6 March 1975.

14. Markides, *op. cit.*, pp. 174-175.

15. *The Sunday Times*, London, 21 July 1974, p. 15.

16. Stern, *op. cit.*, p. 107; Jesse Lewis, *The Strategic Balance in the Mediterranean* (Washington, D.C.: American Enterprise Institute, 1976), p. 32.

17. Stern, *op. cit.*, p. 86.

18. Cuneyt Arcayurek, *Cankaya'ya Giden Yol, 1971-1973* (Ankara: Bilgi, 1985); Roger Nye, "The Military in Turkish Politics: 1960-1973" (Ph.D. dissertation, Washington University, St. Louis, Missouri, 1974), pp. 153-165.

19. Arcayurek, *op. cit.*

20. *Disisleri Bakanligi Belleteni*, Nos. 60/61 (Sept.-Oct., 1969), pp. 47,48.

21. Omer Kurkcuoglu, "Turkiye'nin Orta Dogu Politikasindaki Son Gelismeler," *Dis Politika*, Vol. I, No. 2 (June 1971), pp. 26-27.

22. Van Coufoudakis, "American Foreign Policy and the Cyprus Problem, 1974-1978: The Theory of Continuity Revisited," Theodore Couloumbis, John Iatrides, eds., *Greek American Relations* (New York: Pella, 1980), p. 107.

23. Michael Turner, "The International Politics of Narcotics: Turkey and the United States" (Ph.D. dissertation, Ohio, Kent State University, 1975), p. 106.

24. James Spain, "The United States, Turkey and the Poppy," *The Middle East Journal*, Vol. XXIX, No. 3 (Summer 1975), p. 297.

25. *Disisleri Bakanligi Belleteni*, No. 89 (Feb., 1972), p. 109.

26. *Disisleri Bakanligi Belleteni*, No. 71 (Aug., 1970), p. 128.

27. U.S. Congress, House, Committee on Foreign Affairs, *Foreign Assistance Act of 1971*, 92nd Congress, 2nd Session, 27 Apr. 1971, in Turner, *op. cit.*, p. 225.

28. Turner, *op. cit.*, p. 129.

29. *Congressional Record*, 92nd Cong., 1st Sess., Vol. 117, pt. I, 1 Feb. 1971, p. 1214.

30. *Disisleri Bakanligi Belleteni*, No. 81 (June 1971), pp. 137-140.

31. Spain, *op. cit.*, p. 299.

32. *Ibid.*, p. 305.

33. Turner, *op. cit.*, p. 228.

34. Spain, *op. cit.*, p. 301.

35. Bulent Ecevit, *Dis Politika* (Ankara: Ajans Turk, 1976), p. 18.

36. *Ulus*, Ankara, 10 July 1968, p. 7.

37. *Ibid.*

38. Ecevit, *op. cit.*, p. 11.

39. *Foreign Broadcast Information Service* [Hereafter: *FBIS*], *Middle East*, 23 May 1974, p. Q4.

40. *Ibid.*

41. M. Ali Birand, *30 Sicak Gun* (Istanbul: Milliyet, 1975), p. 36.

42. *FBIS, Middle East*, 9 July 1974, p. Q3.

43. U.S. Congress, Senate, *Turkey's Problems and Prospects: Implications for U.S. Interests*, Report Prepared by the Congressional Research Service of the Library of Congress for the Subcommittee on Europe and the Middle East of the Committee on Foreign Affairs, 3 March 1980, p. 52.

44. *Ibid.*

45. *FBIS, Middle East*, 5 June 1974, p. Q1.

46. Sadun Tanju, *Tepedeki Dort Adam* (Istanbul: Gelisim, 1978), p. 172.

47. *FBIS, Middle East*, 21 June 1974, p. Q1; 28 June 1974, p. Q1; *Hurriyet*, Istanbul, 26 July 1975.

48. *Milliyet*, 2 Feb. 1974, p. 7.

49. *FBIS, Middle East*, 23 May 1974.

50. Haluk Ulman, "Neden ve Nasil Federatif Sistem," *Milliyet*, 22 April 1974.

51. Bulent Ecevit, "Kibris ve Amerika," *Milliyet*, 30 March 1965, p. 1.

52. *Hurriyet*, Istanbul, 25 July 1975.

53. *FBIS, Middle East*, 9 July 1974, p. Q1.

54. *FBIS, Middle East*, 8 July 1974, p. Q2.

55. Turner, *op. cit.*, p. 252.

56. *Department of State Bulletin*, Vol. LXXII, No. 1857 (27 Jan. 1975), pp. 110, 111; Spain, *op. cit.*, p. 308.

57. U.S. Congress, House, *Turkish Opium Ban Negotiations*, Hearing Before the Committee on Foreign Affairs, 93rd Cong., 2nd Sess., 16 July 1974, p. 1.

58. Turner, *op. cit.*, p. 261.

59. *Turkish Opium Ban Negotiations*, p. 6; Pete Hamill, "Act of War," *New York Post*, 8 July 1974.

60. Stern, *op. cit.*, p. 94.

61. U.S. Congress, House, *U.S. Intelligence Agencies and Activities*, Hearings before the Select Committee on Intelligence, 94th Cong., 1st Sess., Sept/Nov. 1975, p. 1293; see also Michael A. Attalides, *Cyprus: Nationalism and International Politics* (New York: St. Martin's Press, 1979), p. 167; Stern, *op. cit.*, p. 99.

62. *U.S. Intelligence Agencies and Activities*, p. 1536.

63. *Ibid*.

64. Stern, *op. cit.*, p. 100.

65. *U.S. Intelligence Agencies and Activities*, p. 1289.

66. *Ibid*., p. 1297.

67. *FBIS, Middle East*, 10 July 1974, p. 1.

68. *U.S. Intelligence Agencies and Activities*, p. 1540.

69. Christopher Hitchens, *Cyprus* (London and New York: Quartet Books, 1984), pp. 87-88.

70. *Time*, 28 Feb. 1977 in Stern, *op. cit.*, p. 105.

71. John G. Stoessinger, *Henry Kissinger: The Anguish of Power* (New York: W. W. Norton, 1974), p. 139.

72. Stern, *op. cit.*, p. 101.

73. *U.S. Intelligence Agencies and Activities*, pt. 2, p. 759.

74. Hasan Cem, *Kibris Antlasmalarinda Ecevit'in Savunmasi* (Istanbul: Aktuel Yayinlari, 1974), p. 94.

75. *The New York Times*, 2 August 1974; Taki Theodoracopulos, *The Greek Upheaval* (New Rochelle, N.Y.: Caratzas Brothers, 1978), p. 36.

76. Stern, *op. cit.*, pp. 101-102.

77. Attalides, *op. cit.*, p. 170.

78. *FBIS, Middle East*, 15 July 1974, p. 01.

79. *FBIS, Middle East*, 16 July 1974, p. 03.

80. Stern, *op. cit.*, p. 79.

81. See Halley, *op. cit.*, p. 19; Hitchens, *op. cit.*, pp. 93-94; Markides, *op. cit.*, p. 131.

82. *Cyprus Mail*, 17 July 1975, in Necati M. Ertegun, *The Cyprus Dispute*, (Oxford: The University Press, 1981), p. 35.

83. Makarios' speech before the U.N.: Security Council, *Official Records*, 1780th Meeting, 1974.

84. *Ibid.*

85. *FBIS, Middle East*, 19 July 1974, p. 07; Rauf R. Denktash, *The Cyprus Triangle* (London and Boston: Allen & Unwin, 1982), pp. 146-147.

86. U.S. Congress, House, *Cyprus, 1974*, Hearings before the Committee on Foreign Affairs and Its Subcommittee on Europe, 93rd Congress, 2nd Sess., August 1974, p. 53.

87. *Ibid.*, p. 74.

88. Stern, *op. cit.*, p. 111.

89. *Facts on File*, Vol. XXXIV, No. 1758 (20 July 1974), p. 571.

90. Tad Szulc, *The Illusion of Peace: Foreign Policy in the Nixon Years* (New York: Viking Press, 1978), p. 795.

91. Henry Kissinger, *Years of Upheaval* (Boston: Little Brown & Co., 1982), p. 1190.

92. *Ibid.*, p. 1191.

93. *Ibid.*, p. 1192.

94. Birand, *30 Sicak Gun*, p. 29.

95. *Ibid.*, p. 28; *Cumhuriyet*, 22 July 1975, p. 4.

96. *Cumhuriyet*, 15 July 1975, p. 4.

97. Birand, *op. cit.*, p. 30.

98. Birand, *op. cit.*, pp. 35-36.

99. *Ibid.*, p. 40.

100. *Ibid.*, p. 40.

101. Cuneyt Arcayurek, *Yeni Democrasi, Yeni Arayislar 1960-1965* (Ankara: Bilgi, 1984), p. 283.

102. Birand, *op. cit.*, p. 40.

103. *Ibid.*, pp. 31,53; *Hurriyet*, 20 July 1975; Necmettin Erbakan, *Milli Gorus* (Istanbul: Dergah Yayinlari, 1975), p. 362.

104. Birand, *op. cit.*, pp. 31,53; *Hurriyet*, 20 July 1975.

105. *Cumhuriyet*, 25 July 1975, p. 4; *FBIS, Middle East*, 15 July 1974, p. Q5; Birand, *op. cit.*, p. 83.

106. Birand, *op. cit.*, p. 54; Stern, *op. cit.*, p. 114.

107. Haluk Ulman, "Geneva Conferences," *Foreign Policy*, (Ankara), Vol. IV (1974), p. 50.

108. Ecevit, "Kibris ve Amerika," p. 1.

109. *Hurriyet, Milliyet, Gunaydin, Tercuman, Cumhuriyet*, 16-20 July 1974.

110. *Cumhuriyet*, 17 July 1974, p. 3; 19 July 1974, p. 3; *FBIS, Middle East*, 19 July 1974, p. Q3.

111. "Ecevit'in Aciklamalari," *Milliyet*, 30 June 1976.

112. *Ibid.*

113. *Hurriyet*, 20 July 1975.

114. *Ibid.*

115. Kissinger, *op. cit.*, p. 1191.

116. U.S. Congress, House, *Suspension of Prohibitions Against Military Assistance to Turkey*, Hearing before the Committee on International Relations, 94th Congress, 1st Sess., 10 July 1975, p. 16.

117. *FBIS, Middle East*, 19 July 1974, Q10.

118. *Ibid.*, p. 20; Birand, *op. cit.*, p. 87.

119. Birand, *op. cit.*, p. 87; Stanley Karnow, "Tough Turkey: Premier Ecevit's Perspective on Cyprus," *The New Republic*, 5 Oct. 1974.

120. *Hurriyet*, 21 July 1975.

121. Karnow, *op. cit.*

122. *Ibid.*

123. Ecevit, *Dis Politika*, pp. 64-65.

124. *Hurriyet*, 21 July 1975; *Cumhuriyet*, 18 July 1975.

125. Karnow, *op. cit.*

126. *FBIS, Middle East*, 21 July 1974, p. 012; *Cumhuriyet*, 17 July 1975, p. 4.

127. *Ecevit'in Aciklamalari, 1976* (Ankara: [ ], 1976), p. 97.

128. Ecevit, *Dis Politika*, p. 65; Birand, *op. cit.*, p. 140.

129. U.N. Security Council, *Official Records*, 1793rd Meeting (15 August 1974), para: 110.

130. Birand, *op. cit.*, p. 59.

131. *FBIS, Middle East*, 30 July 1974, p. 012.

132. Birand, *op. cit.*, p. 165; *Hurriyet*, 21 August 1974.

133. *Ibid.*, p. 235; *Economist*, London, 10 Aug. 1974; *FBIS, Middle East*, 22 July 1974, p. 04.

134. *FBIS, Middle East*, 20 July 1974, Q20; *Cumhuriyet*, 20 July 1974; *Milliyet*, 21 July 1974.

135. *FBIS, Middle East*, 22 July 1974, pp. Q4-Q5.

136. Tanju, *Tepedeki Dort Adam*, p. 43.

137. *The Sunday Times*, 21 July 1974, p. 14.

138. *FBIS, Middle East*, 21 July 1974, p. Q17.

139. Kissinger, *op. cit.*, p. 1191.

140. *Ibid.*

141. *Ibid.*

142. *The Washington Post*, 22 Nov. 1974; Stanley Karnow, "Greece in Transition: A Passel of Problems to be Solved," *The New Republic*, 21 Sept. 1974.

143. *Hurriyet*, 21 July 1975.

144. *U.S. Intelligence Agencies and Actions*, p. 1552.

145. Birand, *op. cit.*, p. 171; *FBIS, Middle East*, 22 July 1974, p. Q2.

146. *Hurriyet*, 23 July 1975.

147. Kissinger, *op. cit.*, p. 1192.

148. *Department of State Bulletin*, Vol. LXXI, No. 1833 (12 Aug. 1974), p. 257.

149. *FBIS, Middle East*, 6 Aug. 1974, p. Q4.

150. U.S. Congress, House, *Congressional-Executive Relations and the Turkish Arms Embargo*, Committee on Foreign Affairs, Print, June 1981, p. 14.

151. *FBIS, Middle East*, 22 July 1974, p. Q9.

152. *FBIS, Middle East*, 24 July 1974, p. 01.

153. Ulman, "Geneva Conferences," p. 55.

154. *Economist*, 10 Aug. 1974; Denktash, *op. cit.*, p. 70.

155. *FBIS, Middle East*, 22 July 1974, p. 04; Birand, *op. cit.*, p. 237.

156. *FBIS, Middle East*, 29 July 1974, pp. 014, 015; Ulman, *op. cit.*, p. 55.

157. Birand, *op. cit.*, p. 305; *FBIS, Middle East*, 29 July 1974, p. 016; Ulman, *op. cit.*, p. 55.

158. Birand, *op. cit.*, p. 344.

159. Art. 4 of "The Geneva Declaration of 30 July 1974" reprinted in Ertekun, *op. cit.*, p. 249.

160. *Ibid.*, Art. 5; See also: Polyviou, *op. cit.*, p. 189.

161. U.S. Congress, Senate, *World Hunger, Health, and Refugee, Problems, Pt. 5*, Hearing before the Subcommittee to Investigate Problems Connected with Refugees and Escapees, of the Committee on the Judiciary, 93rd Cong., 2nd Sess., 20 Aug. 1974, p. 12.

162. *FBIS, Middle East*, 7 Aug. 1974, p. Q3.

163. *Milliyet*, 3 Aug. 1974; *FBIS, Middle East*, 5 Aug. 1974, p. Q5; Necmettin Erbakan, *Milli Gorus* (Istanbul: Dergah Yayinlari, 1975), p. 389.

164. *Cumhuriyet*, 5 Aug. 1974; *FBIS, Middle East*, 6 Aug. 1974, p. Q1; *FBIS, Middle East*, 12 Aug. 1974, p. Q3.

165. *FBIS, Middle East*, 6 Aug. 1974, p. 03.

166. *FBIS, Middle East*, 5. Aug. 1974, p. 013.

167. Birand, *op. cit.*, pp. 374-375.

168. *FBIS, Middle East*, 9 Aug. 1974, p. 012.

169. Ulman, *op. cit.*, p. 47.

170. *FBIS, Middle East*, 1 Aug. 1974, p. P3.

171. *FBIS, Middle East*, 11 Aug. 1974, p. 06.

172. Polyviou, *op. cit.*, pp. 330-331.

173. Ulman, *op. cit.*, p. 59.

174. *Ibid.*

175. Birand, *30 Sicak Gun*, p. 423; M. Ali Birand, *Diyet: Turkiye ve Kibris Uzerine Pazarliklar, 1974-1979* (Istanbul: Milliyet Yayinlari, 1979), p. 27.

176. Birand, *30 Sicak Gun*, p. 426; *FBIS, Middle East*, 20 Aug. 1974, p. 014.

177. Polyviou, *op. cit.*, p. 176.

178. *Ibid.*, p. 183; *FBIS, Middle East*, 13 Aug. 1974, p. 013.

179. Polyviou, *op. cit.*, p. 196.

180. *Ibid.*, p. 197.

181. Ulman, *op. cit.*, p. 49.

182. Birand, *30 Sicak Gun*, p. 402.

183. Birand, *Diyet*, p. 40.

184. Karnow, *op. cit.*

185. *FBIS, Western Europe*, 23 July 1975, p. T4; *Hurriyet*, 25 July 1975.

186. *FBIS, Middle East*, 7 Aug. 1974, p. 07.

187. *Hurriyet*, 25 July 1975.

188. *FBIS, Western Europe*, 23 July 1975, p. T4.

189. Birand, *Diyet*, p. 34.

190. *Department of State Bulletin*, Vol. LXXI, No. 1837 (9 Sept. 1974), p. 354.

191. *Ibid.*, p. 367.

192. Polyvios G. Polyviou, *Cyprus: In Search of a Constitution* (Nicosia: Nicolaou & Sons, 1976), p. 327.

193. *FBIS, Middle East*, 21 Aug. 1974, p. 015; *FBIS, Middle East*, 5 Sept. 1974, p. 08; Hitchens, *op. cit.*, p. 44; Salih, *op. cit.*, p. 186.

194. *FBIS, Middle East*, 20 Aug. 1974, p. Q12.

195. Ecevit, *Dis Politika*, pp. 83, 95.

196. Ahmad, *op. cit.*, p. 344; *Ecevit'in Aciklamalari*, p. 95.

197. Birand, *Diyet*, p. 42; *Ecevit'in Aciklamalari*, p. 95.

198. Ahmad, *op. cit.*, p. 345.

199. *Congressional Quarterly Almanac*, Vol. XXXI (1975), p. 327.

200. Arthur M. Schlesinger, *The Imperial Presidency* (Boston: Houghton Mifflin Co., 1973), pp. 282-283.

201. Richard Haass, "Congressional Power: Implications for American Security Policy," *Adelphi Papers, No. 153* (London: The International Institute for Strategic Studies, 1979), p. 7.

202. John Spanier, "Congress and the Presidency: The Weakest Link in the Policy Process," in *Congress, the Presidency and American Foreign Policy*, p. xxv.

203. Joseph Nogee, "Congress and the Presidency: The Dilemma of Policy-Making in a Democracy," in *Congress, the Presidency and American Foreign Policy*, p. 191.

204. Haass, *op. cit.*, p. 8.

205. Spanier, *op. cit.*, p. xxv.

206. *Orthodox Observer*, New York, 7 Aug. 1974, pp. 1, 3.

207. Russell Warren Howe and Sarah Hays Trott, *The Power Peddlers* (New York: Doubleday & Co., 1977), p. 443.

208. Hicks and Couloumbis, "The Greek Lobby . . .", p. 75.

209. *Ibid.*, p. 76.

210. *Ibid.*, p. 76.

211. Howe, *op. cit.*, p. 450; Hicks, *op. cit.*, p. 80.

212. *National Herald*, New York, 29 Sept. 1974; *Congressional Record*, Vol. 121, Pt. 24 (Nov. 1974), p. 11; in John Paul, "A Study in Ethnic Group Behaviour: The Greek Americans and Cyprus" (Ph.D. dissertation, University of Denver, 1979), p. 204.

213. Paul, *op. cit.*, p. 204.

214. Ethnic vote ratios are derived from: Michael Barone, et. al., *The Almanac of American Politics, 1974* (Boston: Gambit, 1974).

215. Hicks, *op. cit.*, p. 88; Paul, *op. cit.*, p. 282; Keith Legg, "Congress As Trojan Horse: The Turkish Embargo Problem, 1974-1978," in *Congress, the Presidency and American Foreign Policy*, p. 126.

216. Legg, *op. cit.*, p. 126.

217. Hicks, *op. cit.*, p. 84.

218. Paul, *op. cit.*, p. 189.

219. *Foreign Military Sales Act, Statues at Large, 82, Section 4 (1968); Foreign Assistance Act of 1961, Statues at Large, 75, Section 505 (1961).*

220. *Congressional Record*, 24 Sept. 1974, Vol. 120, Pt. 24, p. 32430.

221. *Cyprus-1974*, p. 62.

222. *Congressional Record*, 24 Sept. 1974, Vol. 120, Pt. 24, p. 32429.

223. *Ibid*., p. 32433.

224. *Ibid*.

225. Marry Russel, "Turkey Aid Terms a Victory for Greek-Americans," *The Washington Post*, 25 Oct. 1974, p. A5.

226. *Military Aid Cutoff to Aggressor Recipients of Foreign Military Assistance*, A Study by the Library of Congress, reprinted in: U.S. Senate, Subcommittee to Investigate Problems Connected with Refugees and Escapees of the Committee on the Judiciary, *Humanitarian Problems on Cyprus*, 26 Sept. 1974, p. 39.

227. *Ibid*., p. 37.

228. *Congressional Record*, Vol. 121, Pt. 19 (24 July 1975), pp. 24490-24491.

229. Raymond Celeda, "Waiver Authority Under Section 614 a, Foreign Assistance Act of 1961, As Amended, 2 U.S.C. 2364 a, 1974," The Library of Congress Research Service, 20 Sept. 1974.

230. *Congressional Record*, Vol. 120, Pt. 25 (30 Sept. 1974), p. Q5.

231. *FBIS, Middle East*, 30 July 1974, p. Q5; Cem, *op. cit*., p. 54.

232. Kissinger, *op. cit*., pp. 1192-1193.

233. David Rudnik, "Death of an Embargo," *The Round Table*, No. 272 (Oct. 1978), p. 358.

234. Legg, *op. cit*., p. 129.

235. K. J. Holsti, *International Politics: A Framework for Analysis* (Englewood Cliffs, N.J.: Prentice-Hall, 1983), p. 149.

236. Robert Dahl, *Modern Political Analysis* (Englewood Cliffs, N.J.: Prentice-Hall, 1976), p. 33.

237. Kissinger, *op. cit.*, p. 1190.

238. *Ibid.*, p. 1191.

239. David A. Baldwin, "Inter-Nation Influence Revisited," *The Journal of Conflict Resolution*, Vol. XV, No. 4 (Dec., 1971), p. 481.

240. David Singer, "Inter-Nation Influence: A Formal Model," in *International Politics and Foreign Policy*, ed. by James N. Rosenau (New York: The Free Press, 1969), p. 386.

241. *Ibid.*, p. 387.

242. Carl J. Friedrich, *Constitutional Government and Democracy* (New York: Harper and Brothers, 1937), pp. 16-18.

243. Carl J. Friedrich, *Man and His Government: An Empirical Theory of Politics* (New York: McGraw-Hill, 1963), p. 205.

244. Singer, *op. cit.*, p. 391.

V. Conclusion

This study set out to find how an influence relationship between two unequal allies works during regional crises. The Cyprus crises of 1964, 1967 and 1974 were discussed to understand how the respective parties desired the crises to end and why their efforts were or were not successful. The examination of the three case studies indicated that geopolitical, domestic, and functional factors affected the American-Turkish influence relationship and determined the outcomes of the Cyprus crises.

Before 1964 Turkey had assumed that its geopolitical and regional interests were identical with those of the U.S. Both post-World War II leaders, Inonu and Menderes, considered Turkey's alliance with the U.S. essential for Turkey's security, and hence tried to cooperate with the U.S. even in areas thought unimportant to Turkish national interests. For example, Turkey eagerly associated itself with American Middle East policies. During the 1950s Turkey was also anxious to coordinate its Cyprus policy with that of Britain and the U.S., because it shared the American view that a Turco-Greek conflict over Cyprus would destabilize NATO and play into the hands of the Soviet Union.

The 1959 Zurich-London Agreements were a welcome development for both Turkey and the United States. The U.S. was pleased because the settlement seemed to have eliminated a serious friction point in the relations of three of its allies and saved the viability of the southeastern flank of NATO. Turkey was satisfied with the agreements because they provided constitutional guarantees to Turkish Cypriots and granted Turkey the right of intervention if the *status quo* in Cyprus came under attack. Since Turkey had never seriously considered annexing the island, it easily accepted the 1959 settlement. During the following three years, Turkey avoided any actions that might destabilize the fragile Republic of Cyprus.

After the December 1963 intercommunal clashes broke out, Prime Minister Inonu faced a difficult choice. He had to choose to either militarily intervene or ask the U.S. to work for a peaceful settlement. He chose the latter. Before making his decision Inonu took into account several factors. One of them was the geopolitical factor, or the condition of Turco-Soviet relations. Despite some minor Soviet overtures, the Turkey-Soviet relationship in 1963 still reflected Cold War tensions and neither country seemed enthusiastic about a rapprochement. Moreover, Khrushchev had announced publicly that the U.S.S.R. would assist Makarios if a Turkish intervention took place.

Prime Minister Suleyman Demirel faced a similar crisis in 1967. Turkey's position *vis-a-vis* the Soviet Union was, however, much different than in 1964. The new Soviet leadership which ousted Khrushchev in 1964 was anxious to improve Turkey-U.S.S.R. relations; much of this improvement had occurred in the past three years. The Soviets, furthermore, no longer opposed Turkey's Cyprus thesis, i.e., the existence in Cyprus of two different national communities. During the 1967 crisis there were also reports that the U.S.S.R., which opposed the Greek junta's attempt to annex the island, consented to Turkey's use of force in Cyprus. Regardless of the reliability of these reports, it is fair to assume that Demirel had less reason than Inonu to be concerned about a hostile Soviet reaction.

The Soviet tilt toward Turkey continued during the 1974 crisis. Before both the first and second Turkish offensives the Soviets chose to remain silent about Turkey's intervention preparations, indicating that they did not oppose it. In addition, before the first offensive the U.S.S.R. privately approved Turkey's action provided Turkey respected Cyprus' independence and nonalignment.

As Inonu later confirmed, he decided not to intervene in 1963-64 partly as a result of Soviet opposition to any Turkish move in Cyprus. In 1967, although the Soviets were not as threatening as they were in 1964, Prime Minister Demirel had already made up his mind to first try peaceful methods. When the Vance Mission brought a compromise settlement which satisfied his demands to some degree, Demirel gave up the intervention option. In 1974, Ecevit was pleased with the Soviet acquiescence in the Turkish landing. Thus, he had one more reason to initiate the intervention.

Another factor taken into account by all three leaders was the reaction of world public opinion to a possible landing. This element especially worried Inonu who was aware of Turkey's international isolation. As he confided to his close friends, he was afraid that if Turkey's motivation for an intervention were misunderstood, Turkey could be faced with United Nations involvement and forced to withdraw its troops in humiliation.

Demirel, and especially Ecevit, had less reason to fear a U.N. move against Turkey because as a result of its multi-faceted foreign policy, Turkey's isolation had diminished. Since 1964, the Soviet bloc countries and several Western and Third World countries had chosen to abstain from voting in favor of anti-Turkish U.N. resolutions. Demirel and Ecevit knew that Turkey still could not count on a majority of U.N. General Assembly votes, but they did not fear that the U.N. would send its own forces to Cyprus or impose sanctions against Turkey. In both 1967 and 1974 neither the U.S. nor the U.S.S.R. spoke against a Turkish landing, nor did they threaten sanctions. Thus, a U.N. Security Council consensus against

Turkey was less likely in 1967 and in 1974 than it was in 1964.

The functional factor, or Turkey's ability to conduct a successful naval and aerial landing in Cyprus, also affected the decisions of the three Turkish prime ministers. In 1964 Inonu took into account the fact that the armed forces were not prepared to undertake a landing on the island, even though the commanders insisted that if necessary, they could accomplish the operation by using fishing boats. Especially after the arrival of 20,000 mainland Greek troops in Cyprus in the spring of 1964, Inonu believed that Turkey's intervention not only would encounter a formidable force, but that the engagement of mainland Greek and Turkish forces would possibly lead to an all-out war between Greece and Turkey. Inonu indicated that this latter possibility forced him to insist on a peaceful solution.

In 1967 the readiness of the Turkish armed forces remained essentially unchanged. Despite the public and official campaigns to build a landing force during the three years prior to 1967, the landing force would still have to rely on makeshift means of transportation, and the arrival of mechanized units would have to await the capture of a suitable harbor. Military unpreparedness also influenced Demirel to postpone the intervention in favor of the Vance Mission. In 1974, however, Turkey's landing force was capable not only of invading Cyprus, but also of capturing some of the Aegean islands if Greece declared war on Turkey. Thus, Ecevit's assertiveness before and during the 1974 crisis stemmed in part from Turkey's military readiness.

The domestic factor, which included the influence of the Turkish and American policymaking processes, had an equally if not more important effect on the outcomes of the three crises than did the above mentioned factors. During the 1964 crisis, especially during the second half of the year, there was strong public pressure on Inonu to send forces to Cyprus. There were frequent public demonstrations, and most newspapers urged Inonu to assert Turkey's rights boldly. The commanders of the armed forces, who also favored intervention, did not hesitate to pressure Inonu.

Inonu opposed the idea of military intervention for most of the 1963-64 crisis. Only in June 1964 did he seem to favor intervention, but when faced with President Johnson's disapproval he changed his mind. Inonu's reluctance to send forces to Cyprus was largely a result of the above mentioned lack of military readiness, the Soviet promise of assistance to Makarios if Turkey undertook an invasion, and Turkey's apparent inability to convince world public opinion that its cause was just. Inonu's disinclination to use force also reflected his cautiousness. It should be stressed that the unfavorable geopolitical and functional conditions, combined with the U.S. opposition to a Turkish intervention, significantly fostered Inonu's conviction that Turkey first should exhaust all the peaceful alternatives. Thus, he enthusiastically accepted American mediation efforts.

In 1967 there was again strong public pressure on Demirel to send forces to Cyprus. As in 1964, citizens staged large demonstrations, and the press advocated intervention. Military commanders once more prevailed upon the Government not to miss another opportunity to settle the dispute once and for all. Despite the fact that he initially seemed to have agreed to an intervention, Demirel enthusiastically embraced the outcome of the Vance Mission.

Cyrus Vance's mediation brought a settlement which only partly favored Turkey. Greece accepted the withdrawal of its illegally introduced troops from Cyprus. Yet despite the provisions of the Greece-Turkey agreement, Makarios refused to abolish the unconstitutional Greek Cypriot National Guard. Consequently, Demirel still could have insisted on the complete implementation of the agreement, and if Makarios continued to refuse to abide by it, Turkey could have intervened in Cyprus. Instead, Demirel chose to portray the Vance mission as a big success in Turkey. Demirel believed that once the Greek troops evacuated the island, Makarios would realize the futility of achieving *enosis* through intercommunal fighting and opt for a negotiated settlement.

Demirel's conduct during the 1967 crisis conformed with his overall management of crises throughout his public life. Demirel, who shunned rushed solutions, was satisfied with a partial success in 1967, because he believed that in the long run common sense would prevail; therefore, there was no reason to insist on an immediate constitutional settlement.

In 1974 the domestic factor also played an important role. Public opinion once again favored intervention, especially after Greece was clearly identified as the instigator of the Sampson coup. In contrast to its attitude in the earlier crises, however, the Government was as enthusiastic about an intervention as were the people. Ecevit was a believer in the virtue of assertiveness. This characteristic had exhibited itself in his well-known impatience with prolonged negotiations. Ecevit considered Inonu's cautious and Demirel's pragmatist approaches to have failed in the previous two crises. He thought that Turkey could afford to be more assertive in Cyprus because not only were the geopolitical and functional conditions favorable, but the U.S. had lost its once paramount role in regional if not world affairs, and would therefore be forced to acquiesce in Turkey's action to avoid harming the southeastern flank of NATO.

U.S. policies in support of or opposition to Turkey's goals significantly affected Turkey's decisions during the three Cyprus crises. This factor not only played an important role in restraining or provoking Turkey *vis-a-vis* Cyprus, but it also shaped the U.S.-Turkey influence relationship. Moreover, Turkey's frustrations at the U.S.'s "partiality" toward Greece led the Turkish policymakers to adopt a more "flexible" foreign policy, which in the long run could have significant consequences for the NATO alliance and Turkey's role in the Middle East.

The U.S.-Turkey influence relationship throughout the three Cyprus crises could be explained by several influence variables discussed earlier. The propositions that not all power is usable or convertible to influence and that "the amount of influence a state wields over others can be related to the capabilities *mobilized* in support of *specific* foreign policy objectives"[1] were verified by the facts of our case studies as described earlier.

The case studies also verified that if A, the influencer provides an alternative besides prohibiting B's, the influenced state's proposed action, B would very likely try the alternative rather than ignore A's advice.[2] For example, Inonu's decision to cancel the June 5, 1964 intervention plan was influenced by the threat of U.S. passivity in the event of a Turco-Soviet war and by the positive incentive of U.S. assurance of speedy negotiations.

In 1967, the U.S. did not need to threaten Turkey because Demirel had not yet opted for a military intervention. Therefore, U.S. envoy Cyrus Vance only had to urge restraint on Demirel and promise that he would succeed in convincing the Greek junta to withdraw its troops from Cyprus. Vance's influence attempt thus was directed toward Greece rather than Turkey. Vance's prevention of a Greek-Turkish war and the solution of the immediate crisis emphasizes the importance of providing alternatives to influenced states.

In 1974, despite Kissinger's attempts, the U.S. was unable to *mobilize* its capabilities in support of *specific* objectives. These objectives were, first, the prevention of the Sampson coup, and later, of the Turkish intervention. The U.S. failed in both of these goals because it did not effectively use its *resources* as documented in chapter IV. The U.S. also provided no alternative solution or a positive incentive, but instead, simply asked Turkey not to intervene, thereby restricting the chances for success of its influence attempt.

The examination of the Cyprus crises also enables us to test the validity of the propositions that influence is partly determined by the responsiveness of the influenced to the requests of the influencer,[3] and that "[w]hat often seems to be influence turns out instead to be joint interests of the two parties."[4] In 1964, the U.S. seemed to have successfully influenced Inonu, but it was also Inonu's responsiveness, or readiness to accept a U.S.-mediated solution, which rendered the influence attempt successful. In 1967, Demirel likewise responded positively to U.S. interference, because he also believed that American mediation could lead to a peaceful resolution of the dispute. In 1974, most Turkish political parties had concluded that accepting a U.S.-mediated solution in Cyprus would eventually result in an unfavorable settlement for Turkey. Ecevit's intractability shows that Turkey no longer was responsive to U.S. demands concerning the Cyprus question, even though Turkey continued to be as responsive as before with regard to the East-West issues and other aspects of U.S.-Turkey relations.

Another influence variable discussed was that B's, the influenced state's, expectation of A's, the influencer's, potential reaction to B's compliance or non-compliance with A's wishes affects B's decisions.[5] Even if B thinks that A opposes B's actions and would threaten punishments, it may go ahead with its original plan if it attaches a high value to the outcome.[6] In 1964, Inonu decided not to intervene in Cyprus, partly because he believed the operation would be too costly if at all possible. This calculation caused Inonu to attach less value to the Cyprus issue. Since Inonu also believed that the U.S. reaction to Turkey's non-compliance with U.S. mediation would hurt Türkey's national interests, he chose not to move. In 1967, Demirel likewise did not perceive the stakes as high enough to risk Turkey's involvement in a regional war. Thus, he opted for the U.S. mediation even though there were few signs of potential U.S. sanctions.

In 1974, Ecevit knew that the U.S. opposed a Turkish intervention, but he thought the U.S. would not be able to "punish" Turkey if he went ahead with it. Ecevit also attached a high value to the Cyprus crisis, maintaining that unless Turkey intervened, Cyprus would be unified with Greece, dangerously compromising Turkey's national security interests. It is thus not surprising that Ecevit did not hesitate before deciding for the so-called "peace operation."

The examination of the three Cyprus crises also indicates that policymakers take into account two additional dimensions: *utility* and *probability*. Decision-makers differ "in the degree to which they emphasize either the probability or the preference element in their appraisal of an outcome."[7] Moreover, policymakers tend to exaggerate the probability of an outcome if they value it highly. "Conversely, when a probability looks very low, the tendency will be to downgrade the attractiveness of the associated outcome."[8]

Inonu stressed the preference element. For a number of reasons discussed earlier, he preferred an American-mediated settlement of the 1964 crisis. Therefore, he further downgraded the probability of the intervention's success. In 1967 Demirel took a dim view of the prospects of a military action. Hence, he also downgraded the attractiveness of a military solution. In 1974, Ecevit's conviction that an intervention was necessary led him to exaggerate the probability of a favorable outcome.

The so-called "rule of anticipated reactions"[9] also proved to be relevant to the three Cyprus crises. This influence variable suggests that many times state B behaves in a way desired by state A even though A has not tried to pressure B. Sometimes, however, states fail to anticipate the reactions of other states due to "possible errors in anticipation, . . . to oversight, incomplete information, lack of insight, and the like . . ."[10]

In 1964, Inonu behaved several times in a way desired by the U.S. Administration even though the U.S. had not tried to make its wishes known. This was the case in December 1963 and January 1964 when the U.S. avoided assuming responsibility and asked Britain to mediate the dispute. Inonu opposed intervention for most of the crisis period, but he based his reluctance in part on his anticipation of U.S. opposition to Turkey's landing.

Similarly, in 1967, Demirel believed that the U.S. was against a landing, and procrastinated in making a final decision, anticipating that the U.S. would eventually mediate between Greece and Turkey. The Vance mission which came after only one week of hostilities proved that Demirel's expectation of U.S. reluctance to tolerate a prolonged crisis was correct.

In 1974, Ecevit accurately anticipated the response of the U.S. Administration to Turkey's two-part intervention. As expected, Kissinger did not threaten Turkey with economic or military sanctions, nor did he demand an immediate withdrawal of Turkish forces from Cyprus. Ecevit did not, however, accurately predict the reaction of the U.S. Congress, which moved quickly to impose an arms embargo on Turkey, a move enthusiastically supported by the Greek Lobby.

Kissinger's reluctance to forestall Turkey's intervention bears out Robert Dahl's proposition that these are variations in the skill or efficiency with which statesmen use the resources. Second, there are variations in the extent to which individuals stress influencing others.[11] Kissinger apparently weighed the costs and benefits of challenging Turkey and opted not to do so because the costs would outweigh the benefits. This finding corroborates David Baldwin's argument that "A will continue to apply resources to influencing B only up to the point in which [its] estimated marginal return equals his estimated marginal cost."[12]

During the first two crises, however, the Johnson Administration was convinced that the benefits of preventing a Turkish landing outweighed the costs. Hence, in both cases, but especially in 1964, the U.S. concentrated its resources on keeping the Turkish forces at home. Since the U.S. was unsuccessful in providing a satisfactory negotiated settlement to the dispute, the main problem remained. The resources of influence were most effective when used negatively to veto or deny a specific outcome.[13] In both 1964 and 1967, the U.S. succeeded in solving the immediate crisis, but did not achieve a lasting settlement.

The three Cyprus crises significantly altered the Turkish perceptions of U.S. importance to Turkish national security. Ecevit noted that after 1964, Turkish policymakers

> realized that [their] one-dimensional national security approach did not cover all contingencies. [They] began to discuss whether Turkey's membership in NATO contributed to Turkish security or actually increased dangers. [They] also realized that [NATO's commitment] would be useless if [Turkey's] friends changed their minds [and did not stand up to their commitments.][14]

As a result, Turkey started to improve its relations with the Soviet Union, regional states and other Third World states, striving to decrease its dependency on the U.S. When the 1974 crisis occurred Turkey had gone a long way toward breaking its isolation. The U.S. arms embargo of 1974 highlighted the point that Turkey's dependency on American military assistance contradicted Turkish national interests. Turkish statesmen were particularly offended that, in their view, a small ethnic minority could dictate U.S. foreign policy toward Turkey. In an interview, former Prime Minister Ecevit argued that the Greek Lobby played a big role in the imposition of the arms embargo, and that therefore, "as a country, which is in a critical geopolitical region, Turkey is no longer in a position to thrust its national security into the hands of the U.S."[15]

Hence, Turkey continued its efforts to lessen its reliance on the U.S. In 1975, Turkey decided to eventually manufacture most of the military equipment its forces need. Since then a number of factories have been established to produce at least the basic needs of the armed forces.[16] Although Turkey remains far from self-sufficient in armaments production, it is continuing the effort in that direction with the same momentum as in 1975.

Another example of Turkey's attempts to pursue a more flexible foreign policy since 1974 is the "Political Document on the Principles of Good-Neighborly and Friendly Cooperation between the U.S.S.R. and Turkey" signed in June 1978. This agreement, though it falls short of a non-aggression pact, is another indication of Turkey's desire to reduce its defense burden.[17] It stresses the belief, now widely popular with the Turkish people, that Turkey's defense system

> should be compatible with [its] continued membership in NATO, but certainly [its] contribution to NATO in the future would be and should be commensurate with NATO's contribution to Turkey's security. At the same time [Turkey believes] that [its] contribution to NATO in the future should not constitute a serious risk for Turkey by rendering [it] provocative in the region where [it] is situated."[18]

The transformation of Turkish foreign policy continues and it is still too early to determine exactly how the Cyprus crises will change the Turco-American influence relationship in the long run. Clearly, Turkey still considers its membership in NATO a basic pillar of its foreign and defense policies, but as suggested many times throughout this study, it no longer believes that its NATO-membership is a panacea for all security contingencies. The findings of this study suggest that Turkey's search for a new identity will go on until Turkey establishes a balance between its geopolitical security commitments, i.e., containment of the U.S.S.R., and its need to deal with the Turco-Greek problems more assertively. Turkish policymakers are aware that assertiveness toward Greece would hurt Turco-American relations and that these relations will not improve as long as there are Turco-Greek disputes over a number of issues.

NOTES

1. K.J. Holsti, *International Politics: A Framework for Analysis* (Englewood Cliffs, N.J.: Prentice-Hall, 1983), p. 149; Hans J. Morgenthau and Kenneth W. Thompson, *Politics Among Nations* (New York: Alfred A. Knopf, 1985), p. 33.

2. David Singer, "Inter-Nation Influence: A Formal Model," *International Politics and Foreign Policy*, ed. by James N. Rosenau (New York: The Free Press, 1969), p. 391.

3. Holsti, *op. cit.*, p. 153.

4. Alvin Z. Rubinstein, *Red Star on the Nile: The Soviet Egyptian Influence Relationship Since the June War* (Princeton, N.J.: Princeton University Press, 1977), p. xvii.

5. Singer, *op. cit.*, p. 386.

6. *Ibid.*

7. *Ibid.*

8. *Ibid.*

9. Carl Joachim Friedrich, *Man and His Government, An Empirical Theory of Politics* (New York: McGraw-Hill, 1963), p. 203.

10. Friedrich, *Man and His Government*, p. 205.

11. Robert Dahl, *Modern Political Analysis* (Englewood Cliffs, N.J.: Prentice-Hall, 1976), p. 33.

12. David A. Baldwin, "Inter-Nation Influence Revisited," *The Journal of Conflict Resolution*, Vol. XV, No. 4 (Dec., 1971), p. 481.

13. Karl W. Deutsch, "On the Concepts of Politics and Power," *International Politics and Foreign Policy*, ed. by James N. Rosenau (New York: The Free Press, 1969), p. 260.

14. Bulent Ecevit, "Donum Noktasi," *Milliyet*, 26 Apr. 1965.

15. *Milliyet*, 30 June 1976; See also: Bulent Ecevit, "Turkey's Security Policies," *Survival*, Vol. XX, No. 5 (Sept., 1978), p. 204; *The Guardian*, 30 Sept. 1975, p. 2.

16. *Cumhuriyet*, 30 June 1975, pp. 1,8; *The Pulse*, Ankara, No. 3522 (25 July 1977), p. 1; Michael Boll, "Turkey's New National Security Concept: What It Means for NATO," *Orbis*, Vol. XXIII, No. 3 (Fall 1979), p. 614.

17. V. Alenik, "Soviet-Turkish Ties Today," *International Affairs*, Moscow, No. 4 (April, 1979), pp. 14-19; Alvin Z. Rubinstein, *Soviet Policy Toward Turkey, Iran and Afghanistan* (New York: Praeger, 1982), p. 41.

18. Ecevit, "Turkey's Security Policies," p. 203.

Bibliography

PUBLIC DOCUMENTS

Great Britain

Her Majesty's Stationary Office. *Conference on Cyprus: Documents Signed and Initialed At Lancaster House on February 19, 1959.* Cmnd. 680, London, 1959.

_____. *Cyprus.* Cmnd. 1093, London, 1960.

_____. *Cyprus: Statement of Policy.* Cmnd. 455, London, 1958.

_____. *The Tripartite Conference on the Eastern Mediterranean and Cyprus.* Cmnd. 9594, London, 1955.

_____. *Treaty of Peace with Turkey.* Cmnd. 1929, London, 1923.

Turkey

Disisleri Bakanligi Belleteni ("The Bulletin of the Foreign Ministry"). Ankara, 1964-1973.

Millet Meclisi Tutanak Dergisi ("Official Records of the National Assembly"). 1952, 1960-1974.

United Nations

Official Records of the General Assembly. 9th Sess., 1st Committee, 749th meeting, 14 Dec. 1954.

_____. 11th Sess., 1956-1957, Annexes, Vol. II, Document A/C.1/788.

_____. 1956-1957, Agenda Item 55.

_____. 1958/1959, Annexes, Agenda Item 68.

_____. 1532nd Plenary Meeting, 22 June 1967.

Report of the Secretary General. Doc. S/6569, 29 July 1965.

Report of the Secretary General. Doc. S/8248, 1967.

Report of the Secretary General. No. S/5950, 10 Sept. 1964.

U.N. Resolutions. Series No. I, Vol. XI (1966-1967).

U.N. Security Council Official Records. 1095th Meeting, 18 Feb. 1964.

_____. Res. 186 in Document No. S/5575, 4 March 1964.

_____. 1096th Meeting, 19 Feb. 1964.

_____. 1153rd Meeting, 17 Sept. 1964.

_____. 1383rd Meeting, 24-25 Nov. 1964.

_____. 1793rd Meeting, 15 Aug. 1974.

Yearbook of the United Nations, 1955. New York: Columbia University Press, 1956.

Yearbook of the United Nations, 1965. New York: United Nations, 1965.

United States

Celeda, Raymond. "Waiver Authority Under Section 614 a, Foreign Assistance Act of 1961, As Amended, 2 U.S.C., 2364 a, 1974." The Library of Congress Research Service, 20 Sept. 1974.

Congressional Quarterly Almanac. Vols. 30-31 (1974-1975).

Congressional Record. Vols. 120-121 (1974-1975).

The Defence and Economic Cooperation Agreement: U.S. Interests and Turkish Needs. Washington, D.C.: GPO, 1982.

Department of State. Bureau of Public Affairs. *Current Policy.* No. 18, May 1978.

_____. Bureau of Public Affairs. *Current Policy*, No. 6, Sept. 1975.

U.S. House of Representatives. *Authorization of Appropriations for the Board for International Broadcasting and Partial Lifting of the Turkish Arms Embargo.* Hearing before the Committee on International Relations on S.2230, 94th Cong., 1st Sess., 17 Sept. 1975.

_____. *Congressional-Executive Relations and The Turkish Embargo.* Foreign Affairs Committee, Congress and Foreign Policy Series, No. 3, Washington, D.C., June 1982.

_____. *Controlled Dangerous Substances, Narcotics and Drug Control Laws.* Hearings before the

Committee on Ways and Means, 91st Cong., 2nd Sess., 20 July 1970, p. 247.

_____. *Cyprus-1974.* Hearings before the Committee on Foreign Affairs and Its Subcommittee on Europe, 93rd Cong., 2nd Sess., 19 and 20 Aug. 1974.

_____. *Suspension of Prohibitions Against Military Assistance to Turkey.* Hearing before the Committee on International Relations, 94th Cong., 1st Sess., 10 July 1975.

_____. *Turkish Opium Ban Negotiations.* Hearing before the Committee on Foreign Affairs, 93rd Cong., 2nd Sess., 16 July 1974.

_____. *U.S. Intelligence Agencies and Activities.* Proceedings of the Select Committee on Intelligence, 94th Cong., 1st Sess., Sept./Nov., 1975.

National Security Council History File: Cyprus Crisis. L.B. Johnson Library, Austin, Texas.

U.S. Senate. *Crisis on Cyprus: 1974.* A Study Mission Report for the Use of the Subcommittee to Investigate Problems Connected with Refugees and Escapees of the Committee on the Judiciary, 93rd Cong., 2nd Sess., 14 Oct. 1974.

_____. *Humanitarian Problems on Cyprus, Pt. I and II.* Hearing before the Subcommittee to Investigate Problems Connected with Refugees and Escapees, 93rd Cong., 2nd Sess., 26 Sept. 1974 and 17 Dec. 1974.

YEARBOOKS AND DOCUMENTARY COLLECTIONS

Blaustein, Albert P. and Flanz, Albert H. *Constitutions of the Countries of the World: Cyprus.* Dobbs Ferry, New York: Oceana Publications, 1972.

Department of State Bulletin. Vol. XXXIII (1955); Vols. LXXI-LXXII (1974-1975).

Hurewitz, J.C., ed. *Diplomacy in the Near and Middle East: A Documentary Record, 1535-1956.* Princeton, N.J.: Van Nostrand, Vol. II (1956).

"Inonu's Letter to Johnson, 13 June 1964." *The Middle East Journal*, Vol. XX, No. 3 (1966).

"President Johnson's Letter to Prime Minister Inonu." *The Middle East Journal.* Vol. XX, No. 3 (1966).

University of Ankara. *Turkish Yearbook of International Relations, 1963. Ankara University Press, 1965.*

NEWSPAPERS AND PERIODICALS

The Ahepan (Greek American], 1956, 1964.

Akis, Ankara, 1958, 1967.

Aksam, Istanbul, 1963-1964.

Atlantis [Greek-American], New York, 1954, 1958.

Cumhuriyet, Istanbul, 1960-1975.

The Current Digest of the Soviet Press, Vol. XV (1963); Vol. XVI (1964).

Dis Politika, Ankara, 1971, 1974.

Facts on File, Vol. XXV (1965).

Foreign Broadcast Information Service, M. East, 1974.

Foreign Broadcast Information Service, W. Europe, 1975.

Hurriyet, Istanbul, 1974-1975.

Keesings Contemporary Archives, 1963, 1964, 1967.

Milliyet, Istanbul, 1963-1976.

National Herald [Greek American], New York, 1964-1974.

The New York Times, 1948, 1956, 1958, 1962, 1963-1964, 1967, 1974.

Observer, London, 1961.

Orthodox Observer [Greek-American], New York, 1974.

Tercuman, Istanbul, 1974.

The Times, London, 1961, 1963-1964.

Turkish Yearbook of International Relations, Ankara, 1964-1974.

Ulus, Ankara, 1961, 1964-1974.

The Washington Post, 1964-1974.

BOOKS, PAMPHLETS AND DISSERTATIONS

Adams, Thomas W., and Cottrell, Alvin J., *Cyprus Between East and West.* Baltimore: The John Hopkins Press, 1968.

Ahmad, Feroz. *The Turkish Experiment in Democracy: 1950-1975.* London: C. Hurst & Company, 1977.

Arcayurek, Cuneyt. *Demirel Donemi, 12 Mart Darbesi, 1965-1971.* Ankara: Bilgi, 1985.

_____. *Cankaya'ya Giden Yol, 1971-1973.* Ankara: Bilgi, 1985.

Attalides, Michael A. *Cyprus: Nationalism and International Politics.* New York: St. Martin's Press, 1979.

Aydemir, Sevket S. *Ikinci Adam.* Vol. I. Istanbul: Remzi Kitabevi, 1976.

Bachrach, Peter, and Baratz, Morton S. *Power and Poverty.* New York: Oxford University Press, 1970.

Ball, George. *The Past Has Another Pattern.* New York: W.W. Norton, 1982.

Birand, M. Ali. *30 Sicak Gun.* Istanbul: Milliyet, 1975.

_____. *Diyet: Turkiye ve Kibris Uzerine Pazarliklar, 1974-1979.* Istanbul: Milliyet, 1979.

Bitsios, Dimitri S. *Cyprus: The Vulnerable Republic.* Thessaloniki: Institute for Balkan Studies, 1975.

Borowiec, Andrew. *The Mediterranean Feud.* New York: Praeger, 1983.

Cem, Hasan. *Kibris Antlasmalarinda Ecevit'in Savunmasi.* Istanbul: Aktuel Yayinlari, 1974.

Couloumbis, Theodore A. *The United States, Greece, and Turkey: The Troubled Triangle.* New York: Praeger, 1984.

Crawshaw, Nancy. *The Cyprus Revolt.* London: George Allen & Unwin, 1978.

Cyprus Question and Greek Extermination Plans. Turkish Federated State of Cyprus: Public Information Office, 1977.

Dahl, Robert. *Modern Political Analysis.* Englewood Cliffs, N.J.: Prentice-Hall, 1976.

Denktash, Rauf R. *The Cyprus Triangle.* London and Boston: Allen & Unwin, 1982.

Deutsch, Karl W. *The Analysis of International Relations.* Englewood Cliffs, N.J.: Prentice-Hall, 1968.

Ecevit, Bulent. *Dis Politika.* Ankara: Ajans-Turk, 1976.

Ecevit'in Aciklamalari. 1976. Ankara: [ ], 1976.

Ehrlich, Thomas. *Cyprus, 1958-1967.* New York: Oxford University Press, 1974.

Erbakan, Necmettin. *Milli Gorus.* Istanbul: Dergah Yayinlari, 1975.

Erden, Deniz A. "Turkish Foreign Policy Through the United Nations." Ph.D. Thesis, University of Massachusetts, 1974.

Erim, Nihat. *Bildigim ve Gordugum Olculer Icinde Kibris*. Ankara: Ajans-Turk, 1975.

Ertekun, Munir N. *The Cyprus Dispute*. Oxford: The University Press, 1981.

Foley, Charles. *A Legacy of Strife*. London: Penguin, 1964.

_____. *Man and His Government: An Empirical Theory of Politics*. New York: McGraw-Hill, 1963.

Hass, Richard. *Congressional Power: Implications for American Security Policy*. Adelphi Papers. No. 153. London: International Institute for Strategic Studies, 1979.

Halley, Laurence. *Ancient Affections: Ethnic Groups and Foreign Policy. New York: Praeger, 1985.*

Harris, George. Troubled Alliance. Washington, D.C.: American Enterprise Institute, 1972.

Hill, Sir George. *A History of Cyprus*. Cambridge: The University Press, 1952.

Holsti, K.J. *International Politics: A Framework for Analysis*. Englewood Cliffs, N.J.: Prentice-Hall, 1983.

Howe, Russell W., and Trott, Sarah H. *The Power Peddlers*. New York: Doubleday & Co., 1977.

Ince, Nurhan. "Problems and Politics in Turkish Foreign Policy, 1960-1966." Ph.D. Thesis, Kentucky: University of Kentucky, 1974.

Ipekci, Abdi, and Cosar, Sami. *Ihtilalin Icyuzu*. Istanbul: Milliyet Yayinlari, 1965.

Kissinger, Henry. *Years of Upheaval.* Boston: Little Brown & Co., 1982.

Kuchuk, Fazil. *Cyprus: Turkish Reply to Archbishop Makarios' Proposals.* Nicosia: [ ], [1964].

Kyriakides, Stanley. *Cyprus: Constitutionalism and Crisis Government.* Philadelphia, University of Pennsylvania Press, 1968.

Landau, Jacob M. *Johnson Letter to Inonu and Greek Lobbying of the White House.* Jerusalem: Hebrew University of Jerusalem, 1979.

Lasswell, Harold, and Kaplan, Abraham. *Power and Society.* New Haven: Yale University Press, 1976.

Leber, George. *The History of the Order of Ahepa.* Washington, D.C.: The Order of Ahepa, 1972.

Macmillan, Harold. *Riding the Storm: 1956-1959.* London: Macmillan, 1971.

Markides, Kyriacos C. *The Rise and Fall of the Cyprus Republic.* New Haven: Yale University Press, 1977.

Morgenthau Hans J., and Thompson Kenneth W. *Politics Among Nations.* New York: Alfred A. Knopf, 1985.

Nagel, Jack H. *The Descriptive Analysis of Power.* New Haven: Yale University Press, 1975.

Nye, Roger. "The Military in Turkish Politics: 1960-1973." Ph.D. Thesis, Washington University, St. Louis, Missouri, 1974.

Patrick, Richard A. *Political Geography and the Cyprus Conflict.* Ontario, Canada: University of Waterloo, 1976.

Paul, John. "A Study in Ethnic Group Political Behaviour: The Greek Americans and Cyprus." Ph.D. Thesis, University of Denver, 1979.

Polyviou, Polyvios G. *Cyprus: Conflict and Negotiation, 1960-1980*. New York: Holmes & Meier, 1980.

Rubinstein, Alvin Z. *Soviet and Chinese Influence in the Third World*. New York: Praeger, 1975.

_____. *Soviet Policy Toward Turkey, Iran and Afghanistan*. New York: Praeger, 1982.

Salih, Halil I. *Cyprus, An Analysis of Cypriot Political Discord*. New York: Theo. Gaus' Sons, 1968.

_____. *Cyprus: The Impact of Diverse Nationalism on a State*. Alabama: The University of Alabama Press, 1978.

Sarica, Murat, et. al. *Kibris Sorunu*. Istanbul: Fakulteler Matbaasi, 1975.

Sezer, Duygu. *Kamu Oyu ve Dis Politika*. Ankara: Ankara University, 1972.

Soysal, Mumtaz. *Dis Politika ve Parlamento*. Ankara: Ankara University, 1964.

Stavrinides, Zenon. *The Cyprus Conflict: National Identity and Statehood*. Wakefield: Stavrinides, 1976.

Stegenga, James A. *The U.N. Force in Cyprus*. Columbus, Ohio: Ohio State University Press, 1968.

Stern, Laurence. *The Wrong Horse: The Politics of Intervention and the Failure of American Diplomacy*. New York: Times Books, 1977.

Tanju, Sadun. *Tepedeki Dort Adam.* Istanbul: Gelisim, 1978.

Toker, Metin. *Ismet Pasayla On Yil, 1961-1964.* [ ]: Burcak Yayinlari, 1969.

Turkes, Alparslan. *Dis Politikamiz ve Kibris.* Istanbul: Kutlug Yayinlari, 1974.

Turner, Michael. "The International Politics of Narcotics: Turkey and the United States." Ph.D. Thesis, Ohio, Kent State University Press, 1975.

Vance, Cyrus. *Hard Choices.* New York: Simon and Schuster, 1983.

Volkan, Vamik. *Cyprus: War and Adaptation: A Psychological History of Two Ethnic Groups in Conflict.* Charlottesville, Va.: University Press of Virginia, 1979.

Wiener, Sharon A. "Turkish Foreign Policy Decision Making On the Cyprus Issue." Ph.D. Thesis, Duke University, 1980.

Wilson, Andrew. *The Aegean Dispute.* Adelphi Papers. No. 155. London: The Institute for Strategic Studies, 1979.

Windsor, Phillip. *NATO and the Cyprus Crisis.* Adelphi Papers. No. 14. London: The Institute for Strategic Studies, 1964.

Xydis, Stephen G. *Cyprus: Conflict and Reconciliation, 1954-1958.* Columbus, Ohio: The Ohio State University Press, 1967.

ARTICLES IN PERIODICALS AND BOOKS

Alenik, V. "Soviet-Turkish Ties Today." *International Affairs*. [Moscow], No. 4 (April, 1979), pp. 14-19.

Baldwin, David. A. "Inter-Nation Influence Revisited." *The Journal of Conflict Resolution*, Vol. XV, No. 4 (Dec., 1971).

Ball, Michael. "Turkey's New National Security Concept: What It Means for NATO." *Orbis*, Vol. XXIII (Fall, 1979), pp. 609-631.

Bilge, Suat. "Kibris Uyusmazligi." *Olaylarla Turk Dis Politikasi*, ed. by Mehmet Gonlubol, et. al., Ankara: Ankara Universitesi, 1977.

_____. "Turkiye-Sovyetler Birligi Munasebetleri." *Olaylarla Turk Dis Politikasi*, Ankara: Ankara Universitesi, 1977.

Campbell, John C. "The Mediterranean Crisis." *Foreign Affairs*, Vol. LIII (July, 1975), pp. 605-624.

Deutsch, Karl W. "On the Concepts of Politics and Power." *International Politics and Foreign Policy*, ed. by James N. Rosenau, New York: The Free Press, 1969.

Dimas, George. "Ahepans in the Forefront for Cyprus." *The Ahepan*, March/April, 1956.

Ecevit, Bulent. "Dis Politika." *Ozgur Insan*, Sept., 1972.

_____. "Turkey's Security Policies." *Survival*, Vol. XX, No. 5 (Sept./Oct., 1978).

Finer, Leslie. "The Colonels' Bid for Cyprus." *New Statesman*, 10 March 1972.

Fulbright, William J. "The Legislator As Educator." *Foreign Affairs*, Vol. LVII, No. 4 (Spring, 1979).

Georgehallides, G.S. "Turkish and British Reactions to the Emigration of Ćypriot Turks to Anatolia." *Balkan Studies*, [Thessaloniki: Institute for Balkan Studies], Vol. XVIII (1977), No. 1.

Gonlubol, Mehmet, et. al. "Tarafsizlarla Iliskiler ve Bandung Konferansi." *Olaylarla Turk Dis Politikasi*, Ankara: Ankara University, 1977.

_____, and Kurkcuoglu, Omer. "1965-1973 Donemi Turk Dis Politikasi." *Olaylarla Turk Dis Politikasi*, Ankara: Ankara Universitesi, 1977.

Hackett, Clifford P. "The Role of Congress and Greek-American Relations." *Greek-American Relations*, ed. by Theodore A. Couloumbis and John O. Iatrides, New York: Pella, 1980.

Harris, George. "Cross-Alliance Politics: Turkey and the Soviet Union." *Turkish Yearbook of International Relations*, Ankara, No. 12, 1972.

_____. "The Causes of the 1960 Revolution in Turkey." *The Middle East Journal*, Vol. 24 (Autumn, 1970), pp. 438-54.

Hicks, Sallie M., and Couloumbis, Theodore. "The Greek Lobby: Illusion or Reality." *Ethnicity and U.S. Foreign Policy*, ed. by Abdul Aziz Said, New York: Praeger, 1977.

Karnow, Stanley. "The Indispensible Man: An Interview with Makarios." *The New Republic*, 14 Sept. 1974.

_____. "America's Mediterranean Blunder." *Atlantic Monthly*, Vol. 235, No. 1 (Feb., 1975).

_____. "Tough Turkey: Premier Ecevit's Perspective on Cyprus." *The New Republic*, 5 Oct. 1974.

Kurkcuoglu, Omer. "Turkiye'nin Orta Dogu Politikasindaki Son Gelismeler." *Dis Politika*, Vol. I, No. 2 (June, 1971).

Legg, Keith. "Congress As Trojan Horse: The Turkish Embargo Problem, 1974-1978." *Congress, the Presidency and American Foreign Policy*, ed. by John Spanier and Joseph Nogee, New York: Pergamon Press, 1981.

Pipinellis, Panayotis. "The Graeco-Turkish Feud Reviewed." *Foreign Affairs*, Vol. XXXVII, January 1959, pp. 306-316.

Rudnik, David. "Death of an Embargo." *The Round Table*, No. 272 (Oct., 1978).

Singer, David. "Inter-Nation Influence: A Formal Model." *International Politics and Foreign Policy*, ed. by James Rosenau, New York: The Free Press, 1969.

Soylemez, Yuksel. "The Question of Narcotic Drugs and Turkey." *Foreign Policy*, Ankara, Vol. IV, No. 4 (June, 1975), pp. 144-155.

Spain, James. "The United States, Turkey and the Poppy." *The Middle East Journal*, Vol. XXIX, No. 3 (Summer, 1975).

Spanier, John. "Congress and the Presidency: The Weakest Link in the Policy Process." *Congress, the Presidency and American Foreign Policy*, ed. by John Spanier and Joseph Nogee, New York: Pergamon Press, 1981.

Stern Laurence. "Bitter Lessons: How We Failed in Cyprus." *Foreign Policy*, Vol. XIX, Summer 1975.

Sundquist, James L. "Congress and the President: Enemies or Partners." *Congress Reconsidered*, ed. by Lawrence C. Dodd and Bruce Oppenheimer, New York: Praeger, 1977.

Tachau, Frank. "The Face of Turkish Nationalism as Reflected in the Cyprus Dispute." *The Middle East Journal*, Vol. XIII, NO. 3 (Summer, 1959).

Tower, John. "Congress Versus the President: The Formulation and Implementation of American Foreign Policy." *Foreign Affairs*, Vol. LX, No. 2 (Winter, 1981/82).

Ulman, Haluk. "Geneva Conferences." *Foreign Policy*, Ankara, Vol. IV, 1974.

_____, and Dekmejian, R.H. "Changing Patterns in Turkish Foreign Policy: 1959-1967." *Orbis*, Vol. XI, No. 3 (Fall, 1967).

Xydis, Stephen G. "Toward 'Toil and Moil' in Cyprus." *The Middle East Journal*, Vol. XX, No. 1 (Winter, 1966), pp. 1-19.